Jeff Pearce was born in the slums of Liverpool in 1953, and from the moment ... ng second ... thes o ... urteen, u... to read or write, he embarked on an amazing journey that would see him make and lose millions in the 'rag trade' before eventually winning the highest accolade the fashion business had to offer. He is retired nowadays and lives on a small farm in Cheshire with his wife, Gina, two Argentinean polo ponies, Susie the dog and Daisy the cat.

To find out more, visit www.jeffpearce.co.uk

Acknowledgements

I am eternally grateful to Kit Knowles, my friend and part-time assistant who has deciphered my hieroglyphics, dotted the 'i's and crossed the 't's patiently over the past years. A special thank you to Lesley, for being on the other end of the phone whenever I needed her input on the family history; and just for being my big sister. Thanks to my good old mates Matt Barr and Danny Tallon, whose enthusiasm encouraged me to keep going and to finish my book. To my agent, Luigi Bonomi, for believing in me, and I cannot thank all at Penguin enough for helping me tell my story to the world.

A Pocketful of Holes
and Dreams

JEFF PEARCE

PENGUIN BOOKS

PENGUIN BOOKS

Published by the Penguin Group
Penguin Books Ltd, 80 Strand, London WC2R ORL, England
Penguin Group (USA) Inc., 375 Hudson Street, New York, New York 10014, USA
Penguin Group (Canada), 90 Eglinton Avenue East, Suite 700, Toronto, Ontario, Canada M4P 2Y3
(a division of Pearson Penguin Canada Inc.)
Penguin Ireland, 25 St Stephen's Green, Dublin 2, Ireland
(a division of Penguin Books Ltd)
Penguin Group (Australia), 250 Camberwell Road, Camberwell,
Victoria 3124, Australia (a division of Pearson Australia Group Pty Ltd)
Penguin Books India Pvt Ltd, 11 Community Centre,
Panchsheel Park, New Delhi – 110 017, India
Penguin Group (NZ), 67 Apollo Drive, Rosedale, North Shore 0632,
New Zealand (a division of Pearson New Zealand Ltd)
Penguin Books (South Africa) (Pty) Ltd, 24 Sturdee Avenue,
Rosebank, Johannesburg 2196, South Africa

Penguin Books Ltd, Registered Offices: 80 Strand, London WC2R ORL, England

www.penguin.com

First published 2011
1

Copyright © Jeff Pearce, 2011
All rights reserved

The moral right of the author has been asserted

Set in 11.5/14.75 pt Garamond
Typeset by Palimpsest Book Production Limited, Falkirk, Stirlingshire
Printed in Great Britain by Clays Ltd, St Ives plc

ISBN: 978–0–241–95107–1

www.greenpenguin.co.uk

In loving memory of Elsie, my mother, for having given me the
greatest gift a son could ever wish for.

This book is also dedicated to three other women in my life, Gina, Katie
and Faye, for all their love, laughter and support over the years;
with particular thanks to Gina, for literally being my writing hand.

Contents

1. The Boss

If only the Boss could have been more of a father. But he wasn't. There were times when he seemed to live in a completely different world to the rest of us. I rarely saw him while I was growing up, and if I did it was when I came home from school, when I would find him shaving over the kitchen sink.

Seeing me standing there, he'd put his hand in his pocket, jingling coins before taking out half a crown. 'Son, go and get me a pack of twenty Rothmans King Size and a packet of Seven O'Clock razor blades,' he'd say. He only smoked Rothmans. Other brands like Woodbines and Senior Service were too common for him.

Getting himself ready for work was an afternoon ritual, with Mum waiting on him hand and foot, treating him as if he was a Hollywood movie star. Dad modelled himself on Clark Gable – so many people had told him he was the mirror image of him. Mum made sure his shirts and collars were freshly laundered, with starched collar and cuffs, and he always wore a tie and a pair of gleaming cufflinks.

And his preparations didn't end with a shave and a clean shirt. He'd blacken his moustache with a cosmetic pencil and apply vast amounts of Brylcreem to his thick black hair, positioning the waves carefully and frequently checking his reflection in the mirror. His vanity needed constant reassurance of his good looks; it was an attention to detail bordering on the obsessive. He'd even turn his shoes over to check that Mum had polished the arch on the sole as well as the uppers! She was very much his 'gentleman's valet'.

Despite his failings as a provider, Mum adored him and dreamt that, one day, he would change, becoming the perfect husband and a good father to his children. But, in reality, my father lived a lie, just pretending to the world that he was an affluent man. He certainly looked the part.

Once he was away from home, his young family ceased to exist. He'd do anything for his 'cronies', as Mum called them, giving them his last penny, knowing full well he'd never see it again; and they would feed his ego with compliments and flattery. They were the ones who nicknamed him 'The Boss', and being the weak person he was, he was easily caught up in their lies. He lived in a make-believe world, playing the part of a wealthy businessman. He refused to grow up, turning his back on his true responsibilities towards his family and his wife.

He part-owned a black taxi cab with one of his best friends, Nobby, who lived a couple of streets away. Nobby worked the day shift while my father did nights. Working out of the clubs on the seedier side of town, he'd chauffeur the prostitutes and their clients to and from the ships that were in dock at the time. It was a lucrative business for him as well as the girls, earning him at least £5 for a return trip.

Besides seeing him in the afternoons, the only other time I occasionally saw him was in the morning when I left for school. He didn't look well groomed and tidy then. He'd be slouched in the chair, stinking of booze and tobacco, and he'd look almost frightening, with bloodshot eyes, his hair an untidy mess and his tie askew. We wouldn't bother talking to him then. He couldn't string a sentence together he was so drunk.

Until I was old enough to work with him, he only took me out on one occasion, and that was because Mum forced him to, pointing out that he never took his children anywhere and that a boy should spend time with his father.

We went to Southport, a coastal resort town famous for its amusement arcades and funfair. Most of the kids in our street had been there, and they told me all about it. We had to make an early start, but I was so excited I was sitting on the front step dressed in my Sunday best eagerly waiting for our special day together. We took the bus to a railway station, where we caught the train. I can't remember much of the two-hour journey. I guess anticipation made the time fly.

When we arrived, I could see the big wheel of the fairground in the distance, slowly going around, the carriages full of people laughing and waving. That would be me soon, I thought to myself, clasping my father's hand firmly in mine. I was terrified of losing him in the crowd.

At the fairground, Dad put me on a couple of the smaller rides, saying we could have a go on the bigger ones later. He bought us each an ice-cream, and I was really beginning to enjoy myself, looking around and planning which ride I would go on next.

While we were walking along, Dad bumped into a man he knew. The man had his three sons with him, all slightly older than me. Like us, they were there for a day out together. We joined them, Dad talking to his friend, me trailing along behind the three older boys, who ignored me. I felt much smaller and younger than them, so I just kept quiet, thinking about the adventures to come.

After a few minutes, we stopped outside a pub. Dad put his

hand in his pocket and pulled out a half-crown. 'Take this, son,' he said. 'I'm going in here for a pint with my friend, so you run along with these lads and have fun. Just be good and don't get lost. Don't worry about me – I'll be in here.'

As Dad and his friend disappeared inside, I turned around to the other boys, but they had vanished. I caught sight of them running into the fairground, and reckoned they must have been so excited at the thought of spending the money their dad had given them they forgot to wait for me. Anyway, I didn't want to be with them, I wanted to be with my dad, just the two of us going on all those promised big rides together. I stood there not knowing what to do, a seven-year-old rooted to the ground, too frightened to move, terrified of getting caught up in the crowds and lost.

My father hadn't mentioned the name of the pub, and even if I'd been able to see the sign, I wouldn't have been able to read it. What if Dad couldn't find me? Or even forgot he'd brought me and left me stranded? I didn't think I could find my way to the train station on my own, and I certainly wouldn't know which train to catch or where to get off.

Waves of panic were beginning to engulf me, and I decided that the best thing to do was to get as close to the pub door I had seen Dad go in and to stay there until he came out.

My half-crown was burning a hole in my pocket, and I kept touching it to make sure I hadn't lost it. I wanted to look at it but felt it best to keep it hidden in case some bigger lad tried to steal it from me. I so wanted to buy something for myself, but I didn't want to lose sight of the pub door, and there were no shops close enough, so I could only wistfully look at the other kids walking past, wearing funny hats, eating sticks of rock and enjoying themselves as kids should on a special day out.

Time passed slowly. It was hot, I was thirsty and I needed to wee. I plucked up courage to nip around the back of the pub, but I had to hurry as I was terrified Dad would come out and find me gone.

The three other lads eventually came back, full of stories of the rides they'd been on. I wasn't interested; I just wanted to get back home to my mum.

When he finally staggered out, it was easy to see that Dad had been drinking heavily. He had to hold on to me for support as we walked along. He had forgotten where the station was. I had to ask for directions. He fell asleep on the train, unaware of the seven-year-old next to him, and his drunken snores were an embarrassment. I remember wishing he was not my dad.

Mum never let him take me out for the day again.

I kept the half-crown hidden for a couple of weeks, and then one day when I knew Mum needed some extra pennies to buy food I gave it to her, telling her it was from my day out with Dad. She always tried to protect us from my father's antics, but we all knew. My brother and two sisters were older and had a greater awareness of what was going on than I did, but there is one memory we all share.

We were the last family in our street to get a television set. Mum couldn't afford to buy one and had gone into debt paying the deposit on a slot TV. You had to insert a shilling into the meter at the back, which made it the most expensive way of viewing, but it was the only one she could afford. She was so proud of it and put it in the best room, our front parlour.

I remember, it was a cold, dark wintry evening, and the four of us were clustered around our 14-inch television, watching a group of acrobats forming a human tower on the screen. Just as the last man was about to be thrown into the air, the door to the parlour opened and we heard a drunken grunt. Without thinking, and as one voice, we chorused a loud 'shush'. As the final acrobat flew through the air, on the point of taking his place at the top of the tower, we all realized who was standing behind us.

'Tell me to shush, will you? I'll show you who's boss in this house.'

Roaring with anger, he lurched over to the television set, picked it up, staggered over to the bay window and hurled it with all his might through the glass on to the street. The noise was horrendous, as fragments rained down on the cobbles outside. Leaping to our feet, we made a bolt for the safety of upstairs. The fact that we all managed to fit through the door at once proved how desperate we were to escape.

As we pounded upstairs, our feet making a loud noise on the brown lino that covered the floor, Mum, attracted by the shouting, dashed out of the kitchen. Wiping her hands on her apron, she cried out, 'What's going on? Will someone tell me what's going on?' She must have gone into the front parlour and seen the window. My father was still ranting, but perhaps he now realized what he had done, as his voice quietened down, and his anger turned to self-justification.

Slowly, I pulled back the curtains from the window above my bed. I saw that the neighbours were out in force: peering from behind their net curtains or being even bolder and standing on their front steps watching and gossiping.

Mum was out in the street, down on her hands and knees

picking up the pieces of the wreckage. I could see the light from the street lamp glinting on the tears streaming down her cheeks. It was typical of our life as a family that for all the good Mum managed to achieve, my father would destroy it in one drunken moment.

My father did a great many unpleasant things regarding my mother, but I believe this was one of the lowest moments of their married life. He knew how proud Mum was of her television. The complete and utter humiliation that he subjected her to has remained with me as clearly as the image of her tears as she knelt in the darkened street.

From an early age, I had a special closeness with Mum and, being the youngest, I accompanied her everywhere while my three older siblings were at school. She was a woman of incredible spirit and courage and, like mothers all over the world, would do anything to protect and provide for her children.

Like so many other kids living in the Liverpool slums, we were often cold, our threadbare clothes providing little or no warmth. In winter we would huddle around the fire in the living room, and when times were particularly hard, Mum would throw anything on it to keep it going – even worn-out old shoes and boots. Mum worked hard as a cleaner and had a good reputation but couldn't always get work. At those times, even as a small child, I could feel the sense of pure desperation that seemed to enshroud her. Without money, she couldn't feed us.

I remember, one bitter February morning, Mum was sitting at the small table in the living room, counting the copper coins in her purse. She seemed to be weighing something up very carefully in her head. I must have made a noise as I approached, as she looked up then got to her feet. 'Come on,' she said. 'We're going to the Co-Op.'

When we got there she took both my hands in hers and looked me straight in the eye, saying, 'James, listen to me. I want you to stay right here. Do you understand? Don't you dare move; I promise I won't be long.' She fussed with my coat and hat and wiped my runny nose with her handkerchief.

I didn't say anything other than, 'Yes, Mum,' but I couldn't understand why she wouldn't let me go in with her. I stood by the front of the store, looking at the traffic going up and down Smithdown Road and all the people rushing around. I started to feel cold and hungry, and wished Mum would hurry up. I seemed to be standing there forever. Each time the door opened I tried to look inside.

I wasn't used to being on my own and became very upset, crying with confusion and unable to stop shivering with cold. A lady knelt down in front of me, concern in her voice.

'What's up, love?' she asked.

'It's me mum. I want me mum. She's in there.'

Standing up, the lady took me by the hand and led me inside. It was warm, so I started to feel a bit better, but then, in the middle of the store, the woman demanded, 'Who does this child belong to?' in a loud voice, and then asked again.

Everyone looked round, and before long one of the sales assistants said, 'He must belong to the woman in the office with the policeman and the manager.'

The next moment, one of the staff took my hand and led me into the office. As the door opened, I caught sight of my mum, sitting on a chair crying. I was crying myself as I ran to her. She put her arms around me and picked me up, placing me on her lap and covering my face with kisses.

'There, there love,' she said, her voice beginning to soothe me. 'I'm so sorry. Everything will be all right now we're together.'

There was a policeman standing next to my mum's chair. He looked at me sitting on Mum's lap and asked her, 'Have you no shame? Theft is a very serious crime, even if it is only a loaf of bread. If I had my way I would be taking you down to the police station right now. You're very lucky the manager has decided not to prosecute. He says you have never stolen from here before, so he is letting you off scot-free.' At the door, he said, loudly so that everyone could hear, 'Don't let me catch you stealing ever again!', and the manager added, 'Don't you ever show your face in here again.'

Mum left the store and immediately turned into the alleyway, heading for home, grasping my hand and willing me to keep up with her. As soon as we were through the back door, she shut it behind us, sighing with relief at being in the safety of her own home.

Then she groaned as the shame of it hit her. 'Has it come to this?' she cried out. 'Having to steal a loaf of bread to feed my children? What in heaven have I done? The neighbours . . .'

She knew that within ten minutes of our leaving the store everybody from streets around would know what had happened. They would have something new to gossip about, and for once it wouldn't be my dad.

My poor little mum. She must have felt so mortified knowing she had brought shame to our home. It was almost too much for her to bear. She broke down, weeping for the longest time as I stood there with my arms wrapped around her knees, trying to comfort her.

I didn't understand much of it then. But it has stayed with me all my life like a bad dream, coming back to haunt me from time to time.

2. The Perfect Couple

It's only with hindsight that I can fully appreciate how my mother struggled to make ends meet. The electricity would go off on a regular basis because the meter was empty, and Mum's purse would be just as bare. When this happened, she would head off on the hunt for my father, taking me with her. Maybe it was for moral support, or maybe she hoped that seeing one of his children would shame my father into putting his hand into his pocket.

Going from pub to pub, she'd stand in the doorway with me in her arms, peering through the crowd of men and cigarette smoke. If she spotted her husband she'd gesture frantically, trying to catch his attention. More often than not this would fail, as he'd be too busy enjoying himself with his mates or too drunk to notice, so she would have to venture in, making her way through the mass of bodies until she reached his side, then tapping him gently on the shoulder. His response would vary depending on how much he'd had to drink. Sometimes he'd give her a shilling for the meter and something extra for food; other times, he'd insist she went home, annoyed with her for disturbing his drinking.

Occasionally, he was harder to track down. If Mum couldn't find him, she'd look for his taxi. Sometimes he'd be on a rank waiting for a fare, but at other times the cab would be empty.

Once, my eldest sister Lesley was with her. After a while they found the cab parked in a dark sidestreet – so dark they couldn't see if there was anyone in it. Mum tried the doors and found them locked. She and Lesley were about to walk away when the passenger door opened and Dad's angry voice rang out across the cobbles. 'What are you doing here?' he demanded. 'Are you spying on me?'

As Mum was explaining that she had no money for the electricity meter, she and Lesley moved closer to the taxi. Through the open door they could see a woman in a state of undress sitting in the back of the cab next to my father.

It was Ruby Brown, Mum's best friend! As young girls and teenagers they'd been almost inseparable, and their friendship had continued throughout the War and after they'd both married. Mum had even asked Ruby to the pub with her and Dad on numerous occasions because she felt sorry for her, with her husband being away at sea a lot of the time.

I can only imagine what my mother must have felt. Mustering as much dignity as possible, she took Lesley by the hand, and turned and walked away.

Mum's life had changed so much. She walked down the aisle a beautiful young bride looking forward to a future of happiness and love – but it didn't turn out like that.

Elsie May Turner was nineteen years old and working in her mother's shop when she first set eyes on my father. Her mother, Mary Louise, was the proud owner of not one but two sweet and tobacco shops on Lodge Lane. Her father, George, worked as a sheet-metal worker for the Gas Board and in his free time helped out in the family business.

Elsie was the sixth of eleven children; and when she was

eleven she became very ill with pneumonia and spent a large part of her childhood in a special home for sick children on the coast. Unable to play outdoors, she turned her mind to reading and writing, and being naturally inquisitive and intelligent, by the time she left, she was years ahead of many of her contemporaries. Her mother, realizing how gifted she was, put her to work in the shop, confident she would soon pick up the trade.

Leslie Pearce was born and grew up in the same area as Mum, in a two-up-two-down terrace. He was the youngest of six, by seven years, and his father, a taxi driver, left home when he was very young to set up home with another woman, and raised a second family. When Les was barely eight, his mother died of thrombosis, and he and Joyce, the youngest of his three sisters, were put into an orphanage. Les and Joyce hated it there and Joyce left on her sixteenth birthday, taking Les, now nine, with her, back to the family home. She and her two sisters raised Les, spoiling him outrageously to try to make up for him losing his parents so young.

Leslie's first job was working for the Liverpool Corporation Highways Department, maintaining the roads, and his work often took him along Lodge Lane. He was sixteen when he first set eyes on Mum. Going into the shop for a packet of cigarettes one day, he saw her, a pretty young girl, petite, with a fabulous smile and warm personality and the most beautiful head of auburn hair. After that day he kept going back, and if the shop was busy he would peer in through the window trying to catch a glimpse of her. Eventually he found the courage to say a few words to her, and a couple of days later asked her out for a date.

Elsie and Les made an attractive couple and started to see a lot of each other, spending most of their time at dance halls. But not long after her twentieth birthday, Elsie found herself pregnant. And in those days, when a young man got a girl 'in trouble', he did the 'right' thing and married her. Les's sisters weren't so keen, because they felt that, at the age of seventeen, he wasn't much more than a child himself, but the couple did marry, at St Bede's Parish Church, on 23 August 1939. Within a matter of weeks, Great Britain had declared war on Germany.

After a long and difficult birth, Pamela was born in February 1940. Unfortunately, she died a few hours later. The young couple were devastated. Les was too young and inexperienced to know how to comfort his wife, let alone deal with his own grief. And they had married to give a home to the baby. I've often wondered whether he felt cheated of his bachelor years after that, and if that was one of the reasons he shied away from being a father to us later.

Within weeks of Pamela's death, the 'Phoney War' came to an end and troops were mobilized overnight. Les had already joined up and had been posted to RAF Brize Norton in Oxfordshire, where he served as a member of the Catering Corps, and Mum, like so many other women with husbands and loved ones away, just got on with her life. She worked in the family shop until it was destroyed in a bombing raid, then found a job at Freemans, a small department store. After that, she joined the Women's Royal Naval Service (WRNS) and was based at the Royal Liver Building on the city's waterfront, working in the Communications Centre, located deep in the basement.

Towards the end of 1944, pregnant for the fourth time (she

had suffered two miscarriages during the war), Elsie was discharged from the WRNS. And in July 1945, Lesley, her first surviving child, was born, in the front parlour of Grandma Turner's house. Mum's joy was immense: for the first time in six long years she was able to hold a beautiful, healthy baby in her arms.

Les returned briefly to England in November 1946, with the result that Barry was born in August of the following year. By this time my father had been demobbed and was at home for the birth.

My mother was to have three more pregnancies. Ian was born in 1949 but sadly died nine days later of hydrocephalus. This was the second time my parents had had to bury a small child, and my mother once again found herself being the stronger of the two in their time of grief.

She gave birth again, to Sheila, in June 1951, and I was born some two years later, on 30 May 1953.

I always say that I was born with a silver spoon in my mouth. Not because I was born into an aristocratic family, but because my birth coincided with the coronation of our new queen, and any child born within a week of it received a commemorative silver spoon to celebrate the official crowning of Queen Elizabeth II.

I was born James Jeffrey Pearce, and after three days in hospital Mum and I were allowed home. I couldn't have chosen a better day: Tuesday 2 June, the day the whole country was celebrating.

My father picked us up from the hospital in his black cab, and my brother and sisters ran to greet Mum and to see me for the first time. Lesley was eight years old, Barry six and Sheila just two. They all gathered around, all the time asking, 'Where is it, Mum? Where is it?' Mum was puzzled.

'Where's what?' she asked.

'The present off the Queen,' they said all together. 'The spoon!'

Mum laughed, taking the precious silver spoon out of her handbag and passing it to Lesley. 'Don't let it out of your sight,' she warned.

Lesley ran off down the street cradling the spoon gently in her hands, and within seconds she was surrounded by children, all of whom were begging for a look at the treasure. 'Look,' she said, pointing to the hallmarks on the back of the spoon. 'That's real silver that is. It was made for the Queen, and she took it out of one of her kitchen drawers to give to us as a special present for our new baby!'

I loved our house and have fantastic memories of growing up there. We had two and a half rooms upstairs and two and a half downstairs, but somehow we all managed to fit in, and even with four children to look after and all the extra jobs my mum had, she still managed to keep the house clean and tidy.

All the women on our street were houseproud, and they spent a lot of time making sure they presented the right outward appearance. Brass door knockers and letterboxes would be polished until they were spotless and reflected like gold, and the women would ache from scrubbing the front steps until they were clean enough to pass inspection from any critical eye. Many a reputation had been ruined by dirt on the doorstep:

'Have you seen the state of her step? It's rotten!'

'Step? Never mind the step. Have you seen her curtains? I feel ashamed for her!'

'It makes you think what the rest of the house is like!'

'No bloody wonder. She's always out gallivanting, that one.'

There was one thing, however, that couldn't be overcome, no matter how clean you kept your home – especially on summer nights. Mum would tuck us into bed with the words 'Good night, sleep tight, hope the bed bugs don't bite,' and would always pop her head in later to see if we were asleep. Sometimes, we weren't, as we were tossing and turning, tormented by a terrible itching. Mum would respond immediately, getting us out of bed to check our bodies for bite marks. Then she'd know what type of insects to look for and where to find them. It was like gathering military intelligence for an attack on the enemy!

She'd tug back the blankets, and three or four bugs would scatter away from the light. Then, like a trained mercenary, she would strike out, grabbing a bug and squishing it between her thumbnails, making our blood squirt out. With split-second precision, she would annihilate our tormentors before they could escape, then she'd roll up the bedding, take it outside to the backyard and give it all a good shake, just in case any bugs had managed to evade her.

The final strike was to take the mattress off the bed, check it and shake bug powder on the metal frame and on the base of the legs to stop the bugs climbing up to the mattress and attacking us all over again.

It was brilliant watching Mum killing the enemy, but most of the time we were too busy scratching, trying to find some relief from the bites and dreading the moment when we had to return to bed. Mum always assured us the bed bugs wouldn't come back, but we knew they would. Nobody on the street ever talked about it, but you knew that everyone had the same problem – no matter how gleaming the brass or spotless the net curtains!

Once a year, the council would send a special truck to fumigate the houses. The residents would have to wait outside on the pavement while some sort of chemical smoke was sprayed into each house. The house stank afterwards, and the smoke made us cough. And it didn't even work: the bugs would return and we'd all be itching again in a matter of days.

And bug annihilation wasn't the only night-time adventure in our house. I'll always remember the trips to the toilet in the backyard. I could handle a wee in the potty up on the landing by myself, but if I needed to go outside, the job of taking me would fall to Lesley, as I was too small to go on my own, especially on dark winter nights.

I had to wake her up, and she'd take me downstairs to the kitchen, and wrap herself up in Dad's old RAF coat. She'd place me on her hip, holding on to me with one arm, the other holding a lit candle, and we'd make our way to the brick shed at the end of the yard. Inside, it was very basic: a wooden box with a hole cut in it above a trench which led to the sewers. For toilet paper, Mum would cut up sheets of newspaper and hang them on a piece of string. I'd sit on the cold wooden 'seat', the candle next to me to stop me being scared, my eyes firmly fixed on the ground, hoping and praying that the big slugs that lived in the toilet came nowhere near me.

Lesley would be out in the cold, teeth chattering, hopping around trying to keep warm, and telling me to hurry up. We couldn't wait to get back indoors and would bolt for the warmth of our beds. Lesley would tuck the blankets snugly around me and put Dad's RAF coat on top of me. That jacket certainly saw some service!

3. One Thing after Another

I started attending Lawrence Road Infants School when I was five. I wasn't looking forward to being separated from my mother: we'd been so close and had never been apart. The school was a fair distance, so Mum would strap me into a little wooden seat perched above the rear wheel of her bicycle, and I would hold on tight as the wheels bumped over the road's cobble setts.

Mum knew I wasn't happy there, so she'd come and see me at lunchtime, bringing me a buttie. I always knew when she was about to leave: she'd wet the corner of her handkerchief with the tip of her tongue and wipe my mouth. Then she'd kiss me through the railings and cycle away, waving her arm in the air, as she disappeared into the traffic.

I found school difficult. I was so inquisitive and really wanted to learn, but when they started teaching us to read, no matter how hard I tried, I just couldn't make any sense of the letters and words. They'd just jump around before my eyes and get all jumbled up. And I felt even worse because I sensed that the teachers were unhappy with my progress and thought I wasn't trying.

As ever, Mum did her best to help. At first, thinking I couldn't see the blackboard properly, she asked my teachers to let me sit at the front of the class, and when that didn't work she arranged for me to have my eyes tested and I was given glasses.

I hated them! They were too big for my face, had heavy dark

frames and made my ears stick out, but Mum insisted that I wore them, even though they didn't make any difference. With or without glasses, the words just got mixed up. I'd sit for hours after school with Mum teaching me simple spellings like c-a-t, h-a-t, m-a-t and d-o-g. I'd memorize the words, but minutes later, when I saw them on paper again, I would have no idea what they were.

One of the most important words which I couldn't spell was my first name, James. When it came to writing it down, the five different letters all became jumbled up. One day, Mum must have had enough as she decided there and then that I was going to be called Jeff. And so it's been ever since.

Mum was always there to meet me at the school gates, but one afternoon it was Lesley who came to pick me up. As we got nearer our house I ran ahead, bursting through the kitchen door, happy to be home. Mum was sitting in an armchair in the living room, rocking backwards and forwards and holding a large white handkerchief to her mouth.

Going over to her side, I leaned forward so I could see her face better. 'What's wrong, Mum?' I asked. 'Are you feeling sick?' Silently, she shook her head from side to side. I was getting worried. This wasn't like Mum. I could feel a note of panic welling up in my voice and tears starting to form at the back of my eyes. 'Please, Mum, tell me what's wrong.'

Looking at me properly for the first time, she lowered the handkerchief from her mouth and I caught a glimpse of blood on the white cotton.

Jumping away, my voice almost hysterical, I cried, 'Who did it, Mum? What happened?' I looked at her mouth in horror. She'd had beautiful teeth, with a gap between the front two, just like I had. She'd always said it meant we would be wealthy one day. But now all that remained were red gums.

She was trying to answer me, but she sounded like a different person, muffled and old. It just wasn't the Mum I knew. 'I hate you!' I shouted. 'I don't love you any more. Who's done it? Who's done it?' Dashing out of the room and slamming the door behind me, I ran upstairs.

Throwing myself on my bed, I sobbed my heart out. I was frightened and confused. What had happened?

Lesley was sent upstairs to calm me down. She sat on my bed, gently stroking my head.

'What's wrong, Jeff?' she asked.

My face buried in my pillow, I uttered a muffled, 'Go away, leave me alone.' But Lesley didn't give up so easily. 'I don't love Mum no more, she hasn't got any teeth, she can't even talk properly!' It all rushed out in one long sentence.

Lesley explained that a disease had made Mum's teeth so painful the dentist had taken them all out, but that he was going to make Mum some beautiful new teeth. I understood then, but my poor mother was so upset.

Years later, she told me that me saying I didn't love her that day had caused her more pain than the loss of her teeth.

There was a well-worn path from our house to the top of Smithdown Road. Three pairs of feet regularly headed that way: my father's, on the way to the Boundary pub, and Mum and one of us kid's, on the way to the doctor's surgery.

My best friend when I was a kid was Ian Watt, who lived a few doors down from us. We always played together, often on one of the sites that had been bombed during the war. We would play at being soldiers, making dug-outs for ourselves and using stones and broken pieces of brick as ammunition and hurling them through the air with cries of '*whoosh!*' and '*kaboom!*' as if they were hand grenades.

I'd finished throwing my missile and was crouching down, waiting for Ian to counterattack. I seemed to be waiting forever, so being impatient, I stood up, breaking cover. His rock flew silently through the air and struck me right smack in the middle of my forehead. It was a direct hit, and I keeled over backwards, landing on a pile of rubble. Wiping my eyes free of the blood that was streaming down my face, I staggered to my feet. Ian took one look at me and ran like hell, doubtless knowing he was in big trouble.

Howling loudly, I too ran home, calling out for Mum all the way. She must have heard the racket because, as I entered the backyard, she appeared at the kitchen door. She stopped dead in her tracks when she saw me – her small son, dirty, bedraggled and covered in blood. She must have been thinking the worst, as my bloodied hands were clamped to my head, and the noise I was making couldn't have left her in any doubt as to the pain I was in.

'What . . .?' She couldn't find the words. 'Come here. What have you done? Who did this?' She drew me closer to her and led me inside so she could look at my head.

'Ian Watt did it, Mum,' I said, in between loud sniffs and whimpers of pain. 'Ian Watt threw the grenade.' One look at my head and she knew she'd have to take me to the hospital. As we sat on the bus going to Sefton General, I'm sure she was planning what she'd do to Ian Watt when she got her hands on him!

Six stitches later, a bandage wrapped around the top of my

head like a turban, I was allowed to go home. Mum had other plans, however: after we got off the bus she marched me straight to Ian's house and banged loudly on the door. Mrs Watt opened it.

Mum wasted no time on pleasantries. 'Look what your son has done to him!' she exclaimed angrily, thrusting me in front of her. 'I've had to take him down the hospital. Three holes in his head to stitch up. Your son did this. Six stitches he's had!' She was furious.

Ian's mother was none too happy either. 'Ian, get yourself here now!' she shouted. His head appeared cautiously around the edge of the door. When he saw me standing there like a half-wrapped mummy, he looked terrified. For all he knew, he'd nearly killed me and it was a miracle the doctors had been able to save my life! His mother grabbed him and cuffed him around the head, and my mother, now apparently satisfied, gave strict instructions that I was never to play with Ian again.

Of course, the next day, when I went out to play, I went straight to Ian to tell him about my adventures at the hospital. We were best mates again within minutes!

Our street was a fantastic place to play, and football was the boys' favourite. The street was lined with glass from windows that had fallen victim to a flying football, and I managed this on numerous occasions myself, pretending that I was playing for England in the World Cup, which was all we talked about at the time.

This particular day I was Bobby Charlton, about to take a very important corner kick. I took a long run-up to the ball, kicked it as hard as I could and watched the ball leave the ground at great speed. Smash! The sound of breaking glass falling on to the pavement was the signal for all the kids to run like mad into their own houses, while I stood there frozen to the spot, waiting for the trouble to begin. Within seconds, a woman came out of the house, shouting, 'Who the hell did that?'

By this time I was the only child left in the whole street. 'It was you, you little get!'

Neighbours were now appearing at their front doors or peering through their net curtains. Straightening the headscarf around her head, the woman advanced in my direction. She wasn't going to let me escape! Tight-lipped, she grabbed me by the ear, dragging me towards our house. Banging on our front door, she shouted, 'Your son has smashed my windows! What are you going to do about it?'

Mum opened the door, listening to what the neighbour had to say, then offered to pay for the damage. Once I was inside, however, she was furious. 'How am I going to find the money to pay for that?' she shouted. 'Why is it always you?'

Mum was right: no matter how hard I tried to be good, I was always the one who caused her the most problems. I was ridiculously accident-prone.

Durden Street was one of a series of narrow streets nestled between Smithdown Road and Earl Road, both being main roads leading in and out of the city, and teeming with traffic and activity. There was every type of shop you could imagine, and a pub on every other street corner. There'd often be some thirty kids playing out on our street, aged from about three to ten, and we all had nicknames. Mine was 'Red', because of the colour of my hair.

We played all sorts of games – skipping, ball games, marbles, and conkers. The older boys would make their own carts out of old wooden planks and pram wheels. The 'driver' would sit at the front, steering with a long piece of old rope attached to the front wheels, while a second boy pushed the cart from behind, running along until the cart built up speed. Then he'd leap on the back, holding on to the driver's shoulders for dear life as they rattled along.

There was no grass or trees growing in our streets, so we would make our way to Sefton Park, the nearest public park, which was about an hour's walk away. Mum encouraged us to go there during school holidays and sunny Sundays so we could play and get some fresh air. She'd make us jam or banana butties and give us a large bottle of tap water to quench our thirst. Being the youngest, I had to wait until last before I could have a swig, and by then there would be bits of bread floating around in the water. It didn't bother me, though. We were all family and friends, after all.

4. In the Blood

Looking back now, I think I was born to trade. I remember being about six and sitting with my feet in the street gutter watching the other kids play. A horse and cart loaded with old bikes, bits of metal, huge bundles of rags and boxes full of old bones left over from the stockpot came down the street, and I heard the man driving the cart shouting, 'Any old rags! Any old bones! Any old iron!'

He pulled his horse to a stop, and most of the kids ran off to their houses, coming back within minutes, their hands full of old clothes, clothes which were almost beyond repair, rags in the truest sense of the word. The children formed a queue, passing their bundles up to the man. He inspected the contents carefully before deciding whether or not they were worthy of a balloon tied to a piece of string. He looked so stern and grumpy no one ever argued.

As he was nearing the end of his collection, I noticed Mum standing beside the cart talking to him. They seemed to be coming to some arrangement. Then she got up on the back of the cart and began rummaging through the rags. After a while she got down with an assortment of jumpers and other clothes. Still negotiating, she opened her purse and took out a few coppers, passing them up to the rag-and-bone man.

Heading towards our front door, she called out to me, 'Come on, Jeff, we have work to do.' I followed after her, leaving my friends and their balloons behind.

We went through to the small kitchen at the back, and Mum carried two small metal buckets full of boiling water into the backyard and emptied them into a larger tub – the dolly tub. Then she swirled the clothes around with a dolly peg, cleaning them before any fleas or lice could invade the house. Once they were dry, she sat and darned through the night so she could sell them on the market.

Some of my earliest memories are of Great Homer Street – Paddy's – Market. Its nickname derived from the huge number of Irish immigrants that had settled in the area many years before. Most of the stallholders sold second-hand items and, like Mum, would rent a small space for a few shillings.

Apart from the rag-and-bone man, we also got our stock from 'going on the knocker' – knocking on rich people's front doors asking for any unwanted clothes. Sometimes we even got things Mum could pawn. On one of our better days, Mum and I were out calling on the grand houses overlooking Sefton Park. Mum stood by the gate waiting and watching while I walked up the footpath to the front door, standing on tiptoe and stretching as high as I could to reach the knocker. After a few moments the door opened.

'Please, missus, any old rags?' I piped up.

The lady standing in front of me was beautifully dressed, and smelt really nice. She smiled down at me. 'Wait there,' she said, and turned back into the house, closing the door behind her.

I stood there for what seemed like ages, then the door reopened and a large bundle, too big for me alone to carry, was placed at my feet. I was almost speechless, but managed to stammer a thank you.

Mum had quite a task carrying the bundle to the bus stop,

even with me helping as best I could. At home, she carefully undid all the knots, and gasped.

'Look, Jeff,' she exclaimed, pulling out the first item. 'A fur coat!' Slipping it over her shoulders, she span around the room as if she was dancing with Fred Astaire.

'Mum, you look fantastic,' I laughed, caught up in her excitement.

'Mink!' Her voice was brimming with joy. 'Mink is worth a fortune. And this is a real mink coat!'

The next item was a man's overcoat, a camel-hair Crombie. Running her hands over the material, she said, 'Oh, Jeff, this will fit your father. He'll look so handsome in it!' By now her voice was almost a whisper. 'Can you believe our luck? All this wonderful stuff. We can make so much money from it . . . and it didn't cost us a single penny!' She looked at me, gently resting her hands on my shoulders. 'God has been so good to us today. If you are a good person in life, then He will always look after you.'

Later that afternoon, Mum sent my older sister Lesley to the pawn shop with the mink coat – and she came back with not one but two £10 notes! Mum held the money to her chest, then turned and looked at the two of us standing there. 'We're rich! We're rich! This is what I was telling you about; this is a great day!' It was also one of those rare moments when I saw Mum happy and laughing.

Mum would prepare for the Saturday markets the night before, and showed me how to sort out the different categories of clothing and tie them into small bundles. Up and dressed in record time, Mum and I would be on our way by six o'clock in the morning, Mum pushing an old-fashioned pram laden with our wares while I almost jogged alongside her, my little legs finding it impossible to keep up at times.

Hiring a table for the day, she would arrange all the items for a shilling on top of it and everything that was a tanner (sixpence) on a tarpaulin on the ground before starting her spiel: 'Come on, folks! Everything a shilling on the table and a tanner on the floor!' I also remember her calling out, 'Here, Johnny, Johnny, lookee, Johnny, Johnny! Here, Johnny, Johnny!'

'Johnny' was the name given to the Lascars, Indian seamen from the cargo ships that visited Liverpool docks. Paddy's Market was very popular with them, and they'd buy umbrellas and hats – lady's hats and men's trilbies in any colour and condition, so long as they were cheap. Mum told me they took the hats back to their loved ones, who used them to protect themselves from the heat of the sun.

Johnnies always moved around the market in groups of at least three or four, forming a line, one behind the other, so close that the man behind was almost a part of the man in front, moving as one with a shuffling sort of dance step. They stacked the hats up ten high on their heads, and they'd tower over the crowds around them and tilt in different directions, and their arms would be adorned, too, with umbrellas, eight or nine on each one. Mum said that travelling in groups made them feel safe – the one in the middle always held the money.

I asked Mum why they were called Johnnies. She told me that, over the years, when anybody asked their name, they would always say 'Johnny'. In response, the market traders would laugh, and joke that 'They must all be called Johnny in their country,' and so the nickname stuck.

After a couple of years I had become a regular trader on the market with Mum. I loved it, particularly first thing in the morning when the traders were getting their stalls ready. The atmosphere was great and humming with energy, buzzing with the calls of the traders: 'All right, Gert? Tess? Dave? Alice?' 'The best of luck to you today. Have a good'un – hope you take lots of money.'

One day we had a small hand-operated sewing machine to sell. Mum had to go to the toilet and left me in charge, and a lady came over and asked how much it was. Mum had told me earlier how much she wanted to sell it for, but I couldn't remember. Not wanting to lose a sale, I quickly came up with a figure.

'£5 that, missus,' I replied. 'Just £5.' (Mum always said 'just' before the price.)

Tousling my hair, the lady smiled. 'You're very grown-up for your age, young man,' she said, and gave me the money, a big, crisp £5 note. I folded it up into a small square and hid it deep in my pocket.

Mum got back and immediately noticed that the machine was gone.

'Where is it?' she asked, a note of worry in her voice.

'Sold and paid for,' I replied.

'Did you get the £3 I was asking for it?'

'No.' I paused. 'I got £5.' Pulling the note out of my pocket, I passed it over to her. Mum was lost for words; she pulled me into a big hug and squeezed me tightly.

'Well done, Jeff! You're a real market trader now, and that's official!' Then she handed me a shilling and told me to go and buy a big bag of sweets to celebrate.

After that, I felt I could handle anything. Seven years old, selling by myself, and £5 in one go! My confidence soared. I had now found something I was good at!

As I got older, I was always on the lookout for 'business' opportunities. One day, I was up in the bedroom I shared with my parents. I was bored, so I decided to investigate my father's chest of drawers.

Opening the bottom drawer, I found some of his clothes: ties, socks, handkerchiefs – nothing of any great interest. The second drawer was pretty much the same, so I moved on to the top one. When I pulled it open, the runners slightly sticking, the contents were much more promising: tins, a jar of Brylcreem, belts and braces, and a wooden box, full of big cigars. My father bought them from the sailors and sold them on to the nightclub owners.

Taking one out of the box, I stood in front of the mirror posing, the cigar between my lips. The image of an eight-year-old with red curly hair grinned back at me. 'My mates would love this,' I thought to myself, and I decided to take it into school the following day.

The next day, sitting behind my desk, I waited until our teacher had his back to the class and pulled the cigar out of my pocket. Giving Raj, who was sitting next to me, a quick nudge, I showed him my 'surprise', sticking the cigar in my mouth and pretending to smoke it.

Word spread through the class, and all the boys were quietly sniggering at the sight of me sitting there 'puffing' away like a miniature Winston Churchill. The teacher turned around, but before he could catch me, the cigar had disappeared back into the depths of my blazer, and I was all innocence.

Hissed requests of 'Show it me' and 'Let's see it again' came from every direction, but I just mouthed, 'Later,' gesturing with my finger towards the classroom door. Come playtime, my mates were in for a treat!

When the bell rang, I was one of the first out, followed by an impatient gang of lads. Heading for the block of toilets in the playground, I found myself surrounded by about ten of them, all eager for a look at my cigar. We had all tried smoking a Woodbine at some stage, but a cigar was different. It was big and fat and smelled of rich tobacco. It was so grown-up.

A couple of the lads asked me if I was going to light it, others if they could have a smoke. I said the cigar was for look-see only.

'I'll pay yer for a puff,' said one lad.

'Me too,' said another. 'A penny for a puff – I've got the money here.' He put his hand in his pocket and pulled out a coin. I couldn't believe it. With the ten boys in the toilets with me, and the guy on dixie (lookout) by the toilet entrance, I could make nearly a shilling!

I arranged the 'Big Smoke' for the next day, managing to bring in with me some matches from a box Mum kept in the kitchen. At playtime we all made our way to the toilets, making a dash for it one at a time, trying to avoid the attention of the teacher on playground duty. We all gathered around one of the cubicles and I produced the cigar.

Striking a match on the wall and holding the flame to the end of the cigar, I puffed once or twice, lighting the tobacco as everyone watched in fascination. The end started to glow and a plume of smoke rose in the air. Everyone sniffed. We had all seen adults with cigars, or one of our heroes in the movies, but we'd never been this close to the real thing before. Puffing a few more times to make sure that the cigar was well lit, I held it out for the first lad to have a go.

The cubicle was already filling up with smoke, the taste in my mouth was awful and my eyes were watering. And after everyone had paid their penny and taken their turn, there were ten of us with streaming eyes, all coughing and feeling slightly queasy, but very grown-up.

Everyone agreed it was worth a penny, though I think the thought that, at any moment, a teacher could walk in and catch us was more enjoyable than the actual cigar. And we'd only smoked a small amount of it. I knew I had a money-spinner on my hands, so you can imagine how careful I was when I stubbed it out.

After that I became a bit of a hero to the other boys, and my reputation spread quickly throughout the school. Before long, there were loads of boys queuing up for a puff on my cigar. The money was rolling in, and I was able to give Mum quite a few shillings, telling her it was winnings from a game of marbles. But the cigar was getting smaller and smaller, and so was my business venture. I wasn't going to chance another one. I knew it would only be a matter of time before I was caught.

Sure enough, right in the middle of our last smoking session, dixie sounded the alarm. A teacher was coming! We all scrambled hastily in the direction of the nearest urinal, unzipping our flies as we went. Jonesy was in the middle of his puff and was left in the cubicle. He panicked, slamming the door shut and locking it just before the teacher burst into the toilets. 'We're done for!' I muttered to myself.

Mr O'Reilly stood blocking the entrance, scrutinizing each boy before walking down the row of doors. He moved quietly, taking one step at a time, pausing outside each door, pushing on it and watching it swing back and hit the tiled wall with a loud bang. To Jonesy, the slams must have sounded like the heavy footsteps of an approaching executioner. Then Mr O'Reilly came to the one door that was locked. We all stood there, a long row of boys facing the urinals, holding our willies and pretending to pee, acting as if nothing was wrong.

'Come on out,' O'Reilly called, banging on the cubicle door. 'I know you're in there, and I know what you're up to.'

'I'm on the toilet, sir,' Jonesy squeaked.

'No you're not. I know what you're doing. Open up at once!'

Jonesy was stalling for time. 'Honest, sir, I'm still sitting on the toilet. I'm not finished yet.'

'Not finished?' O'Reilly bellowed. 'By the time I'm finished with *you*, you won't be able to sit on anything for quite some time! Now open up!'

There were a few moments' silence, broken by the sound of a toilet being flushed. We all turned to look as the cubicle door opened. A thick cloud of smoke billowed out. It was so dense we couldn't see a thing, and for a moment it looked as if Jonesy had vanished into thin air! But there was no escape, and when Jonesy emerged, O'Reilly, coughing and waving his hand about to clear the air, took hold of him by the ear. Not letting go, he peered into the cubicle looking for evidence and saw it – a small brown object floating in the toilet bowl. The cigar had refused to cooperate!

Jonesy was frog-marched off to the headmaster's office while everyone else got on with spreading the news. Smoking at school could mean expulsion. And I knew Jonesy wouldn't last long under interrogation.

I was right: he cracked. I was summoned to the headmaster's office and asked where I had got the cigar. He wanted to make sure that it hadn't been stolen from a shop. Once I admitted that it was my father's, I was sent home to fetch my mother and told to come back with her as quickly as I could.

The journey from the house back to school was made in near silence. My mother's face was grim and her footsteps were very determined. I sat outside the office for what seemed an eternity, until she finally came out, the look on her face giving me a clear indication how angry she was.

We returned home, again in silence, but as soon as the door was closed, Mum went ballistic, shouting at me for stealing the cigar and for even looking in the drawers in the first place. She said I should have been expelled and that she was ashamed to have been asked to the school because of my bad behaviour. She was furious that she'd had to plead on my behalf and made to promise that I would never misbehave again if I was allowed to stay on.

Mum didn't speak to me for days afterwards, or even look at me. It was as if I didn't exist. And that was the worst punishment by far.

Several days later, she was doing some ironing and I was sitting at the kitchen table drawing, when she turned to me and asked, 'How much did you charge for a go on that cigar?'

'A penny a puff, Mum,' I replied.

'A penny a puff?' She almost sounded pleased, and when she looked away I could see the hint of a smile at the corners of her mouth.

5. Money for Old Rope

Money was often short, but Mum was very inventive and came up with all kinds of ways of making some, most of which involved us kids.

In the winter, we'd collect firewood from sites nearby that had been flattened by the Luftwaffe. The four of us would set off with Barry's steering cart and load it up again and again, and the following day, Mum would oversee a production line in the backyard. She and Barry would chop the wood into chips, Sheila and I would place them in a clamp and tie them into bundles with a thin piece of wire, then Lesley would stack them in the cart. Once it was full, myself and my two sisters would go knocking and sell the bundles door to door for tuppence each. There was just one simple rule: we were not allowed to sell our firewood on our street. Mum didn't want the neighbours knowing our business.

Another winter money-maker was shifting snow. If it snowed heavily during the night Mum would get us up early the following morning, wrap us up warmly and arm us with shovels and stiff brooms. We'd offer our services to the shops first, letting the shopkeepers set the price. They'd often throw in little extras, like an apple each or a bag of sweets.

All the other kids would be out playing in the snow, but it didn't bother us – we had a laugh while we were working, and we were helping Mum. At the end of the day we'd give her all the money we'd made and she in turn would reward us with pennies to go and buy ourselves some sweets.

In summer, Mum had us collecting jam jars and old newspapers. We'd tell people we needed them for painting at school, but we sold them to the rag-and-bone yard off Smithdown Road for a penny for four jars. On a good day we'd collect around sixty and make half a crown. The newspapers we gave to the nearest chippie in exchange for portions of chips. Smothered in salt and vinegar, to us, they tasted like the best chips in the whole wide world.

Mum often found work in the large houses in the posher parts of the city. As well as cleaning, she'd iron and make up fires; she could turn her hand to anything. There was one particular lady Mum cleaned for who would hide half-pennies underneath the ornaments. By doing this, she would know if Mum had been thorough dusting and also find out if she was honest or not. Mum was wise to it from the start, though. She'd go from room to room collecting all the coins and stacking them on the grand mantelpiece in the main room so the lady of the house would see them straight away. You couldn't fault Mum's honesty, but whether she actually went back and dusted underneath everything is debatable! The woman did appreciate Mum's work and her honesty, though, and was very generous to her and us kids, giving us all sorts of things to eat.

Mum could make a feast out of nothing. I remember my mouth would water at the smell of Scouse, the famous Liverpool dish, bubbling away on the cooker. Sometimes we'd just have a jam buttie, or a mug of Oxo with a chunk of bread to help it down, but it all tasted great. My favourite was 'pobs' – chunks of bread floating in a bowl of hot milk with a sprinkling of sugar on top.

Mum's greatest gift, however, was that you loved being at home with her: the house always seemed warmer and safer when she was there. Even though she had to do everything – bringing us up, taking care of the house and earning the money to support us – she still managed to give us more love than most other children got from both their parents.

We all learnt from Mum at a very early age that if we wanted something in life we had to work for it. Nothing came for free. As I grew up, I inherited jobs from my older siblings – it was almost a family tradition, passing jobs along like hand-me-down clothing.

My first job was running errands for Mrs Gilbert, who lived at the bottom of our street. Every afternoon after school I'd rush home and change out of my uniform. I had to be quick, as Mrs Gilbert expected me to be at her house no later than quarter to five. Otherwise I'd be too late to get her shopping done before the shops closed.

Mrs Gilbert was large – we kids reckoned she must have weighed about 25 stone – and found it very difficult to move around. As a result, she never left her house. She even left her front door ajar for me so she didn't have to get up to let me in. I had to take a deep breath before entering, because her house stank. It was the cats. No one knew how many she had, and they never went out. That deep breath was so important: the longer I could hold on to it, the better it was for me. I'd dash down the hallway and into the living room, grab the money and the shopping list and speed out the front door and into the fresh air. It always took me a couple of lungfuls to recover.

And the stink wasn't the only problem. I'd have to ask Mum or one of my sisters to decipher the shopping list. It could have been written in double Dutch for all I could make out. After a while, however, I got used to her handwriting, and when I realized she always wanted the same things, I found ways to manage it myself.

I did Mrs Gilbert's shopping Monday to Friday for three years, and was paid two shillings and sixpence a week. Of course, the money helped, but by making us work, Mum was also keeping us out of trouble!

Her own mother was a real character, and another task that had been passed down through us kids was asking Grandma Turner for a loan when money was scarce. She was a known money-lender in the neighbourhood and knew that our visits were predominantly 'business related', so I'd go in and call out, 'Hi, Grandma! Mum has sent me to borrow half a crown.'

She'd always be sitting in a large armchair in front of her fire, her skirts up around her knees, stirring the coals with a long poker. She would listen to my request, pull a disapproving face and 'tut-tut' several times. Then, slowly raising herself out of the chair, she would heave a big sigh before starting the most extraordinary ritual.

Once on her feet, she'd lift up her black, ankle-length skirt, revealing several grubby petticoats underneath. She would then slowly raise each petticoat, holding it with one hand, using her free hand to peel back the next one until she reached the final layer. She wore old flat black shoes and a saggy pair of socks, faded to dark grey and wrinkled around her ankles. Her legs, blotched with chilblains from the heat of the fire, came to an abrupt halt as they disappeared up into a long pair of bloomers.

Digging into the pockets of the small 'pinny' she wore on top of her bloomers, she would pull out a small book, letting the roll of petticoats drop to the floor. The book had a short length of pencil attached to it by a piece of string. Putting the tip of the pencil into her mouth, she would lick the lead, then turn to the 'Elsie' page, where she would make another entry.

'Tell your mother that she needs to come and see me,' she would instruct. 'She hasn't paid me for a long time. Are you listening to me?'

'Yes, Grandma,' I would reply. 'I'm listening.'

'This borrowing has got to stop. She has to pay me back the money and all the interest she owes me or she can't borrow any more. Do you understand?'

'Yes, Grandma,' I would say, feeling uncomfortable and just wishing she would give me the money so that I could get back home to Mum.

Book-keeping done, the whole process of raising the petticoats would start all over again, until the pinny was found and she could return the book to its safe place. Then she'd pull out a small purse, extract the money and place it firmly in the palm of my hand, closing my fingers over the coin. 'Take care of this now,' she would warn. 'Don't go losing it, because I won't be giving your mother any more.'

Clutching the money tightly and with Grandma's message firmly imprinted on my brain, I would run off as fast I could. I always felt so guilty, as if I was the one personally borrowing the money. Talk about shooting the messenger!

When I was nine, I inherited a new job, taking over from Barry after he'd started his first proper job. I was only small, and I wasn't really old enough, but my new job was to be a 'security guard' at the local wash house. The swimming pool and public baths were in the same place, and the swimming baths were very popular with the children, especially if you could swim four lengths without stopping. If you managed this, you got a free yearly pass. Mum encouraged us all to go to the baths, and Lesley and Barry taught Sheila and me how to swim. I'm sure Lesley was a much gentler teacher with Sheila than Barry was with me. He just pushed me in at the deep end when I was about five, watched as I floundered to the edge and told me to get on with it. And get on with it I did. It wasn't long before I was swimming as confidently as the others.

The public baths were for anyone and everyone who wanted a hot bath. For a shilling you could soak in a large tub full of steaming hot water – a real luxury, because there was no running hot water in the houses in that area. If you wanted a bath at home you had to boil kettle after kettle until you had enough hot water to fill a large metal hipbath. Every house had one, hanging on the backyard wall. But because bathing at home took so much effort, one bath would often be shared by the whole family.

Friday nights at the public baths were a hive of activity. Shop and factory girls, and men from the building sites and the docks – everyone would congregate there between five and seven o'clock. Although the bathing areas were segregated into male and female, before and after the bath was a great time to meet and chat. Many a marriage started at the baths, and many a friendship.

The wash house, before anyone had washing machines, was the public laundry, a place where women did their weekly wash. As most of the women had large families, with some members of the family doing very dirty jobs, it could take all day. The women came from miles around, with large bundles of washing tied up in a sheet and balanced on top of a pram.

At seven o'clock every Saturday morning, the busiest time of the week, I would be there, come rain or shine. My job was to guard the prams while the women did their laundry. At 7.15, the doors would open, and twenty women would go in. An hour later, another twenty would be allowed in, and so it went until midday.

The women had an hour to do their washing, and then they had to move to the wringers, passing the clothes through large mangles to wring the water out. This could take another hour. The washing was hung out to dry in a room heated by the hot-water pipes running from the boilers to the wash house and the public baths. While everything was drying, the women would escape from the heat and the steam of the drying room to the fresh air outside, smoking a cigarette or two and gossiping. And I would be standing outside too, keeping guard over all the prams.

Gangs of young lads were always on the lookout for wheels and other bits and pieces to make steering carts, so the prams were a target. Barry had shown me how to tie them together to stop them being stolen, attaching a long rope around a cast-iron railing at one end, threading it through the front two wheels of each pram and tying the other end to another railing. On Saturday mornings, knowing the prams would be lined up on the pavement, lads would turn up in groups, some as many as six, like hyenas prowling for prey.

They would laugh at me and taunt me, shoving me from side to side. I had to keep my distance so they couldn't actually grab me. If I fell into their trap, I'd be finished, and the prams would be nicked. So I'd dodge their lunges, moving all the time, edging closer to the main entrance. When it all got too much for me, and it often did, I would dart inside and call out for help. 'Quick, missus, quick. They're robbing your prams. Help, missus, I need some help.'

Like a stampeding herd of wildebeest, the nearest women would charge towards the door. Emerging into the daylight, sleeves rolled up above their elbows, they'd shout and scream at the lads outside, 'Get your hands off those prams, you little thugs!'

It was an awesome sight: sweat dripping off red faces, their hair tucked up under white mop caps, they were definitely not women to be argued with! I stood there feeling invincible; a pint-sized general with an army behind him, watching my enemies disappearing like rats down sewers.

I looked after those prams until I was twelve and made good money week after week – threepence a pram every Saturday morning. Pockets jingling, I would then return home happy, knowing what a difference it would make to Mum.

6. Sun, Sea and Scrap

My father's continual drinking and irresponsible behaviour were a source of constant worry to Mum. The uncertainty of the future plagued her, and she knew that as long as my father did night shifts in the taxi the problem wouldn't go away.

Something had to change, so Mum started thinking of a new business for him. In post-war Britain, there was a high demand for scrap metal, and there was plenty of it around with all the bombed-out sites. It was a relatively simple business, requiring a wagon, a driver and some 'sales skills'. Dad could handle the last two, so all we needed was a wagon. Mum borrowed some money from her sisters, enough to put a deposit down on a second-hand wagon with a long flat-bed and drop-down sides.

The blue Bedford had a covered cab at the front with two seats, and in between them a metal cover concealing the engine. Dad put an old blanket over it, and that is where Barry and I would sit. Dad would drive the wagon with Jack, his friend, who had experience and contacts in the scrap business and who, like Dad, could talk his way in and out of anything. Mum even had a telephone installed (the only one in our street) and some smart business cards printed: L. N. Pearce & Sons, Scrap Merchants. She was so proud of how professional they looked. We were now officially in business.

Setting off each morning, Dad and Jack would drive around Liverpool looking for scraps of abandoned metal. It could be anything: an old bicycle or pram, or debris from buildings – anything they could get their hands on. Meanwhile, Mum was contacting small companies and arranging for Dad to do pick-ups and deliveries.

Another little earner was selling wooden blocks. Mum had won a contract to remove and dispose of small oak blocks that had been used as paving on roads but were now stored in a large yard near the city centre. They'd been laid in tar, and Dad soon discovered that they burnt for ages and made great firewood! So every morning, we loaded up the wagon and went selling them. Barry and Jack would go knocking on doors calling out their sales spiel: 'We have served the Duke of York, the King of Cork and all the Royal family. Get your burning blocks now, ten for a shilling.' Dad would be driving the wagon slowly along the streets, beeping his horn. I would be on the back of the wagon, stacking them into piles of ten. It would take us all day to empty one wagonload but we didn't stop until every last one was sold. It was dirty work, and we were as black as tar ourselves by the time we were finished.

Listening to Dad and Jack talking, though, we soon learnt that it was worth all the hard work. On a good day we could make as much as £5 or £7 profit, which, considering the average weekly wage back then was £4 to £5, made it very good money.

Come the end of the day, Dad would announce that he had to 'take his medicine'. This meant driving to the nearest pub, where he would sup pint after pint. Barry and I would remain outside looking after the wagon, with a bottle of lemonade and a packet of crisps to keep us happy. 'Taking his medicine' could last up to three hours, and the pubs were often in the roughest parts of the city. On such occasions the two of us would be fighting for our lives, or so it seemed, against gangs of lads on the mooch looking for anything to steal.

Armed with long sticks, supposedly to intimidate them with, we must have been a bizarre sight – two small boys guarding a wagonful of goodies as if it were the Crown Jewels. Sometimes there were only three or four in the gang. We could handle that. Any more, and we'd be battling against half the gang while the others helped themselves. We couldn't even go for help, as Dad was not to be disturbed once he got into the pub. We hated every minute of those lonely nights. If it had just been Dad's drinking money, it wouldn't have mattered so much, but it was Mum's money too.

Financially, things started to improve, and Mum started to take us on more days out, one of our favourites being New Brighton on the ferry across the River Mersey. The huge open-air swimming pool there was one of my favourite places. It had a fifty-foot diving board, reaching high up into the sky. But while Lesley and Barry were brave enough to leap off the higher boards, Sheila and I would only jump off the lower ones.

On one occasion, Dad joined us on a day out at the baths and announced that he was going to dive off the top board. We all watched nervously as he climbed the steps to the top platform. Standing at the end of the diving board, he waved to us, a seemingly small figure in the distance, a hero about to take flight. He certainly seemed like a hero to me – no one ever dived off the top board. The pool was busy that day, and a hush fell over the crowd as thousands of pairs of eyes turned towards him. All that could be heard was the drone of insects in the heat of the summer sun.

Perfectly balanced at the end of the board, his arms outstretched, his toes gripping to the edge, Dad looked ready to dive. As I watched him push off and fly through the air, I was so proud – that was my dad! But when he landed in the water seconds later, the watching crowd gasped and groaned in sympathy. He had done the most perfect belly-flop from fifty feet in the air. He hit the water so hard that it splashed out of the pool, soaking all the sunbathers. His head broke the surface of the water, and he made his way to the steps at the side.

Slowly, he emerged, sheepishly pulling himself up the steps. Everyone could see his bright-red chest and belly, and the tops of his legs were crimson from the impact with the water as he hobbled towards us. He sat down beside us, and Mum looked at his chest and grinned. 'You daft thing,' she said. 'I thought you said you could dive?' We all burst out laughing, including Dad.

In the summer months, Dad and Jack would drive to North Wales. It was only fifty miles away, but with its rolling green mountains and sandy coastline it was a world away from city life. They didn't go for leisure though. They would visit farms scouting for disused equipment, doing a deal with the farmers before loading up the wagon and taking their collection to the scrap-metal yard.

Mum decided that, as Dad was spending so much time there, the family was also going to Wales, but this time for a holiday. It would be our first family holiday. She booked a small caravan near Prestatyn for two weeks. The holiday was the most amazing experience, with wide open spaces and green fields to run in, sand dunes to climb on and beaches that seemed to go on for miles.

One afternoon, the four of us were out exploring the fields around the campsite. We were walking in single file along the top of an old dry-stone wall, arms spread out on either side like tightrope walkers. Barry and Lesley were in front, followed by Sheila, while I lagged behind. Afraid they were going too fast and would leave me behind, I started to quicken my pace, trying to catch up with them. Suddenly a loud scream broke the stillness of the summer afternoon. The others turned, but there was no sign of me anywhere. Turning to retrace their steps, Barry noticed that the tops of the stinging nettles growing on one side of the wall were moving and a muffled yelping was coming from underneath.

'I think he's in there!' Sheila said, pointing at the nettles. 'What are we going to do?'

'I'm not getting in to pull him out,' said Barry. 'No way!'

Eventually, and after much coaxing from Barry and Lesley, I slowly made my way to the wall, crying out with every step. Taking my hands, Barry pulled me up. I was a big red lump, covered in so many blotches they seemed to be all joined as one. The pain was horrible. It felt like my body was on fire, and as the tears ran down my face, the saltiness of them made the rashes on my cheeks sting even more.

My mother, needless to say, was horrified when she saw me, and immediately sent the others off to find as many dock leaves as they could. She crushed them in her hands and rubbed them gently over my skin. When the initial stings had subsided, she smothered me in calamine lotion. I spent the next few days looking like a little pink shrimp.

Mum loved watching her children playing together and having a good time. She didn't stop smiling all the time we were there, and before leaving she arranged another holiday for the following year, negotiating six weeks' rental on a small wooden hut across the road from the campsite.

That second summer was the best holiday we ever had. We fell in love with our hut from the moment we opened the door. It was very basic, with a main room containing two sets of wooden bunks on facing walls, and a table and four chairs. In one corner, there was a small table with a gas stove sitting on top and shelves arranged above it. A sink attached to the wall beside it completed the living room-cum-kitchen. One other small room contained a double bed, ideal for Mum (and Dad when he came to stay). Toilet and washing facilities were available at the campsite across the road.

Most of our time there was spent playing and having fun, but we did occasionally resort to ways and means of earning money – some ideas more imaginative than others.

Near the beach was a shop that sold buckets and spades, ice creams, sweets and lemonade. At the end of a hot summer's day we would walk along the beach collecting empty lemonade bottles. The lady who ran the shop would give us a halfpenny for each bottle, with which we would then buy sweets.

It didn't take Barry and Lesley long to realize that the empty bottles were stacked in crates at the rear of the shop. If we hadn't collected enough bottles to buy sweets that day, they'd sneak around the back and remove some of the empties from the crates to make up the numbers.

Sadly, one day, it all went wrong. We were just about to walk up the hill back to the hut, already chewing our sweets, when I noticed some full bottles of lemonade by the door of the shop, this wonderful place where, like magic, Lesley and Barry would produce sweets out of nothing. With the innocence of a six-year-old, I thought everything in this magical place was free, so picking up two bottles, one each for Barry and Lesley, I set off at a steady pace behind them.

But as they got to the top of the hill, Lesley heard somebody shouting. Looking back down the hill, they saw me, struggling to keep hold of the bottles, with an irate shop owner chasing after me, waving her fist in the air and shouting, 'Put them down, you little thief.' In a flash, Barry was racing down the hill towards me. He grabbed the bottles from my hands, placed them carefully on the ground, picked me up and threw me over his shoulder, turned and ran up the hill.

They made me promise not to tell Mum, cross my heart and hope to die, and to swear I would never do anything like that ever again. I had spoilt everything, as we couldn't go back to the shop any more in case we were reported to the police.

The holiday eventually came to an end. We'd had the most fabulous six weeks; even Mum enjoyed herself. Sadly, we never holidayed again as a family – our six weeks of sunshine was only the second holiday we had ever had, and it was the last.

Once back home, life carried on as normal; a million miles away from the sea and sand and the simple happiness of our little hut by the beach.

Our scrap business was doing well, although Dad did have problems finding somewhere to park the wagon, and one morning he woke up to find all six tyres had been let down. What finally killed it, though, was when Dad slipped a disc lifting a heavy piece of scrap iron on to the wagon. He was taken to hospital he was in so much pain, and ended up spending two months in traction sleeping on a wooden board before he was allowed home.

Mum tried to keep the business going by employing a driver to work alongside Jack. Unfortunately, it didn't work out, and as she couldn't keep up the payments on the wagon, it was repossessed by the finance company.

The scrap business had been good to us while it lasted. We'd had two fantastic summer holidays out of it, and we'd also had a taste of family life as it could be, where money or the lack of it was not the overriding concern. Mum started to think of new business ideas and Dad returned to the taxis.

Old habits die hard, and the ritual of getting ready for a night in his cab was resumed. But this time there was a new layer to be added: he now needed a corset to provide support for his back. He had selected this garment with care, choosing a corset 'worn by the stars'. Occasionally, we'd catch a glimpse of him putting it on. As he held it in place, Mum would be behind him, pulling the laces as tightly as she could while he emitted grunts of protest. And all the while she'd be smiling broadly, from the safety of behind his back.

7. Tears and Torment

I remember the day I started at junior school, aged seven. Mum thought Barry's school was too rough and that the boys there would pick on me, especially as I still couldn't write my own name, so she chose Sefton Park secondary school, a little further away.

I was very nervous that first day. It was a big school, with about a hundred boys to every year, split into three bands. Band A was for the bright sparks, B for the average Joes and Band C for 'the thickies'. Although I was a confident young lad in many ways, I was always apprehensive about school, and my first two days were made even more horrible because we had to sit exams so they could decide which band we'd be in.

Exams were pure torture. I'd find myself staring at a piece of paper, my eyes darting all over it as I tried to pick out words that were familiar to me. The tick of the clock was deafening, and as I got more tense and more panicky, even those words would seem to vanish from the page. I'd glance at the boys on either side, as if for reassurance that I was not alone.

By copying their actions and flicking through pages, or resting my head on my hand while I pretended to study the question before me, I created an image of being in control, while in reality I felt I was drowning. If only there'd been a calming voice or a helping hand to lead me through, to take the edge off my tension, it might have been different. As it was, I was alone in my misery, feeling like the only stupid person in the whole world. The excitement of a new school and new friends to meet was overshadowed by the horror of those first two days, and I cried myself to sleep both nights. Only Mum knew what I was going through.

I was placed in Band C, with thirty-three other boys. We were a bunch of misfits – no-hopers. Some were from what we called in those days 'broken homes', and had no father and no discipline in their lives at all; for others, English was their second language. But rather than being singled out for assistance, we were shunted to one side. We weren't worth the time or trouble.

Although small, I was quite popular in my class, as I had a lot of confidence and could think on my feet. After a while, I enjoyed my time at Sefton Park Juniors, if only because I became a member of the football and swimming teams. The reading and writing didn't get any easier though. Some teachers did try to help, but they quickly gave up, unable to understand how it was that somebody who could talk so well and seemed so bright just couldn't get the simplest words when they were written down. One or two got angry with me and said I was lazy and showed no interest. They would stand me in the corner of the classroom facing the wall with a tall dunce's hat on my head. It didn't encourage me to try harder, it just made me feel worse.

One teacher in particular really had it in for me and said if I didn't try to improve I would be sent to a special school for backward children. I had seen groups of mentally handicapped children waiting for the bus to collect them in the mornings, and the thought frightened the life out of me.

There wasn't much research into dyslexia back then, and a lot of schools didn't know anything about it. Some people thought it was a form of mental illness while others believed it was just an excuse for laziness. It wasn't until the mid-1960s that it was recognized as a difficulty resulting from a reduced ability to associate visual symbols with verbal sounds. Up till then it was referred to as 'word blindness', and confined to the domain of medical specialists. Although it's a lifelong condition, with the right help it can be overcome and dyslexics can learn to adapt to their limitations, but in my case, and that of thousands of other children at the time, that help was just not available.

At school, I did put my other talents to use, however. I certainly wasn't Mr Goodie-Two-Shoes. The playground was perfect for developing my entrepreneurial skills, and I'd sell single cigarettes and marbles, and set up bets on games of conkers.

Marbles were the best business for me. I played well, so my pockets were always full of them. A bag from the sweetshop cost tuppence, whereas I cannily charged half the price, ensuring a good turnover. The ironic thing was that many a boy who lost his marbles to me during a game ended up buying them back the following day.

Mum was constantly tired, and it worried me. She was becoming more irritable, snapping at everybody and shouting at me for the slightest thing I did wrong. It just wasn't like her.

I'd lie in bed at night listening to Mum and Dad yelling at each other downstairs. It went on for weeks, then one afternoon I found out what the problem was. I was coming downstairs and overheard Lesley and Sheila talking in their bedroom. Mum was having a baby.

Hurtling down the rest of the stairs, I ran into the kitchen, straight over to Mum. 'Is it true, Mum?' I asked. 'Are you going to have another baby?' She stopped what she was doing and bent down to give me a big hug.

'Yes, Jeff, it's true.' We stayed there for a few minutes, our arms around each other. 'The baby is due in November. Just think, you'll have a little brother or sister to play with this Christmas. Santa is coming early.'

All the shouting I had overheard over the past few weeks was Mum reading Dad the riot act, which must have paid off, because he was around much more, and although he still smelled of alcohol in the mornings, he was nowhere near as drunk as before. This lasted for several months, which made for a much happier atmosphere at home.

Months passed, and all the kids on our street and around were parading their guys around to raise money for fireworks on Bonfire Night. It was 4 November, and I was out collecting firewood for the next night when I heard Barry shouting for me. When I got in the house, Lesley told us that Mum had been rushed to hospital. 'She's going to be all right,' she said, 'but you all have to be good, as I'm in charge while Mum is away.'

Lesley allowed Sheila and me to join all our friends at our street bonfire at 6.30 that evening. We stood in a circle watching the flames licking their way up towards the guy on the top. By the time he started to burn, the bonfire was taller than the houses, the sparks shooting out in all directions, crackling and spitting. Fireworks were popping and cascading beautiful colours into the night sky – it was perfect! Keeping our promise to Lesley, the two of us were home by nine, happy, tired and smelling of woodsmoke. And once our heads hit our pillows, we quickly fell asleep.

In the early hours of the following morning, Mum gave birth to a perfect little baby girl, June Karen Pearce. When she came home a few days later, bringing our little sister with her, Mum told us that it was the sound of the fireworks that had woken little June up, which is why she was born when she was!

8. On the Never-Never

Despite the financial difficulties of winter, Mum always made Christmas the most magical time of year – she would pay for it later. Debt after the festive season was part of the tradition – a custom, almost like Christmas trees and chocolate Santas. With no savings or extra money to spend, there was one option available, and that was to apply for credit from companies who specialized in 'helping out'. The Provident was one of the best.

In the weeks before Christmas, a rep from the Provi would be out knocking on doors asking if you needed any help over the festive season. The answer was always yes. A sum would be agreed – anywhere between £20 and £40 – and then the interest, always high, was added and the total weekly repayment worked out. Within a week the salesman would come by again, bringing you your 'Provi cheque'. It was the difference between Christmas feast and Christmas famine, but it was so hard to pay back. Mum would spend most of it on new school uniforms for each of us and, most importantly, new shoes. She'd also make sure that we all had one good Christmas present each.

Another form of credit was available from a most obliging Jewish gentleman called Harry Shapiro. Harry didn't offer cheques but called at doors laden with items no housewife could do without: warm blankets in the middle of winter, or a beautiful tablecloth, just as the final touches were being put to the Christmas decorations.

'You can have them, Mrs Pearce,' he would say, 'for ten shillings, and you can pay me only a shilling a week until you are clear.' It was a good deal. Within two weeks, he would be back with something else, and another deal would be struck. And so it went on, like a form of rolling credit, and you didn't pay off what was owed for many, many years.

Harry Shapiro would call every Friday without fail to collect his money. Sometimes, Mum didn't have it for him so she'd tell me, 'When he comes, don't open the door. Just say, "Me mum's not in." Do you understand?' Rolling my eyes with exasperation, I'd tell her I understood.

One Friday the knock came and I shouted down the hall in what I thought was a grown-up voice, 'Me Mum says to tell you she's not in.'

After a few moments the letterbox flap was raised, and Harry Shapiro's eyes peered at me. Then he moved his head so that his mouth was framed by the letterbox and said, 'Go and tell your mother she *is* in and I want my shilling.'

I went down the hallway to the kitchen and relayed the message to Mum. 'All right,' she replied. 'Tell him I'll give him his bloody shillings next week. I promise.'

Traipsing down the hall once again, I repeated Mum's message under my breath several times so I wouldn't forget it. I leaned towards the letterbox flap, and as if by magic it lifted and I found myself looking Harry Shapiro straight in the eye. 'Me Mum says you'll get your shillings next week. Oh and she bloody promises.' He looked at me for a moment before dropping the flap, then I heard his footsteps walking away, no doubt going to the next house to go through the ritual all over again!

The Co-Op man would call once a week, too, for a penny

payment towards funeral insurance, and the 'Pools man' would come to collect the weekly coupon for the Littlewoods Football Pools. Mum used to say that winning it would get us out of this mess one day. The streets were a buzz of activity on Friday afternoon and early evening, as all the different debt collectors were out knocking on doors trying to collect their money. Even some local shops offered credit: our favourite was Mary's.

Mary was a middle-aged woman who ran a small shop just around the corner from our house. The shelves reached to the ceiling and were stacked with dry provisions such as tea and sugar and tinned goods, and she also sold milk, butter and bread. But best of all were the jars full of sweets – lemon sherbets, Drumsticks and Refreshers, wine gums and Everton mints – prominently displayed so that children of all ages and heights could see them. Some were sold by weight, tuppence a quarter, but you could also get a penny mix.

Mum would send us there for groceries, telling us to ask Mary to put it in the book. There were quite a few occasions, however, when she would refuse, telling me to go back and tell Mum that we couldn't have anything else until our 'account' had been settled. We then had to steer clear of Mary's for a while, until Mum had enough money to pay the bill.

Mum was good at teaching me how to trade, but it was Dad who showed me the art of selling.

Christmas was only six weeks away, and this year it was going to be different. Mum had come up with another of her clever business ideas. With a little financial assistance from Aunty Joyce and Mac, her gentleman friend, Mum put her plan into action: Dad and Mac were going into business selling stockings on

Saturdays outside T. J. Hughes, a large department store in the heart of Liverpool. Mum organized everything, from where to buy the stock to how it should be sold and for how much. Then she wrapped the stockings in cellophane and packed them into an old suitcase.

That first Saturday morning, I, aged eight, was sitting on the stairs listening to my parents discuss what they were planning to do. It sounded so exciting, and after a while I built up enough courage to say, 'Dad, can I come with you?'

'It would be very good for him, you know, Les,' said Mum. 'A son should spend time with his father, and he'd be an asset to you. I've taught him lots on the markets, and he learns very fast.'

Dad shook his head from side to side, a clear 'no' in any language, but then he stopped and smiled. 'Of course you can, Jeff. Go and get your coat. And I might even buy you a pint on the way home.'

Mum's response to this last comment was very clear: 'Don't you even think about it!'

That Saturday morning, the street was busy even when we arrived, with barrow boys setting up their carts. The barrow boys were 'legal' and had street-trading licences, usually passed down from generation to generation. These were like gold dust. We were 'illegal' traders or fly-pitchers. If we were caught by the police, it would mean instant arrest, confiscation of property and a court appearance, with a fine anywhere between £10 and £20, so the stakes were high.

Dad and Mac discussed the best position and the getaway strategy should the 'bizzies' (police) show up. There was a free spot just inside the corner entrance of T. J. Hughes, so while

Mac acted as lookout on the opposite corner, where he could see up and down the road, Dad took up position. Dressed in his camel-hair Crombie, with his signature starched collar and wearing a bright-yellow tie, he looked as if he owned the department store. And not only did he have the looks, he had bags of charm, too, a way of talking to people that made them feel important. Listening to his words was like collecting pearls of wisdom. And he could twist people around his little finger.

So there we were on a cold winter's morning, Pearce, Son & Associates, ready to do battle with the elements, the authorities and potential customers. Now it started: 'Here we are, ladies, here we are.' Dad's patter rolled off his tongue. 'Nineteen-denier stockings, two pair for half a crown . . . All perfect, just like me!' Women of all ages soon gathered around to have a look.

'Me old man's on nights,' said one. 'I wouldn't mind a bit of company, if you know what I mean.'

'Hey, handsome, I'll take four pair off yer, if you'll put them on for me,' called out a very large lady in a loud voice. Everyone laughed at this, which got the day off to a fine start.

There was no doubt about it, Dad could sell. And I could see the effect his charm and good looks had on the female customers – and how they looked at him. I'm sure if I'd understood half the things they said to him, I would have been shocked. But I was only eight. I'd mention what they said to Mum when we got home, but she would just laugh and say, 'They can look at him all they want as long as they keep on buying.'

Before we started, I'd been told how important my job was. I had to kneel down on the ground in the doorway next to the open suitcase and pass the stockings up to my Dad for each customer. Above all, I was to do what I was told. If Mac saw a policeman, he would give Dad a warning nod, then Dad would tell me and I was to close the suitcase and casually stroll into the store, drawing as little attention to myself as possible. Afterwards, I was to meet him at the side entrance and we'd join Mac in the café across the road until the coast was clear. Then we'd take up position again and continue trading.

We soon got into a routine, and after a busy Saturday's trading, we'd head to the café at about five o'clock. Dad ordered a large pot of tea, and he and Mac talked to the other traders. Dad would empty his pockets and split the money with Mac, passing any left-over small change to me as my wages. Dad always stopped off at the pub on the way home for a couple of pints, while I waited outside with the obligatory bottle of lemonade and a packet of crisps.

In the run-up to Christmas, we started selling wrapping paper too, and everything was going well. We were eating good food and we had warm clothes. We also had enough money for coal and even the occasional treat. We felt very proud of ourselves – the Pearces were coming up in the world!

Then, one Saturday morning, I got a nod and a kick from Dad. There was a policeman heading towards us, and I panicked. I snapped the suitcase closed, lifted it over my head and dashed into the store. All that would have been visible to the shoppers inside was a large suitcase on top of a pair of skinny little legs running straight at them.

Due to my mad dash, a path quickly opened up, like I was Moses parting the Red Sea. But my escape abruptly ended when I collided with the large belly of a man wearing grey trousers and dirty boots – all I could see of him. The suitcase bounced back off his stomach, flying through the air. When I looked up, I saw the angry red face of a store detective staring down at me.

He grabbed me by the arm, picked up the suitcase and frog-marched me to the manager's office. I kept trying to pull away, but the more I tried, the redder his face would become and the tighter his grip. Hauling me into the office, he plonked the suitcase on the floor and turned to the manager sitting behind the desk.

'Here he is, sir, one of the culprits who sell right outside our shop.' Lifting the suitcase on to the desk, he went to open it, as if I had just robbed the Bank of England and he was going to find hundreds of pound notes inside. The manager looked first at the large suitcase, then at me. I could tell he was thinking I was small enough to fit inside the case myself.

He had just begun to ask me who my accomplices were when the door was thrown open with so much force it nearly flew off its hinges, and Dad appeared. He looked like a cross between Hopalong Cassidy and Flash Gordon as he burst into the room. 'That's my son,' he yelled, lifting me up with one hand. 'And that's my suitcase,' he added, grabbing the case up off the desk with the other. 'I will thank you to leave them both alone!'

The store detective leapt forward as if to stop him, but Dad swung the suitcase in his direction, making him retreat to safety behind the manager's desk. The manager started shouting at Dad: 'We don't want you outside our shop selling. Not *ever* . . . you got that?'

Turning his back on the two men, Dad merely replied, over his shoulder, 'I'll make a note of that. And you know what I'll do with it then . . . don't you?'

Nobody ever bothered us again. That corner entrance to T. J. Hughes department store became Dad's pitch. And he sold his wares from there, chatted up ladies and successfully avoided the bizzies for many years to come.

9. Silver Blades

I was now eleven, and it was time to move up to the seniors. I wasn't looking forward to it, and neither were any of my classmates in Band C. The only saving grace was that I was not going to be alone this time. My mates and I would be together. We had shared our lives for four years in the juniors and knew each other's strengths and weaknesses. We knew we could rely on each other. What's more, for the first time, we could wear long trousers, something which certainly set us apart from the littl'uns, and made us feel more like men.

The other thing that made all the difference was Mr Beesley, the sports teacher; he was an inspiration to hundreds of pupils. He knew how to get the best out of us all, finding a strength in each individual child, making each one of us feel that he had something worthwhile to contribute. He was a small man and looked so young he had to wear a moustache so as not to be mistaken for one of the pupils. He drove a little yellow three-wheeled Reliant, and would take us to matches and sporting events in it. With three boys crammed in the back, another boy sitting next to him in the front, and the boot and any spare space stuffed with our sports kit and equipment, we would chug along to our destination.

It was amazing how much we could fit into that car. But it was vulnerable to wind, and the slightest gust would catch under the front, raising the front wheels off the road and the bonnet up in the air so that all that could be seen through the windscreen was the sky. Whenever this happened, Mr Beesley would call out to us, 'Lean forward, boys! Lean forward!', so we'd do as he said, until the front wheels bumped back down on to the road again. It must have been quite a sight in a gale-force wind – a little car bouncing up and down as it drove along, full of schoolboys bobbing about inside.

Mr Beesley organized all types of sporting activities, and many of them meant you missed classes. As a result, he had many keen sportsmen, me being one of them, signing up for anything we could.

I loved swimming, and we were fortunate to have a pool in the school basement, which the swim team used every lunchtime for training. It was quite small, but it enabled us to build up our technique and speed, which paid off once we started swimming against other schools. We won more and more.

Occasionally, Mum and June would come along to watch and support me. Mum was always proud of me, no matter how poorly or well I did, but of course she loved it when I won. We would walk home laughing and talking about the competition, with me narrating every second of my race and June tagging along, listening with a big smile on her face.

After one of these occasions, another boy, Paul Cole, started to tease me in the playground. He had a reputation for being a 'hard case', which translated into being a good fighter. 'Who's a mummy's boy then?' he taunted. 'I saw yer last night, walking home with your mummy!' His friends were all laughing and teasing me, shouting out 'Nancy boy' and 'Mummy's pet', and nasty things about my mother. I could take his taunting me, but bringing my mother into it was a different matter!

I saw red. Without stopping to think, I ran straight at him, hitting him in the stomach, knocking him to the ground. Landing on top of him, I continued to hit out, and within seconds we were rolling around on top of each other. Suddenly the school bell rang. And as the other boys pulled us apart and we got to our feet, he shouted, 'I'll have you at four o'clock, Pearce.'

The school grapevine worked fast: within a couple of hours the whole school knew that Cole and Pearce were having a fight at hometime. I didn't want to fight Cole, but there was no way out. He had laid down the challenge, and unless I wanted to be looked down on as a coward, I would have to face up to him.

Our crowds of supporters started to build, splitting the school in two. Both sides wanted blood. Cole was ranked as fourth 'cock' of the school, i.e. the fourth-best fighter. As for me, I was just a nobody.

As four o'clock drew nearer, my supporters were crowding round to give me advice. From the way they were going on, anyone would have thought they were professional trainers, but I couldn't recall any of them having been involved in a fight themselves. They were filling my mind with nonsense, my stomach was churning with nerves, and there was nothing I could do except put on a brave front as the minutes ticked away.

When the school bell announced the end of the day, almost as one, hundreds of boys burst through the school doors, swarmed across the playground and out to the 'field of honour' – a wide alleyway nearby. Any teacher watching must have realized that there was something afoot, but as soon as we were out of sight we were out of their minds.

I was swept along, surrounded by my supporters, pressed in on all sides by helpful advisors. Cole and his crowd were ahead of us, and the lads kept on turning back to continue their taunting. When we got to the alleyway a circle started to form, one half made up of Cole's followers, the other half mine. Hands were pulling off my blazer, and the advice came thick and fast. 'Cole is going to *kill* Pearce,' someone shouted. 'Cole is history. He's a wimp,' came the retort from my side. 'Pearce is gonna knock him out!' 'Pearce is dead!'

While the two crowds hurled abuse at each other, I stood there almost paralysed, staring at Cole, who was punching the air with his fists, looking like a professional featherweight. I wanted to turn and run. I wanted to say to them all, 'I'm sorry, lads, but I have to go and do Mrs Gilbert's shopping.' But by this stage, there was obviously no chance of that working.

If they had wanted blood before, they really wanted it now. And they didn't care whose it was. There was no way I was going to risk disappointing them. To chants of 'Oooh, Oooh, Oooh' and 'Fight, fight, fight,' I found myself being pushed into the middle of the circle, face to face with Cole, a few inches away. I knew he was two years older and was bigger than me, but it was his reputation that was scary. I'd been in a couple of small scraps before, but nothing like this. This was my first real fight, and it would determine my whole future at school. The adrenaline was rushing through my body, and I found myself feeling exactly the same as I had when I was on the back of Dad's wagon, or standing in front of the wash house guarding the prams.

Barry's words rang through my head, as clearly as if he was standing next to me: 'Attack, Jeff. Attack is the best form of defence.' Then I just steamed in, hitting Cole as many times as I could in the face, the ribs, the chest – anywhere I could land a punch. As my knuckles made contact with his nose, pressing it flat against his face, I felt the warm stickiness of his blood on my fist. It spurred me on, and I continued to lash out until suddenly he fell to the ground, curling up in a ball to protect himself, his arms around his head.

'Kick him! Kick him!' the spectators urged. 'Kick him hard, Pearce!'

But Cole had had enough and was crying out, 'No more! No more!' The fight was over. Out of breath, I stood there, looking down at Cole on the ground. I couldn't quite believe it – it really was all over! I was unscathed, not even one punch hitting me, while Cole lay in a small huddle at my feet. My supporters crowded around me, raising my hands into the air, as if I was the victor in a world-title fight.

After defeating Cole, I automatically replaced him in the pecking order as fourth cock, but although I liked the title, I didn't want to have to fight every other day to keep it, preferring to keep my head down. I got into enough trouble, both in and out of school, and I wasn't planning on looking for any more!

One thing that really did save me from getting into trouble was ice skating. Dad's oldest sister, Aunty Doris, worked at the Silver Blades ice rink, which was about three miles from our house, and one afternoon she came by with two free tickets for Sheila and me. The following Sunday, the two of us entered a whole new world, and we both fell in love with it. Seeing how much we enjoyed it, after that, Aunty Doris tried to get us tickets as often as possible. It certainly stopped me spending so much time just hanging around on street corners with a gang of lads, just looking for something to do.

The poorer areas of Liverpool, like any big city, were also the roughest, where crime flourished. Smaller boys were encouraged to follow in the footsteps of the older lads, starting with petty theft before graduating to more serious crimes. It was almost an accepted part of growing up, and the lads I knocked around with were no exception. We started off with unlocked cars and the backs of lorries, on the lookout for anything worth nicking, then it'd be small shops. If you managed that, it meant promotion to the more profitable targets – people's houses.

I was pulled in too, on a couple of occasions, but I had a permanent sick feeling at the bottom of my stomach whenever we were up to no good. I liked my friends and wanted to be accepted as part of the gang, but this wasn't the way it was going to happen. It just wasn't for me. If the truth be known, the prospect of being found out and punished by my mother was far more terrifying than being bullied by the kids on the street for not joining in!

Sheila and I started to make new friends at the ice rink, which made going there even more fun. I teamed up with a boy called Bernie Snagg who, like me, had been on the verge of falling in with the wrong crowd. He and I would meet up there on Sunday afternoons and Wednesday nights. I still kept all my jobs, running errands for Mrs Gilbert every afternoon after school and working Saturday mornings at the wash house. Even if I had wanted to, with all this going on, I wouldn't have had time to get into trouble!

We would have skated all day every day if we'd had the money, but because the ice had to be resurfaced and refrozen at intervals throughout the day, there were three sessions at weekends and during school holidays, so to skate all day, you had to pay three times. It took us a while, but we came up with a plan.

There was a balcony on the first floor that ran the whole way round the rink, and Bernie and I had found a door at the back of it leading into an old changing room. There was hardly ever anyone on the balcony and the room was only used by the speed-skating team, on Tuesday and Thursday nights, so we decided to hide in there between sessions and hopefully remain undiscovered.

The first Sunday we put our plan into action we were nervous wrecks. As 12.30 approached, I told Sheila I was going to Bernie's house and would see her later. I couldn't tell her what I was really up to, particularly with Aunty Doris working at the rink. It would have been too embarrassing – for all the family – if we were caught. As quickly and as quietly as possible, we made our way upstairs to the changing room, then sat down and waited. There were benches and a row of metal lockers, so we decided that, if we heard anyone coming, we'd hide in them. Hardly breathing, let alone whispering, in case anyone heard us, the time seemed to drag so slowly, every creak or sound becoming a warning that we'd be discovered.

Finally, we heard the organ music for the beginning of the next session starting up and knew we had almost succeeded. Now all we had to do was to get back down on to the ice without being detected. We tiptoed to the door, pausing at the slightest noise. Then, opening it slightly, we peered through the narrow gap to make sure the coast was clear.

Fortunately, there was no sign of the dreaded Mr Kay, the rink manager, a man who seemed to have eyes in the back of his head. Still crouching, we made a dash for it, skates clutched to our chest so they wouldn't bump against anything and make a noise.

The relief of success made our enjoyment of being back on the ice even greater, and as we laughed and skated around, Bernie and I felt like two stowaways who had crossed the Seven Seas!

For at least the next eight or nine Sundays, we managed to pull this off, each time spending the whole day at the rink and only paying once. Then something happened which changed it all.

A man named Hughie ran the ice-rink-maintenance gang, and Bernie and I had been pestering him for months for a job. One afternoon, we had emerged from our hiding spot and were about to head out on to the ice when a hand landed on my shoulder. Startled, I turned to find Hughie standing behind me with a solemn expression on his face. I immediately thought that Bernie and I had been found out and were about to be punished. As the weight of the hand bore down on my shoulder, I began to imagine all the different types of punishment that awaited me. Public humiliation in front of everyone (including Aunty Doris)? A lashing at the hands of Mr Kay, watched by my friends and family? Or something even worse – being banned for life from the ice rink, never to skate again? I was finished; it was all over for Bernie and me. But before I could say anything, Hughie spoke: 'Lads, I need to talk to you in my office.'

Bernie and I looked at each other, fear written all over our faces. Letting go of my shoulder, Hughie started walking in front of us, with Bernie and me following. Our legs were shaking so badly we could hardly keep up and we were frantically signalling to each other. Bernie was forming a hangman's noose with his hands – yes, we were dead men!

In his office, Hughie sat down at his desk before continuing. 'You know those jobs you two have been on at me about? Well, they're now available. What do you think? Do you still want them?' I was so overwhelmed with relief I nearly wet my pants. Seeing I had lost my voice, Bernie jumped in for us both.

'Dead right we do,' he almost shouted. I just stood there next to him nodding, a big grin on my face.

So we became part of the ice-gang, working for Hughie, and in return we got a small wage, but most importantly, free permanent passes which allowed us to come in and out of the rink whenever we wanted. Our dreams had come true!

I gave up my job at the wash house to concentrate more on my new job at the rink and my passion for skating. Bernie and I literally lived there, skating every free moment we had. In the six weeks of the summer holidays, we never missed a day. It was the best time of our lives. For the first time, we both felt really important, doing proper jobs. And we felt that we belonged to something bigger than the small world we had grown up in.

We soon got the knack of scraping the ice. And we were working there just at the right time. As with everything in the 1960s, times were changing, and Mr Kay announced that he was going to build a discotheque on the balcony to attract more teenagers, so the organist was replaced by a DJ.

It was about this time Bernie and I discovered our hormones. Suddenly girls were mysterious; they smelled nice, they moved differently . . . The girls we knew were changing, developing into young women, and these physical changes fascinated us. Girls were no longer just sisters or friends, they had become objects of desire.

I soon noticed a very pretty young girl called Kim. She was not only about the same age as me but also the same height, which to me made us a perfect match. She had shoulder-length golden-blond hair and big blue eyes. Whenever I spotted her on the ice with her friends I'd start to skate closer to her, casually getting nearer and nearer, then acting surprised to see her there next to me. After doing this a few times I plucked up the courage not only to start skating alongside her but also to talk to her. Of course, when it came to it, I was completely tongue-tied. I had waited all week for this moment, and now I had another week before I could speak again. But that would at least give me more than enough time to practise my lines. And that's how I fell in love for the first time.

I started to wash my hair every day and helped myself to Barry's Old Spice, splashing it all over and leaving the house smelling like a tart's boudoir, and clothes became important to me too. It was all part and parcel of creating the right image to impress Kim: I was going to ask her out on a date. After a great deal of input on Bernie's part and endless speculation on mine, I decided on a very simple plan. Kim caught the same bus home as me but got off a couple of stops before mine. I would just ask if I could take her home after skating.

I was so nervous and, like all young boys, so scared of rejection that it took me several weeks to find the courage to ask her. From the way I was behaving, anyone would have thought I was about to propose!

That day, we had been circling the ice for a good few minutes, and she was on her own, her friends having gone for refreshments — perfect, as there would be no audience to laugh at me if she said no. So taking a deep breath, I launched into my proposal, trying to sound as casual as possible and hoping she wouldn't notice the tremor in my voice. 'Can I take you home after skating tonight?' I asked.

'Yes, she said, smiling at me as if she had known for some time that I was going to ask her this and had rehearsed her answer dozens of times. Was it really that simple? I let out a huge sigh of relief, which I was sure was heard all round the rink. I was amazed. I just had to tell Bernie, so mumbling some excuse, I skated away as fast as I could to look for him. It was official: I was about to have my first date!

So much planning had gone into it that I knew exactly what I had to do. We'd get off the bus together at her stop and then I'd walk her to her front door. After a few minutes' conversation I'd lean forward and give her a kiss goodnight, creating the impression that this was something I had done many times before. Kim would be so impressed she would want to go out with me again.

That evening, when the ice rink closed, we walked side by side towards the bus stop. Kim linked her arm through mine as if it was the most natural thing in the world. I felt like an adult – this whole dating thing was so grown-up. We were more like a couple of sophisticated twenty-year-olds than green thirteen-year-olds.

When the bus came, downstairs was full, so we had to make our way upstairs to try and find a seat. But I couldn't have picked a worse evening: the top deck was almost full, too, with men and women returning home from the pubs around town. The conversation was loud, the air was thick with cigarette smoke, and it didn't look as if there were two seats together. Then I saw two at the very front and, taking Kim's hand, literally dragged her towards them before anyone else tried to grab them. We sat down together, and the pressure was momentarily off. I gave a little sigh of relief to myself before I continued my role of leading man.

A moment or two went by, and then Kim leaned over and whispered in my ear. 'I've lost my shoe,' she said.

'What?' I couldn't believe what I'd heard.

Again she leaned into me and whispered, 'I've lost my shoe, I think it's downstairs.' I looked down in disbelief and saw that she wasn't joking. I looked up at her and frowned. 'Please can you go and get it for me?' she pleaded.

I was starting to feel all hot and bothered, sweating at the thought of pushing through all those drunk people. In my experience, you could never tell what people would do when they'd had a few. I'd seen my father fly off the handle often enough, in a rage over nothing. The last thing I needed was for one of the passengers to have a go at me as I searched the bus – for a missing shoe, of all things. With these thoughts going through my mind, I started to walk back along the bus, holding on to the seat rails to keep my balance as the bus rattled and swayed along the road. I had my eyes pinned to the floor, trying to catch a glimpse of the shoe in amongst all the ankles and trouser legs.

I kept on looking as I walked downstairs. Reaching the platform at the bottom, I could hear everyone laughing. The conductor was standing on the platform with his back to me, facing his audience of passengers. My arrival behind him prompted another, louder outburst of laughter, and I could feel my face burning up. Sensing my presence, the conductor turned to me and, with a bow, held out his hand, revealing Kim's shoe. I stood there, not knowing what to do or say. Should I snatch it from him, or just jump off the bus and leave Kim to it?

'Are you looking for Cinderella's slipper, Prince Charming?' The laughter got even louder.

'Yes,' I gulped as I took the shoe from him. 'Thanks,' I

mumbled before stumbling for the safety of the top deck. But it was not to end there.

The conductor followed me, and as I made my way back to Kim I could hear him broadcasting to all the upstairs passengers what had happened. I could feel everyone looking at me, as he described me as Prince Charming, who had come to find his Cinderella. Kim and I were the centre of attention, with everyone wanting to say something to us or make a comment on our version of the 'romance'. But I didn't need this sort of attention: this wasn't part of my script. No, what I needed was a quiet corner in which I could curl up and die! My first date. And I was the object, not of envy at my good fortune, but of ridicule and amusement. It was too much for a teenage boy embarking on romance for the first time.

As the bus pulled up at Kim's stop, I let her get off, staying firmly in my seat. All my hopes of a tender goodnight kiss were dashed. I think she tried to say goodbye to me, but I just sat in stony silence, head turned towards the window and my face still a burning shade of crimson.

I never asked Kim out again, and in fact I can't really remember ever talking to her again. But Bernie and everybody else who knew me thought it was hilarious and laughed for weeks after.

As for me, I think that in some way it scarred me for life, as I can still clearly remember every embarrassing moment as if it had only happened yesterday.

10. Mum's Perfect Place

Life went on. At the start of 1967, Lesley left home and went to live in London. Within weeks of her arriving there, she met Roy Smith, a young science teacher, and married him shortly afterwards.

Barry was nineteen and doing very well as an assistant sales manager at Johnson Brothers, a television company. He had passed his driving test and was the proud owner of a grey minivan. As for Sheila, she had a job as a sales girl in Sayers, a local confectioners.

I was thirteen, and June was five and growing up very quickly. We got on well, she and I; she was a cheeky little madam but also very special to me. I got to play the older brother and would often put her on my shoulders and take her to the sweetshop, and if she'd been good for Mum and I had the extra pennies, I'd treat her to an ice-cream cone when the ice-cream van came down our street.

Dad was still Dad. We didn't see him much; he still worked nights driving taxis and spent the days sleeping off the effects of too much drink the night before. As for my darling Mum, she was starting to look a lot older than forty-seven. Her constant despair at my father's behaviour and the continual worry about money were beginning to take their toll on her. But, unbeknown to us, she had made plans of her own, and things were about to change dramatically.

We were all sitting around the table having our tea, apart from Dad, who was out in his cab, when Mum broke the news. 'I've got something to tell you all,' she said. We carried on eating but looked up to see what she was about to say. 'We're moving.'

'What?' Barry was the first to speak, his fork suspended in the air in front of his mouth. 'What do you mean, we're moving?'

'We're leaving this bug-infested place and moving to something bigger and better, away from this slum.' There was a note of excitement in Mum's voice.

'What about my job?' demanded Sheila.

I piped up, 'I'm not changing school now!'

Poor Mum. She didn't know who to answer first.

Barry said, 'Dad will go ballistic! He won't move all the way out there, it's miles away!' He was spot on. Dad was going to suffer the most, having to travel to his favourite pubs! However, judging from Mum's reply, that had been her intention all along.

'That's my worry, son, not yours,' she said firmly. She believed that by moving us all further away and extracting Dad from the clutches of his drinking partners at the Boundary, he might start drinking less.

It was a plan she'd had years ago, and she had put our name on the council housing list without telling anyone. It was so long ago I think she'd almost given up on it, but she'd just had notification that a house was available, and after a long trip, involving three buses and several hours, she had viewed this house 'in the country'. Her prayers had been answered and her mind was made up. As far as she was concerned, there was no going back: we were moving to West Derby.

Needless to say, Dad wasn't happy at all and came up with all sorts of reasons and excuses why we shouldn't move. He tried every trick in the book, even adding a few of his own, but Mum stood firm. We were moving whether he liked it or not. She was determined that her children would have a new life, away from the slums where we had lived for so many years.

Although we didn't have much to pack, everything we did have was, in Mum's opinion, a treasured possession. And she insisted that everything was carefully wrapped up in newspaper before being packed away in the old tea chests I had collected. Dad got involved too, by borrowing a van off somebody he knew.

The day of the move finally dawned, and once the van was loaded, there were just the goodbyes left. I ran first of all to Mrs Gilbert, who gave me a half-crown and wished me luck, then to Mary from the sweetshop, who had become my friend.

My mates were all hanging around by the van when I got back, not sure how to react. Ian Watt looked particularly uncomfortable, staring silently down at the pavement. After all, we'd been best mates ever since we'd been allowed to play out in the street. And now I was leaving.

As I shook their hands and said my goodbyes, trying to be as grown-up as I could, I had a lump in my throat from fighting back my emotions and trying not to let any tears show. I promised them all I would come back and see them soon. But a part of me knew I never would. I was moving to a whole new life, and even though it was only a few miles away, I could have been travelling to the other side of the world for all the difference it made.

We all set off in convoy, Barry leading the way in his van, with June sitting on Mum's lap, while Sheila and I followed behind with Dad in the van. It must have taken us an hour or so to get there. As we drove through the city streets, getting closer to

Princess Drive, the scenery started to change dramatically. Instead of grey old buildings there were trees and open expanses of greenery. It was almost like being out in the country and reminded us of our trips to Wales.

West Derby, on the outskirts of Liverpool, had been mainly farmland before the Second World War. After the war, however, as a result of the devastation of the bombing raids, the council built housing estates there to accommodate the families made homeless. The estates also catered for the overspill of people who had lived in derelict houses in the inner-city slums.

Our new house was on a corner, with its own front and side garden. I was the first out of the van, running over to a little white wooden gate in the middle of a privet hedge, then down the path towards the red-painted front door. As Mum searched for the keys in her handbag, my excitement was hard to contain. When she finally managed to open the door we all pushed our way in.

The house was fantastic, with three bedrooms upstairs and a big room with a window looking on to the front garden and a lovely long kitchen downstairs. 'What's that on the wall, Mum?' I shouted.

She smiled. 'That's our new gas fire, Jeff. Just think: no more making coal fires.' And there was running hot and cold water, upstairs and down!

I loved the new house, and every room in it. But my favourite, without a doubt, had to be the bathroom. We had never had one of these before. This was amazing to me, with a long white bath that you could stretch out in and get properly warm without any bits of your body getting cold, and with instant hot water. There was also a sink just for washing your hands and face, and cleaning your teeth, and best of all, a white porcelain toilet with a spotless white plastic seat. This was unashamed luxury.

My feeling of gratitude and love for my mother was overwhelming, and I understood why it had been so important for her to move us here. There was no need for words. As I wrapped my arms around her in a big hug, I knew she understood, and we just stood there for a few moments.

Mum discovered the joys of gardening in that house. If the weather was nice, she would be outside, digging over the soil, weeding the flowerbeds and tending to her roses. For the first time in her life, a few of her dreams had come true. She was a different woman. Dad, however, once again managed to add a sour taste to it all. Mum's plan of moving him as far away as possible from bad influences backfired.

He still met up with his cronies, staying out and drinking, carrying on as if he had no other care in the world, and no family or home to come back to. Some nights he would get back very late, sometimes in the early hours, and sometimes not at all. As I soon discovered, Mum would stay awake through the night, worrying herself sick about him and whether he had got himself into some awful trouble. Other times, I imagine she wished he hadn't bothered coming home, he was such a disgrace and an embarrassment, staggering off the bus near our house. On these occasions, he was so drunk he couldn't stand up and had to be helped indoors. My poor mother seemed to spend half her evenings looking out of the front window every time she heard a bus to see if he was on it. I can only suppose that the alcohol made him totally unaware of how much he was spoiling my mother's hard-won happiness.

Princess Drive was a busy dual carriageway that ran down the middle of a very large housing estate. If you turned right out of our house and carried on for about two and half miles, you arrived in West Derby, which was regarded as well-to-do. But if you turned left, a mile down the road would bring you to Page Moss in Huyton, a council estate that had the reputation of being one of the roughest in Liverpool, if not the UK. After building the Huyton Estate, the city council had relocated the hardened criminal community from the city centre to here.

The Eagle and Child pub in Page Moss, five minutes away, and the Bow and Arrow, almost directly opposite our house, were notorious and known to be two of the most dangerous and violent pubs in Liverpool at that time. Even the police hesitated to enter them. At least Mum had succeeded in keeping my father out of *these* locals – both places would have been far too hazardous for a distinguished gentleman like him!

Oh, Mum, God love her! All she had ever wanted was to bring her children up in a safe environment. She had moved us far away from big-city squalor and crime to the benefits of a more rural setting. What a pity – she had miscalculated by only a mile in the wrong direction! We were now living deep in the heart of criminal country.

11. Wot's-a-Gofer-Do?

Once we moved to our new home, time seemed to fly. Suddenly I was fourteen going on fifteen and was due to leave school in a matter of months, so we were all sent to see the visiting careers officer to discuss our plans for the future.

The careers officer was a rather tubby man dressed in a brown suit. His hair was greasy and his tie had a schoolboy knot instead of a man's Windsor, like Dad always wore. He looked at me with tired, disinterested eyes. 'Well, Mr Pearce, what job would you like to do when you leave school?'

This was the moment I'd been waiting for, the first chance I'd had to discuss my big plans for the future. 'Well, sir, I want to have my own business. Maybe start off on the markets like I did with my Mum, selling all kinds of things. And when I have enough money, get my own shop. I want to be like Mr Marks and Mr Spencer when I'm older and have my own big store like theirs.' I paused for breath and looked to see his reaction, to see any signs of encouragement or inspiration, but I was met with a blank stare. Perhaps he didn't know who I was talking about.

'Mr Marks and Mr Spencer, sir,' I repeated. 'The ones who own all the big department stores. You must know them – they have one of the biggest stores in Liverpool.' There was still no response, so I sat there for a moment, not sure what to say.

The careers officer gathered his thoughts and said, 'You can't live off pocketfuls of dreams, young man,' then picked up some leaflets and passed them to me. 'Here you are, some things for you to look at and have a think about. Next,' he shouted loudly, and I got to my feet and slowly walked out of the classroom.

I couldn't read any of the words on the leaflets, but there were pictures of soldiers and sailors. What was this all about? I wasn't interested in being a soldier or going to sea. I'd told him about my ambitions and what I wanted to do with my life, and he hadn't listened to a word I'd said. I left the room feeling very let down and confused. Why hadn't he taken me seriously? Was it because he knew I couldn't read or write? Had my teachers told him that I didn't even try to learn and not to bother with me?

Mum, as ever, did her best to cheer me up, saying that she would find something special for me to do, and sure enough, not long afterwards, she told me she'd found me a proper job and had arranged a meeting with the headmaster to discuss it. In his office, she explained that she'd found me a much sought after job as an apprentice TV engineer, and that the position was available immediately. She knew the school year wasn't yet over, but with my poor academic ability, with all the competition, it would be difficult for me to find something if I left at the same time as all the other boys. Could I leave school before the official end of term so I could start work as soon as possible? The headmaster was very helpful and contacted the Local Education Authority, who after much deliberation gave their permission.

On my last day, I said goodbye to all my friends. Obviously, they were all envious of my early departure; I had all the luck! My form teacher, Mrs Jones, was less congratulatory, saying it had been a waste of time trying to teach me and no good would come from my mother's efforts. In her professional opinion, there was no hope for me.

When I walked out of the school gates that last afternoon, I felt very scared. The thought of my new employer discovering that I couldn't read or write made the safety of school appealing despite the harsh comments of teachers like Mrs Jones. I was fourteen years old, just a boy, about to enter the world of adults.

Mum soon vanquished all my misgivings. She told me that televisions were the thing of the future, that there would always be work installing and repairing them, so I'd always be able to earn a good living. She was so enthusiastic I couldn't help but feel excited at the prospect of my new job – the way Mum described it made it sound very manly and adult.

The company I was joining was Johnson Brothers, where Barry worked as an apprentice sales manager. They were a privately owned TV and radio business, with six shops in and around the Liverpool area, and also sold and repaired other appliances. My job was in the service department.

My first Monday morning that summer of 1968 was memorable. I arrived on the dot of nine, trying to look as mature as possible, but walking through all the hustle and bustle to reception, I began to feel very nervous. I went up to a small square window that was framing the head and shoulders of a lady busy doing something. I had to stand up on my toes to see her, but she was looking down, typing, and didn't see me. I didn't want to jump up and down to get her attention, so instead I cleared my throat.

'Can I help you?' she asked.

'I'm here to fix televisions,' I blurted out.

Her eyebrows shot up as she looked at me – or at a pair of anxious eyes and a nose resting on the ledge in front of her, which was all she could see of me. 'Sorry?' she said. 'What was that again?'

'I'm here for the job.'

'What job?'

'The television engineer job,' I elaborated.

She leaned forward to get a better look at me, and I found myself confronted by an overpowering cleavage that filled the window frame. 'Well, young man,' she said, 'you'd best take a seat, hadn't you?' Then she picked up the Tannoy microphone and, her voice full of laughter, called out: 'Would Frank Johnson please come to reception? Frank Johnson to reception, please. The world's smallest TV engineer is waiting for you.'

Sitting there, my face red with embarrassment, I didn't know what to think. What she was laughing about? I was here for the job.

Moments later, a door opened and a man appeared, a smile on his face. 'You must be the new apprentice,' he said. 'Come on, follow me.'

I had to work hard to keep up with him, my shorter legs doing at least two strides for every one of his as we made our way through a maze of hallways and doors. As we sped along he told me that he was one of the owner brothers and was in charge of the service department. He was going to be my 'big boss'.

We stopped at a large room full of workbenches, all covered with televisions and radios making crackling sounds. About twelve women and four men sat on tall stools, busy with repairs, many of them using soldering irons, which smoked each time they made contact. No one noticed us coming in, so Mr Johnson called for attention and introduced me.

I stood there shyly, feeling nervous and unsure of what to do. Sensing my apprehension, Mr Johnson said, 'It's all right, Jeff. No need to worry. They'll look after you,' but his words fell on deaf ears; while he was talking and once he'd left, everyone just carried on with their work.

After about ten minutes I had built up enough courage to walk over to the woman who had the kindest-looking face. 'Is there anything I can do to help you?' I asked in my politest voice.

'Bloody hell,' she said, almost jumping off her stool at the sudden interruption. 'Who the hell are you?'

'I'm Jeff,' I answered, 'the new apprentice.'

'Oh you *are* here!' she replied. Then she called out loudly to her colleagues, 'Our gofer's arrived!'

'Gofer?' This was a new expression to me, and meant nothing at all. Seeing the look of puzzlement on my face, she smiled.

'Go for this, go for that . . . Come on, I'll show you what you have to do.'

She took me into their 'canteen' and explained that I was to make tea twice a day, take orders for lunch, and clear up after everyone else. Then she left me to it. I just about managed to get the tea ready for the ten o'clock break, and then it was time to take the orders for lunch. I got nervous all over again then, petrified they'd all find out that I couldn't read or write. Luckily, there weren't that many different orders, so I made up a code, using 'fc' for fish and chips, 'skpc' for steak and kidney pie and chips, and so on.

At the end of the week, I received my first wage packet, which contained £3. I'd also received tips from the service engineers, and that amounted to almost £1. I was so proud being able to give Mum all that money. In those days, it was the tradition in Liverpool to give all your first wage packet to your mother, but from then to pay the agreed board and lodging, keeping the balance for yourself. I, however, gave Mum my whole wage packet every week, and in return she'd give me ten shillings to cover the cost of my bus fare. I never had to buy lunch as she always made me sandwiches, and I kept my tips for myself.

After a couple of weeks I had it all down to a fine art, and I soon found myself able to spend more and more time in the workshop, running errands to pick up things like transistors, glass valves and tubes. But the job didn't quite live up to the expectations I'd had when I left school and ventured forth into the big wide world. Making tea and being a gofer for a group of women was not my idea of a career. And when I learnt that I had to start attending engineering college one day a week, I panicked; once again my fear of being found out reared its ugly head.

I began to look for other opportunities, and my attention was drawn to the vans that were constantly coming and going in the yard outside. Surely that would be more interesting and better for me? These were the aerial-rigging vans, and had big aluminium ladders strapped to their roofs which rattled loudly as they drove into the yard. To me, a fourteen-year-old boy, all the drivers were *real* men, tall and muscular, with leather toolbelts strapped around their waists bulging with hammers and spanners. They reminded me of the cowboys I'd seen in films, with their gunbelts slung low around their hips.

Each aerial-rigging team consisted of two men, one who was in charge and drove the van, and an apprentice, who also acted as a gofer. These lads were usually quite big, aged between sixteen and eighteen, and they had to be quite strong, as they were expected to handle the three sixteen-foot-long sections of the ladder.

I found myself watching the riggers every morning as they

came to collect their list of jobs for the day and to stock up and load the van with rolls of cable and shiny aerials. To a kid like me, working outdoors, climbing up and down roofs and wearing a toolbelt around my waist seemed like such a manly job.

One sunny lunchtime, when all the vans and the aerial teams were in the yard, Frank Johnson happened to walk past, and I found myself calling after him. 'Mr Johnson,' I said, 'I would really like to be an aerial rigger, just like them.'

Turning towards me with his usual smile, he said, 'Jeff, I really don't think you want to be like them, out in all kinds of weather, good or bad. Being a TV engineer is a far better job.'

'Mr Johnson,' I replied, 'I really want to be an aerial rigger. I don't want to be an engineer at all.'

'I'm sorry, son, but you're too small,' he answered, but I was adamant. 'Come with me then,' he said, and we walked over to the riggers. 'This young boy wants to be a rigger. What do you boys think?'

They all burst out laughing. 'There's nothing to him, Frank,' said one man. 'There's more fat on a sausage!'

'He needs to grow a bit more,' said another, 'put a bit more meat on him, otherwise he'll be blown off the roof on a windy day.'

'See what I mean,' said Mr Johnson, looking down at me. Upset, I turned away and started to head back to the canteen.

'Wait a minute.' There was a shout from within the group of men behind us. We both stopped and turned around.

'George, what's up?' asked Mr Johnson, directing his question towards a tall young man.

'I'm looking for a van lad, Frank,' he replied. 'This lad could be OK if he can prove himself.' Turning to me, he asked me to follow him. We walked over to his van, Mr Johnson and all the other riggers in our wake.

George took the three sections of the ladder down off the roof and told me that if I could walk over to the gates and back without dropping them I could have the job. The gate was about 50 yards away from his van, so I had to cover 100 yards in total. With my audience watching and laughing at me, I headed off, the ladders balanced on my shoulder. The further I walked, the more difficult it became. The ladders were not so much heavy as difficult to balance, one minute tilting forwards and the next tilting back. But I was so determined, I reached the gates and turned back towards the van. By now I was beginning to feel quite a lot of pain in my shoulder and arms, and my knees felt as if they were about to buckle under me at any minute. The heat of the midday sun and the sheer exertion were making sweat pour down my face and into my eyes.

As I got closer to the waiting crowd, I realized they were all cheering for me, urging me on to complete the task. I kept my focus on the ever-closing distance. About ten yards away from them, I couldn't go on any further. Dropping to the ground, the ladders landing with a metallic crash beside me, I knelt there, my whole body aching. The encouraging cheers had subsided, and all I could hear now was, 'I told you so.'

George came over to where I had stopped, picking his ladders up as if they were as light as feathers before putting them back on the top of his van. I just stayed kneeling, feeling small and dejected and miserable at the thought of another year making tea and running for fish and chips. But then I heard George call out, 'Hey kid, you've got a lot of guts. You weren't frightened to give it a go. I have a mind to take you on.' His words were music to my ears.

'Please, mister, please.' I looked at him imploringly. 'Please give me the job.'

'Hey Frank,' George continued, 'I like this kid and I'm going to take him on.' The other drivers couldn't believe their ears and told him he was making a big mistake – I was too small, not strong enough and too young. Was he mad? I'd never make a good rigger's lad in a month of Sundays. But he just told them to wait and see.

'In six months' time,' he said, 'I reckon he'll be the best lad on the yard!'

Mr Johnson, who'd been watching the whole proceedings, took me to one side. 'Are you sure this is what you want to do?' he asked. I nodded frantically, and after a quick glance at George, he said,

'All right. You can start on Monday. And tell your mother that it was nothing to do with me!'

'I will,' I promised, bursting with happiness.

Mum was a little disappointed when I first told her, but once she realized how keen I was, she accepted the change. Although – knowing full well how accident-prone I was – she warned me to take extra care on the roofs.

12. Up the Ladder

My first morning with George started well. We loaded up the van with all the equipment for the day's work, then I climbed on to the front passenger seat and we set off, me feeling really like a real man. Then he tossed me the daily job slips, pieces of paper bound with a large bulldog clip. I froze. They were covered in writing, a mishmash of letters I had no chance of being able to read.

'What's the address for our first job?' asked George.

I looked over at him. 'I don't know where these places are,' I said, stalling for time. I'd learnt all sorts of ways to try and hide the fact that I couldn't read.

He threw a small book into my lap. 'Look them up in there,' he shouted, 'and be quick about it. We don't have all day.' It was the Liverpool A–Z.

'But I've never used one of these before,' I said. I thought he was going to cuff me he looked so annoyed.

'What's your problem?' he yelled. 'Just find the bloody streets!'

I started to feel cold and shaky, with that familiar sick feeling in the pit of my stomach I always got when I thought I was going to be found out. George's driving was becoming erratic and he was now swearing under his breath. The van veered off the road, mounting the kerb and screeching to a halt as he yanked up the handbrake.

'Are you stupid?' he shouted. 'Can't you bloody read?'

My heart was in my mouth. I just sat there, unable to utter a word. This was my worst nightmare. George was obviously already regretting his decision to take me on. My new job was over before I had even started.

Somehow we got through the day, and at the end of it, I slipped the A–Z into my lunchbox without George noticing and smuggled it home with me to study. Mum was waiting for me, eager to hear how it had gone.

Hanging my coat up, I told her. 'It was horrible, Mum. My new boss got angry with me, shouting and screaming and getting really cross. I think he wants to get rid of me.'

'Why, Jeff? What did you do wrong?' she asked.

'I didn't do anything wrong, Mum. It was what I *couldn't* do,' I answered.

Taking my lunchbox, she said, 'Come on, let's have a cup of tea.' I sat down at the kitchen table, slumped forward with my head buried in my arms. Mum opened my lunchbox and found the A–Z. 'What's this?' she asked.

Raising my head a little, I said, 'That's what wrong with my job.' My voice was flat with despair. 'Mum, why can't I read like everyone else?'

Placing my cup of tea before me, she said, 'I wish I knew, son. What I can't understand is that you're so clever in so many other ways. It just doesn't make sense.'

I explained what had happened, and as ever, she knew just what to say and do. 'Jeff, life is full of obstacles and hurdles, and everyone comes across them from time to time. If you want to achieve things in life, you have to learn how to overcome them, whether it's by tackling them head on or finding a way around them.' She took a sip of her tea. 'What we need to do is work out a way we can overcome this particular obstacle together,' she said, gesturing to the book in front of her. We sat drinking our tea for a few minutes in companionable silence, and my gaze never left her face. I loved watching Mum when she was thinking about things like this.

'I've got it!' she said a few moments later. 'I know how we're going to get the better of this little book!' I couldn't wait to hear what she had to say. 'Every night, I'm going to write down street names and you are going to find them. Start by finding the first two letters of the name in the index, then the third, then the fourth, until there's only one street they could match. With enough practice, you'll be able to find the streets without really having to read their names.'

It was a simple plan, but a good one. For the next week, we spent hours and hours working together at the kitchen table, until I was finding the locations on the maps in a matter of seconds. Not only was I speedy, but I started to enjoy it. That little book was no longer a demon but a friend. And having mastered the art of giving directions from one address to another, I began to plan the whole day's itinerary for George before we set off. He was so impressed at how quick I was in getting us from one job to another, he told all the other drivers I knew Liverpool like the back of my hand!

The next hurdle to overcome was moving the ladders. It wasn't the weight so much as the difficulty of balancing them. I was just about in control, but it must have been the most terrifying sight to any pedestrians walking by: a little lad, well short of five foot, hurrying along with sixteen feet of metal balanced on his shoulder.

The biggest change, however, was that I now had a proper

job. I was part of the adult world, and I soon learnt to toughen up. George was more than happy with my work and how quickly I picked things up, though you wouldn't have known it from the way he treated me. We'd be in the van, driving along, when suddenly I'd feel his clenched fist crashing into my shoulder or my thigh. It hurt, but if I ever asked him to stop, he'd just tell me to stop being such a wimp. He'd been thumped when he was an aerial lad, so that was the way, as far as he was concerned, that aerial lads were 'trained'.

About six months after I'd started working with him, George and I were out on the road. I was making up a lashing kit to fit around the chimney stacks. I usually spent the time in the van getting everything ready, which made the installation process quicker once we got to the job, and I'd almost finished when, out of the blue, I felt George's fist coming into contact with my leg. It was the hardest blow I had received to date. And without thinking, I hit back.

Unfortunately for George, I still had the metal bracket in my hand, and that's what made contact with his forehead, cutting the skin above his eyebrow and making him yell out in pain.

Looking over at him in shock, I saw blood gushing down the side of his face. He let go of the steering wheel and clasped his head in his hands, moaning and swearing. He was muttering over and over again, 'Just wait till I get my hands on you!' I cowered in my corner of the cab, pressed up against the door, desperately trying to work out how I was going to get away from him.

Luck was on my side. The van was out of control, careering across the road and going up on the grass verge dividing the dual carriageway. It lurched forward then ground to a halt, so I opened the door and threw myself out, then scrambled to my feet and ran away as fast as my legs would go. All I wanted was to get as far away as possible. I thought George wanted to kill me! I didn't slow down until I was well and truly out of sight.

It took me two hours to run home, and of course, as soon as I got there, I told Mum all about it. 'I've had enough, Mum,' I said. 'I'm packing it in. Chances are I'll be sacked anyway, for nearly killing him!'

'You did the right thing, Jeff, standing up for yourself like that. I'll have a word with George or Mr Johnson in the morning, and we'll get to the bottom of it all.'

George normally picked me up at 8.30 sharp every morning, but I wasn't expecting him the next day, and there was no way I was going back to work. But the following morning, I heard George beeping the van's horn, as he usually did. I opened the curtains a fraction and peered out into the street below. I could see my mother talking angrily to George, and wagging her finger at him. From what I could see, she was really laying into him.

This went on for a few minutes, then she returned to the house, while George drove away. She had hardly closed the door before I was down the stairs asking what had happened.

'Well, it's quite simple,' she said. 'I told him that if he ever laid a finger on you ever again, I'd swing for him.' I looked at Mum standing in front of me, and an image of her taking on George sprang to mind. Talk about David and Goliath – but there was no doubt in my mind that my mother would be the winner!

When George picked me up the next morning, we weren't quite sure what to say to each other. But once the day's work got underway, we soon started talking, and before long it was almost as if nothing had ever happened. Our relationship had altered subtly, however; George showed me more respect, and he never hit me again. As time passed, we became good friends and enjoyed each other's company, and we worked really well as a team. He took great pleasure in telling the other riggers that I was brilliant at my job, and it was quietly recognized on the yard that I was the best aerial lad. He'd boast that he didn't even have to get out of the van, that I could take care of everything. I was a valuable asset, and George certainly knew it.

My mother's predictions about television proved accurate. Everyone wanted one, and a proper aerial – but not everyone was able to pay the full price. So spotting a gap in the market, George and I went about filling it. We stocked up on the necessary equipment from a small local manufacturer and loaded it into the van alongside the equipment from Johnsons'. George and I were quick at installations, turning jobs around in less than fifteen minutes, so we had more than enough time to do 'foreigners' – a 'foreigner' being a job on the side. Everybody did them in those days, and as long as you met your targets, the bosses just turned a blind eye.

People would see us working and approach us in the street, so there was no shortage of business. And we were making good money. An aerial lad could expect to earn £4 a week working for a company like Johnson Brothers, the foreigners brought in at least an extra £25 a week, so there I was, a sixteen-year-old lad, earning as much as a qualified professional.

That extra money made such a difference, both to Mum and to me. I loved being able to spoil her, and not only was she no longer worried about paying bills and having debt collectors knocking at the door, she could treat herself to little luxuries. She had her hair done once a month, and I'd take her shopping, encouraging her to splash out on something for herself.

As for me, I started to drag Ronnie, my new best friend and next-door neighbour, to the ice rink at the weekends, where we'd meet up with Bernie. Now that we were sixteen, we were allowed into the Beehive disco.

We had one thing on our minds back then – girls! In order to get even to the first post, though, we had to look the part. Bernie, Ronnie and I were all Mods, so we took care with our clothes, and the way we walked, as well as being keen on a certain type of music. *Top of the Pops* at seven o'clock on Thursday evenings was essential teenage viewing in those days. Ronnie and I would watch carefully to see what our favourite bands were wearing and then spend Saturdays in Liverpool, scouring shops like the Army & Navy Stores and the odd boutique, looking for clothes that would fit the image and style. We started to go to a London Road tailor to be fitted for suits. There was nothing off-the-peg about being a Mod.

The most important thing, however, was having the hairstyle. There was a barbershop in Toxteth run by a bloke called Pee Wee, a jovial Jamaican character well known for his skill with a cut-throat razor. His place was *the* place to go, so one Saturday morning, Ronnie, Bernie and I went along. Bernie was called first.

As he sat down in the barber's chair, he looked very small and afraid, and when he asked for a 'skiffle' cut with a 'shaven part', he did it so quietly he could hardly be heard. Pee Wee immediately got to work. Ronnie and I sat there in horrified silence as long chunks of Bernie's hair fell away. Within four or five swipes he was as good as bald, the dark stubble on his head making his head an odd grey colour. Then it got really scary. Pee Wee discarded his trimmer in favour of a lethal-looking cut-throat, sharpening it on the leather strap hanging down from the back of the chair. We could see Bernie's face reflected in the mirror. If he'd looked horrified at his new bald image, he now looked completely terrified.

Pee Wee held his head in a vice-like clamp with one hand while the other scraped a parting line down the left-hand side of his skull with the accuracy and precision of a surgeon. Bernie's eyes welled up with tears, whether from fright or pain we didn't know. We were soon to find out, though, when it came to our turn.

Coming out into the street and the daylight, the full impact of what we'd done suddenly hit us. We all hated our new hair, but none of us had the courage to say so. As I got closer to home a feeling of dread came over me. Grabbing Ronnie by the arm, I towed him up the path to the front door. 'You're coming in with me, mate,' I said. 'I need you there for support.'

Mum was in the kitchen when I walked in. She took one glance at me before slamming the cup she held in her hand down on the table, tea sloshing over the side. 'Jeff, what have you done?' she exclaimed.

'Where are all your lovely curls?'

Ronnie got there first. 'On the floor in Pee Wee's, Mrs Pearce.'

When I was sixteen I developed a new obsession, learning to drive. I wasn't legally old enough, but I didn't want to have to wait another year. After much nagging, George finally relented, teaching me in our van on the quieter back roads of Liverpool and on Southport Beach, places where I could happily and safely drive up and down for hours without getting in trouble with the police.

Dad also had a car, a blue Ford Cortina. It was actually Barry's, but he had decided to leave Liverpool and was going to work his way around Europe. Mum had a real battle convincing Barry to let Dad take over the payments, and although Barry hated the idea, he finally agreed, only because it mattered so much to Mum.

After much persuasion from Mum, Dad agreed to give me the occasional lesson. For the first time, he took an interest in me and what I was doing. And he seemed to be very happy giving me driving lessons. In many ways it was the beginning of a new relationship between us. Having been a taxi driver for years, he was a very good teacher, and it was not long before I was both confident and competent behind the wheel.

In return for the lessons it was agreed that I would give Dad's car a full valet every Sunday morning, checking the oil and water and making sure that it was spotless inside and out. I enjoyed this, my involvement with cars making me feel I had climbed another rung up the ladder of adult life.

Early one sunny Sunday morning, I was out cleaning the Cortina, the radio blaring loudly as I worked away, when Ronnie came over and asked if I fancied going to Southport for the day. 'Sorry, mate,' I replied. 'I have to finish cleaning the car. Perhaps we can go later?'

'No, let's go now. It will be too late later.'

'You know Dad'll go mad if I don't finish it,' I said.

'Come on – we could even take the car,' he said jokingly, patting the bonnet. 'It'll be good for picking up the birds; it'll be a real pose!'

'Forget it. I haven't got a driver's licence,' I replied. 'I'm not old enough to be driving, for one, and for two, Dad would kill me if he found out.'

Ronnie laughed. 'He won't know. He's fast asleep. By the time he wakes up we'll be back!'

The seed had been planted. Before I knew it, we were both dressed in our best gear and on our way to the seaside! The windows rolled down, the latest sounds playing loudly, we felt so cool as we cruised along – two young men on the lookout for some pretty girls.

We were enjoying ourselves, and were only a couple of miles from our destination when the car in front slowed to a halt. After a few minutes I asked Ronnie if he could see what the problem was.

'Can't see a thing,' he said. 'I'll get out and have a look.' After a few seconds, he was back in the car. 'It's trouble; there's a policeman up ahead.'

My face went white. 'What?'

'There's a copper up ahead stopping the cars.'

I looked around me. We were on a narrow country lane, with a car behind and one in front. I wanted to get out of there as fast as I could, but there was no room, and I was nowhere near confident enough to do a three-point turn and didn't want to draw attention to myself by trying. I was stuck, and the only way to go was forward, past the policeman.

Ronnie sat fidgeting beside me, making matters worse. I was becoming more and more anxious. It was ridiculous for someone as small as me to be driving this car. I was bound to get pulled over. I'd lose my licence before I'd even got it! And the thought of having to tell my father was almost too much to think about.

'Ronnie, what am I going to do?'

'Look bigger!' he said. I tried straightening up and puffing out my chest, but the more I tried to sit up, the more my foot kept slipping off the brake.

'This isn't working, Ronnie,' I cried. 'Do something!' Ronnie noticed a checked blanket on the back seat and hastily folded it into a small cushion and shoved it under my backside.

'That's a bit better,' I said, 'but still not enough. I need something else.' By this stage there were only ten cars between me and the policeman, who suddenly gestured for the queue to move forward. 'For God's sake, do something quickly, we're moving.'

Ronnie was now searching around the car. I was staring though the windscreen, my eyes glued to the policeman ahead. Whipping off his jumper, Ronnie shoved it under the blanket.

'How's that?' he asked.

'I still need something else.'

'There's nothing! There's nothing!' he cried. 'What do you want to do, sit on me?' He then had a flash of inspiration and pulled off his shoes, adding them to the bottom of the pile.

I sat there, gripping the wheel as I drove forward. As luck would have it, the policemen held up his hand in front of me. I was so close I could almost see the colour of his eyes.

'Jeff, keep cool,' I heard Ronnie hissing at me. 'Look old, look grown-up!'

'How on earth am I supposed to do that?' I hissed back. The sweat was pouring down my face, my hands were frozen to the wheel, and my legs were beginning to shake as they were stretched out full length so as to reach the brake pedal and hold it down. If my foot slipped, the car would roll forward and the copper would end up spreadeagled across the bonnet.

The seconds ticked slowly by. Ronnie had lowered the sun visor in front of me to try and hide my face, but it didn't make any difference. Suddenly the policeman turned, beckoning me to move forward. I panicked again. What would happen if I stalled the car? Would he come over to see what was wrong?

Trying desperately to remember everything I had learnt, I put the car into gear, eased off on the clutch and gave it some throttle. The Cortina moved forward, slowly and smoothly, and we drove safely by.

Once we were out of sight, I pulled into a lay-by. I opened my door, almost falling off the top of my improvised perch as I got out of the car, the items tumbling to the ground around me. I felt sick and leaned on the bonnet, gulping down huge breaths of fresh air, trying to calm my nerves. Looking up, I saw Ronnie laughing at me through the windscreen.

'Pass me my shoes, mate,' he called out. His request broke the tension. As I picked them up, I realized that his size eights had well and truly saved the day.

I continued my driving lessons with Dad and George right up to my seventeenth birthday, when I could officially apply for my driving test. Mum read the Highway Code to me every night and very soon the big day dawned and I passed with flying colours. I couldn't wait to ask Frank Johnson for my own van.

Going into his office the next day, I felt very confident, like a real adult, so I decided to use his first name, as all the other drivers did. 'Hey Frank,' I said, 'I've passed my driving test. Is there any chance of my own van and my own lad now?'

He almost choked with astonishment. 'You can't be serious,' he said. 'You're only . . . er? How old are you?'

'I'm seventeen, Frank,' I told him proudly.

'No, Jeff, I'm sorry. You need to be at least twenty, if not twenty-one. Just keep on as you are until you're older.'

George told me he wasn't surprised I'd passed my test but that I was expecting too much to have my own van at my age.

But what was the point of passing if I wasn't allowed to drive? There was no way I could wait another four years – I had plans. I carried on working as normal for a couple of weeks, but then I could bear it no longer. Having convinced Mum it was a good idea to start my own aerials business, she agreed to help me by answering the telephone and booking in the jobs.

First, I needed a van. I went to a motor auction out in the suburbs, and bid on an old dark-blue Ford Anglia with a roof rack. It was my first auction and I didn't have a clue what to do, but I watched the other people bidding and by the time the van came under the hammer, I was ready to give it a go.

A few tense minutes and £60 later, the van was mine. I christened her Blue Betty and when I started to drive away, her engine sounded good, and she was driving very nicely. But as soon as I built up speed and put her into fourth gear, she revealed her true personality. She refused to stay in fourth, spitting the gear stick back into neutral with a little clanking noise. It meant I had to physically hold the gear stick to keep it in fourth, and use the other hand to steer.

Finishing work the following evening, I went and bought a good set of second-hand aluminium ladders for £15. They were pretty old but would still do the job, and the bloke I bought them off threw in a box of old tools, too, which would come in handy. Once I'd tied the ladders on to the roof rack, I felt so proud, and stood back to admire my van. It all looked so professional. I was ready to go into business.

13. Postcards from Europe

By the summer of 1972, my aerial business was doing well, and I was enjoying myself, working hard and making good money, but I was beginning to feel a bit restless. Barry, in the meantime, had been planning another trip to Europe with a friend of his. A few days before he was due to leave, however, his friend pulled out and Barry asked me if I wanted to go with him. It came as a bit of a shock, as he and I weren't particularly close, but having heard about his earlier adventures, I didn't take too much persuading, as in the summer months trade went quiet.

Within a couple of days, we were waving good-bye to Mum and June. The last thing I heard as we headed off was Mum calling out, 'Barry, whatever you do, look after Jeff; you know how accident-prone he is. Please bring him back in one piece!'

Barry had bought and fitted out a Land Rover as a very basic mobile home. There was just enough room for the two of us to stretch out full length in the back, our kitchen was a gas camping stove and our bathroom jerry cans of water and a plastic bowl. We headed down to Dover, and looking back at the White Cliffs as the ferry pulled away, I was overwhelmed with anticipation. I'd hardly explored England, let alone anywhere abroad. It was going to be a real adventure.

The age difference between me and Barry had kept us apart when we were growing up, but now that I was nineteen and and he was twenty-five, the gap seemed to have closed and we talked endlessly, learning more and more about each other as the Land Rover ate up the miles through France. Travelling around Europe and stopping off to look for work was the first time we discovered how special a relationship between brothers could be.

We drove on to Lucerne, then turned south towards Spain. Barry had come up with a great idea – to go to Gibraltar. He was sure we'd find work there, as we were English. But Gibraltar was a long way away, and after a few days on the road we decided to stop off in Monte Carlo. The view of the harbour as we drove down through the hills was breathtaking. But it was not until we got out of the Land Rover, having found somewhere to park, that the enormity of the wealth there really hit us.

We just stood and stared. Neither of us had ever seen so many large yachts before, some almost as big as the small cruise liners that had occasionally moored in Liverpool. Looking at the millions of pounds worth of boats, we were completely at a loss for words. This was a far cry from the world we had grown up in.

As we walked along, I noticed a young lady standing on the deck of one of the yachts, polishing the rails. She was very tall and slim and didn't seem to be wearing very much. As we got closer, I realized she was topless! That was unheard of back in those days. And she was not alone – there were five of these goddesses. Like a couple of kids, Barry and I started to laugh, pushing each other about, unable to believe our luck. For two Liverpool lads straight off the boat, this was beyond our wildest imaginings.

We spent the next ten minutes or so slowly walking up and down the harbour front, eyes sharply turned in the direction of the yacht. There was a man with grey hair on it, sitting on a wooden recliner, a glass of champagne on a small table beside him. He was reading a paper, and wasn't really aware of the reaction his 'crew' was having on two lads from Liverpool. One of his girls must have said something, however, because as we walked past for about the tenth time he lowered his paper, loftily peering over the top of the page at us both, one eyebrow slanted in amusement.

Spirits raised, we carried on down the coast of Spain, slowly getting closer to Gibraltar. It was a long, hot and dusty journey, and when we finally arrived at the border, we were told it was closed because of an international border dispute.

Clearly in sight and less than two hundred yards away was what we were now thinking of as a little slice of English heaven. But it might just as well have been hundreds of miles away. The border guard told us that the only way to reach our destination was to drive further south to Algeciras, catch the boat to Tangiers and then a boat from Tangiers to Gibraltar. It took us forty-eight hours.

When we finally got there, we walked around the town enjoying the very English feel of it all, and treated ourselves to a couple of pints of English ale and some fish and chips. There was no work, though, unless we wanted to join the Moroccan gangs of men who were repairing the famous Rock. Sweltering heat and a few pesetas a day was not what we were looking for, so deflated, disillusioned and with our funds running low, we returned to Spain. It had been a long way to come for a couple of pints of bitter and a bag of fish and chips!

Barry and I were beginning to hate that Land Rover. We were sick of spending all our days and nights in it, and it was also a real gas guzzler, only doing around seventeen miles to the gallon. It was eating its way through our funds with alarming speed.

Two weeks after leaving Gibraltar, we pulled up in a small village not far from Barcelona, Lloret del Mar, one of the first package-holiday destinations. We were literally down to a handful of notes by the time we found somewhere to park.

This time there was no casual stroll around the village; we were job-hunting with a vengeance. After visiting several bars asking for work, a Spanish waiter told us of a place further up the sea front that was looking for staff, so feeling a little more positive, we set off.

He was right: there was a notice in the window advertising for an experienced English-speaking barman and a kitchenhand. Before going in, Barry told me to leave all the talking to him, saying he was far more experienced than me and we couldn't afford to make any mistakes.

I'd never pulled a pint in my life, so I spent the first night in my new job standing quietly aside watching the Spanish barman, Carlos, going through his routine – throwing ice cubes and bottles up in the air and garnishing the glasses with slices of orange or lemon. All too soon, it was my turn. Three English tourists came up and one called out, 'Three beers, mate!' This was it!

Picking up a glass and trying to keep my hand steady, I placed it under the beer pump. Trying to remember how I had seen my fellow barman do it, I slowly pulled down on the handle. There was a loud hiss, followed by a series of splattering noises, and beer came spitting into the glass. Froth flew everywhere, followed by droplets of beer, and the three customers sitting in front of me were pebbledashed with frothy flecks of San Miguel. Carlos threw his hand over mine, pushing the pump handle backwards and cutting off the stream of beer that was now flowing everywhere, then poured three beers for the British tourists, saying they came with the 'compliments of the manager'.

Carlos realized that I was an absolute beginner, and quietly told me that he would help me learn without the owner finding out. The rest of the night went reasonably well, and when we finished at midnight, he invited us to a disco.

Barry and I were ready to celebrate our good fortune, and it wasn't long before we were drinking and dancing the night away. The nightclub was full of young people from all over Europe, and my brother and I soon found ourselves going in separate directions. We had earlier agreed that, if we split up, we would meet the following morning at the Land Rover, so I wasn't too concerned about going back to a hotel with the pretty young girl I had met, thinking Barry was most probably doing the same.

My luck ended at her hotel door! So feeling the effects of too much beer, I stumbled my way back to the Land Rover, stripped off down to my underpants, crawled into my sleeping bag and was out for the count within seconds.

Barry, in the meantime, had been a little more fortunate and returned to the Land Rover an hour or so later. He decided that, as it was parked in a very noisy street, he would move it somewhere a little quieter and get a decent night's sleep. Totally oblivious of my presence in the back and thinking I was wrapped up in passion in some hotel room, he decided he would return to the original parking place in the morning.

Leaving the brightly lit streets behind, Barry headed towards the dark outskirts of town, along a narrow winding road and up a steep hill. He realized he was getting too far away but he couldn't turn around on the narrow road and had to keep on driving, in the hope that there was a turning place somewhere near the top of the hill. Finally, the road levelled out, and he found himself in a tiny car park overlooking the town. There were several other cars parked there, with amorous couples in them, enjoying the view through steamy windows!

Cursing his bad luck, Barry decided to do a three-point turn and head back down to Lloret del Mar. Leaning over the steering wheel to see better, he slowly inched the Land Rover forward, taking care to avoid a car parked close by. He put it into reverse, struggling to get the heavy gears to engage, and drove slowly backwards, craning his neck to see where he was going. But in the darkness he couldn't see a thing. Suddenly, he felt the vehicle continuing to move even with his foot hard down on the brake. There was a loud clunk and the vehicle started to groan, and to the accompaniment of a loud grinding noise, he found himself slowly tilting backwards, until he was looking directly up at the stars.

Slamming the gear into first, he put his foot down on the accelerator, but the car didn't move an inch. Totally confused, Barry opened the door to get out – and when he did so, he found himself looking down into a black void with tiny little lights blinking brightly on the valley floor some several hundred feet below! Realizing the full extent of his predicament, Barry slowly lowered himself out of the driver's door, grabbing on to some bushes and whatever other vegetation was there for safety, then pulled himself up into the car park. Turning around, he now saw what he'd done: the Land Rover was half hanging over a cliff, see-sawing backwards and forwards, with the heavy metal chassis groaning under the stress.

Barry stood in horrified silence as the full impact of his narrow escape started to sink in. Within a few minutes, he heard voices as the courting couples emerged from their cars, observing that he seemed to be having '*una problema*'. Even with his limited Spanish, he knew he had a problem!

Surrounded by a group of locals, all offering advice which he did not understand, Barry was not sure what to do. His dazed attention was suddenly caught by the arrival of a blue flashing light as a police patrol car pulled up. The two officers joined the other Spaniards watching the Land Rover as it groaned with pain. Like spectators watching a suicide about to leap off a tall building, they stood there in anticipation, waiting for the vehicle to lose its grip on the edge of the mountain before crashing down into the valley below.

Barry sat down on a rock, his head in hands, thinking, 'What have I done? Everything we own is in there!' Suddenly a thought occurred to him. His mind started to race as he tried to remember, without success, the last time he'd seen me. A deep-rooted panic set in and he leapt to his feet, one finger against his lips, waving with his free hand and calling out, 'Silence, please! Silence, please. Ssshhhhh!' The group of watchers fell quiet, and Barry called out, 'Jeff, can you hear me? Jeff, are you in there?' There was no response other than the creak of the chassis and the sound of a gentle breeze rustling through the bushes on the hillside. By now the sun was coming up, the sky changing colour from dark blue to a golden red. 'Jeff,' he called out again, even louder this time, in desperation, while quietly praying that I was still in town. His voice must have penetrated my sleep, as I mumbled, 'What?'

'Jeff, wake up, it's serious! Listen to me! I want you to slowly make your way to the front of the Land Rover and climb into the front seat. Do you understand?'

By now, I was at least half awake, and realized I was lying in the back of the Land Rover – but not horizontally. 'What's going on?' I called out. 'What's wrong?' The effects of the deep alcoholic sleep made me slow to react, and I was struggling to work out what was happening.

'Jeff!' I could hear Barry's voice clearly now. 'Jeff, listen to me. Climb over on to the front seat, and whatever you do, don't open the back door, or you'll be dead.'

Turning on to my stomach, I pulled aside the curtains that divided the back compartment. The sight which met my eyes paralysed me with fear: twenty or so anxious faces peering down in my direction, with Barry's the most anxious of them all. I could feel that the Land Rover was rocking, caused by my movements, and the extreme urgency on Barry's face was enough to gain my undivided attention. 'Jeff, I want you to carefully open the front windscreen and climb out on to the bonnet,' he said. Not realizing the full extent of the danger I was in, I did as he said, and moved slowly forwards into the front seat. It seemed to take an eternity, and even the smallest movement made the vehicle sway. Raising the windscreen, I crawled through the gap and lay face down on the bonnet.

'Take my hand. Quick, Jeff, come on! Hold on tight.' Leaning forward, Barry grabbed hold of my outstretched hand, pulling me with all his strength. I slid forward across the bonnet until finally I was on firm ground. The crowd spontaneously broke into applause, and Barry gathered me into a bear hug. 'I thought I'd nearly lost you, that you were going down with the Land Rover,' he said, squeezing me tight. 'What would Mum have done if I had come back without you, kid?' Pushing me back to get a closer look at me, he seemed to relax a little. 'Are you all right?' he asked.

'Yes,' I replied. 'Just a bit confused.'

When I looked back at the Land Rover, I couldn't believe my eyes: it was like something out of *The Italian Job*: over half the vehicle was suspended above a long drop to the valley floor below. I really had had a lucky escape.

Some six hours later, and with a lot of help from the police, a crane the size of a small house came crawling up the mountain and lifted the Land Rover to safety. The only damage was to the exhaust – and to our wallets. Barry had to count out every peseta we had left, placing the notes one by one into the crane driver's hand. Everything was gone now – even our 'return home' reserve fund.

Our attitude towards the Land Rover changed after that. Although she was still a gas guzzler, her sturdy build and steel chassis had saved both our lives, and we now felt indebted to her.

We worked at the bar for the rest of the season, and at the end of September; we started to make our way back home. We called that summer of '72 the summer of the S's – sun, sand, sea, sangria and sex – but it was also the summer that Barry and I became the best of brothers. So much so we decided to go into business together erecting aerials.

14. Beloved Mum

At the beginning of April 1973, Mum sat Barry, myself and Sheila down and with her usual directness told us that she had bowel cancer. She was going into hospital in the next couple of days and would be undergoing major surgery. Sitting there listening to her, I felt numb with the enormity of what she was saying. I just didn't want to hear it. This was not happening to us. No one really knew how to respond. We just tried desperately hard to follow Mum's lead, helping her prepare her things for hospital and trying to be as calm as possible.

The morning arrived when, having kissed Mum good luck, she was taken to theatre. We spent the rest of the day waiting and hoping for the best and praying it would all work out to the good. After what seemed like an eternity, Barry, Sheila, June and I returned with Dad to the hospital that evening. We were told by the staff nurse that Mum was doing well but could not be disturbed as she still hadn't come round from the anaesthetic. June's face fell so, taking pity on her, the nurse relented, allowing us all a quick peek at Mum while she slept. Pulling back the screen around her bed, we were all silent as we looked as this tiny, frail person, so beloved by us all, lying in what seemed like an oversized bed, surrounded by all sorts of medical machinery. It was scary.

Reassured, though, by seeing her, that she was doing well, we tiptoed out of the ward. Sheila, June and I went to sit in the waiting room while Barry and Dad went to see the surgeon who had operated on Mum. After some fifteen minutes they emerged, faces as white and as drawn as the sheets that Mum had been lying on. Realizing that something was desperately wrong, we followed them out to the car, again without saying a word. The silence was almost too much to bear; it was worse than all the waiting we had gone through that day.

'What did he say?' I asked Dad. I had to know.

Dad, who was driving, said nothing. Barry turned towards me and looked down at June's hand clasped in mine. After a moment's silence he looked back at me. 'I'll tell you later,' he said.

As soon as we got home, Sheila tucked June up in bed then hurried to the front room, where we were all waiting. The atmosphere was heavy with tension.

'Mum is very ill . . .' Dad started to speak but was unable to continue, so Barry picked up where he had left off.

'They have removed all of her bowel,' he explained, 'and fitted a colostomy bag. But the cancer has spread and there is nothing else that they can do.' Tears streaming down his face, he lowered his head into his hands. 'They have only given her three months to live.'

Sheila let out a cry as if she was in pain. I had to get out of the room, out of the house; I couldn't breathe and needed fresh air. I walked the whole way down Princess Drive as if in a trance, oblivious to the passing people and traffic and to the chilliness of the April evening. It could have been snowing for all I cared; Mum was dying and there was nothing I could do to prevent it. She was only fifty-three, too young to die. I thought she'd live forever. And poor June? She was only eleven! Far too young to be without her Mum. In fact, we all were.

Lesley came home for a few weeks to take care of Mum once she came out of hospital, and having her back with us all made such a difference. Mum, however, couldn't understand what all the fuss was about. She acted as if nothing was wrong: as if there had been some terrible mistake and she had been misdiagnosed; in her eyes, the doctor had no idea what he was talking about. It was hard for her children to know how to respond, and we found ourselves fussing around her, treating each day as if it was her last, which really annoyed her. 'Just you wait and see, I am soon going to be as fit as a fiddle,' was her response, and she'd tell us to pull ourselves together. She insisted that Barry, Sheila and I stopped acting as if something was wrong.

The impact on Dad was phenomenal. He began spending far more time at home, particularly with Mum. And as she started to regain her strength, he took her for days out in the car. June was too young to know what was going on and was simply happy that Mum was back home where she belonged.

It was a very difficult time for us all, particularly for Mum, as she was being so strong and, like always, a tower of strength. She even encouraged Barry and I to go off on our travels around Europe, but there was no way we were going to leave England. So with her blessing, Barry and I went off to spend some time with some good friends of ours, Mick, Tommy and Danny, who were working at Butlin's Holiday Camp in Clacton-on-Sea. It was only a few hours' drive away, which meant that we could come home at weekends. After the worry of the last few months, it was great to see them all again. As we sat around enjoying a pint, they told us about their new jobs working as chefs.

'Chefs!' Barry and I nearly fell off our chairs laughing.

'OK, cooks,' admitted Mick.

'Cooks?' I said. 'What can you lot cook?'

'Anything,' Danny answered. 'It easy, it's all mass-produced, and what's more, it's one of the best-paid jobs on the camp.'

They said they were short-staffed in the kitchen, and if we wanted, it would be easy for us to get jobs working there as well. But Barry and I were having none of it.

'You can't be serious,' Barry said. 'Neither of us can cook.'

Nevertheless, by six o'clock the following morning, Barry and I were dressed and looking every inch the professionals in our blue and white checked trousers and chef's whites. To top it all off, we wore tall white chef's hats which sat stiffly on our heads, as starched as our white jackets. If ever there was a situation when appearances were misleading, this was it.

The kitchen was as huge as a football pitch, but with everything that was going on in it, and the noise, the smells and the heat of the cookers, it seemed claustrophobic. Steam rose up from the tops of the largest saucepans, so big they were more like vats. Two cooks were stirring huge amounts of porridge, while another two were grilling hundreds of kippers, all laid out in neat lines, their fishy odour dominating that area of the kitchen. There was so much going on it was almost impossible to take in. Barry and I just stood there, totally at a loss what to do.

The head chef soon told us. 'Eggs for you two. You're doing boiled,' he instructed Barry, while I was told that I was doing fried. 'Understood?'

'Yes, Chef!' Barry kept his reply short.

'Any questions?' Chef asked, looking at us both.

'How many, Chef?' I asked.

Referring to a piece of paper on his clipboard, he said, 'Three thousand fried. Full quota today.'

He had to be joking.

Danny showed me what to do. I broke the first dozen, and the hot oil spat out and burned my fingertips countless times, but in the end I got the hang of it. After a while I was quite proud of myself, lining up my eggs in professional-looking rows then scooping the cooked results on to the large metal serving trays.

The following morning, when the alarm sounded at 5.30, we both staggered out of bed and back into our whites. We were on time and starting to cook as the clock turned six. I felt sorry for my brother: it was his turn to fry three thousand eggs, while I learnt the art of making porridge.

We ended up staying at the camp, working hard and playing hard, enjoying each others' company and having a good laugh. Every other night we would phone Mum, telling her about the funny things that had happened in the kitchen that day, and every weekend either Barry or I would return home, to spend precious time with her.

Mum, Dad and June even came down for a week, and we pulled as many strings as possible to make their stay perfect. Mum was as proud as Punch of us in our whites, and we were able to cut back on our shifts so we could spend more time with them. We cooked Mum breakfast for the first time ever, too, which gave us both a real sense of pride, as she had been feeding us all our lives.

The night before they left, Mum phoned home to speak to Sheila, who had been unable to get time off work. After the phone call she was very excited and couldn't wait to tell us that Sheila was engaged to be married to a chap from Wales, Keith Jones, who she had met the previous year while on holiday. At the end of the week, although Mum was a little sad to be leaving, she was also looking forward to getting back home and helping Sheila with the preparations for her wedding, which was only a few months away.

When the season ended, Barry and I returned to Liverpool, picking up where we had left off with our TV aerials business. It was now mid-September, and with the evenings getting longer and the weather getting colder, business was once again on the up. Mum continued to help us with the bookings. She seemed to thrive on constant activity, defying the predictions made by her doctor earlier that year. We all of us almost believed that she really would go on for ever.

Sheila and Keith were married on 4 November. The wedding was held at the church just across from our house and was really lovely. Although it was only a small family affair, it was certainly one to remember. Mum, wearing a glamorous big hat, posed with Sheila and Keith outside the church for the photos, Dad standing beside her and June looking pretty in her bridesmaid's dress.

The year drew to a close, and Christmas was upon us. Somehow, we all knew that it was to be the last of its kind, although nothing was ever said. Presents were stacked high, and the kitchen filled with goodies to eat. If there was a time to eat, drink and be merry, this was truly it.

Lesley and her husband, Roy, with their small son David, together with Sheila and Keith, spent New Year's Eve with us. The house was full to overflowing, and as the clock struck midnight, we all held hands and joined in singing 'Auld Lang Syne'. Mum had so far defied the odds; she was a walking miracle, and it was as if our prayers had been answered. I clearly remember her sitting in her favourite armchair with her first grandson on her lap. David had a mop of ginger hair and was the spitting image of me when I was that age. With their heads bent together, as Mum told him familiar stories, it took me back to my own childhood. It's an image I will never forget.

In the spring of that year, 1974, I officially became a man. Mum had established a family tradition, giving each of her children a gold ring of their choice as a twenty-first-birthday present. And as I sit here writing this story more than thirty years later, it rests beside me on my desk.

That summer, Barry and I returned to Butlin's in Clacton-on-Sea, once again working in the kitchens. I went home for a weekend at the beginning of July – the first weekend, to be precise – and I remember it as clearly today as if it had only just taken place.

I got home at around lunchtime and found Sheila in the kitchen. She looked worried and explained that Mum wasn't feeling too well, so she had come home for a few days to help out. 'She's asleep at the moment,' she said. 'Go up and see her later. Just let her rest some more for now.'

I was on tenterhooks, waiting for the time to pass, longing to go and see Mum for myself to make sure she was OK. I feared the worst and wanted to spend as much time with her as I could. Eventually, I couldn't wait any longer so I quietly went upstairs and opened her bedroom door as carefully as possible, not wanting to cause her any disturbance.

'Who's that?' she asked, and her voice sounded so tired.

'It's me, Mum,' I almost whispered.

'Jeff, is that really you?' I could hear the smile in her voice.

'Come over here, son, and help me sit up.' Gently, I put my arms around her, helping her lean forward so that I could rearrange the pillows, then sat her back against them. Mum had always been slender but now she was literally as light as a feather; it was as if she could be swept away by the gentlest of winds. 'That's better,' she thanked me, before asking me to open the curtains to let a little light in the room. She patted the space beside her. 'Come on, Jeff, sit down here and get comfortable. I need to talk to you – there is so much I have to say.'

As I sat at her bedside with her hand in mine, Mum told me the strangest thing. 'You will never guess where I have been,' she said. She was speaking to me as if she was in a dream, her voice soft and gentle. I didn't answer, so she continued. 'I have been to Heaven. God came down and took me with Him for a visit. It's so lovely there. I saw my mother and father, and my brothers who were killed in the war. Everything is so clear up there, you can see it all.'

I was totally unsure of how to respond, thinking that perhaps it was the medication making her talk like this. All I could do was to sit there and listen. As she continued to tell me what she had seen, her voice was getting stronger, and there was a greater degree of urgency about her. 'Jeff, pay attention. I'm being serious; this is important.'

'I'm listening, Mum,' I replied. 'I'm listening to everything you're saying.'

'God is coming to take me soon, and I am going to Heaven. I know it, and I know that I will be so very happy there. I don't want you to worry at all. Everything will be all right. I can watch over you from up there and help you every day.'

I could feel the tears stinging my eyes, and was unable to stop them from welling over and running down my cheeks. This was unbearable.

'Jeff, my dearest son,' she said, clasping my hand in both of hers. 'Please stop crying, I need you to be strong for me. I need you to do what I ask. Do you promise?'

Hardly able to speak, I nodded my response. 'I promise, Mum, I'll do what you want.'

'First of all, let's talk about June. You must make sure that nobody takes her away from this house.'

'I will, Mum,' I told her, making my first promise.

'As for your dad,' she continued, 'as soon I'm gone, he will stop drinking. He will also look after June and be a good father to her. For all his faults, I love him and I always will, and I want you to promise me that you will look after him as well.' This was not such an easy promise to make, but I assured Mum I would take care of them both. 'Now, all that remains is to talk about you.' She smiled at me, squeezing my hand with hers. 'I know that you struggle with your reading and writing, but I also know you are very clever in so many other ways. You will be very happy and successful. I have always believed in my heart that you are destined for greater things in life. You will be famous one day. Don't ever forget that. I will always be watching over you, I promise.'

There was nothing I could say. Wrapping my arms around her, I held her closely against me, and we lay there side by side, not saying a word, for what seemed an eternity. I never wanted to let her go. She was the most important person in my life and I wanted the moment to last forever.

I spent the whole of the next day with her, talking about my childhood and all the things that had happened. We laughed at the trouble I'd got into and the accidents I'd had, the endless doctors and hospital visits, and the stupid things I'd done at school. It was a lovely time, each and every second so very precious.

Before I left that evening, I once again held her close in my arms – this woman who I loved so much and who had given me so much. Cupping my face in her hands, she looked into my eyes, reminding me of what she had said and the promises we had made to each other, before placing a kiss on my forehead. Driving back to Butlin's, I could still feel the touch of her lips on my skin. A part of me wanted to stay with her, yet another part of me could not bear to see her go.

On my second day back at work, I had just arrived in the kitchen when I heard the head chef calling my name. Not giving it too much thought, I made my way towards him. He had a small office and was standing by the door beckoning me.

'There's a phone call for you, Jeff. Take it in here,' he said, and with that he walked back into the main kitchen, shutting the door behind him. I knew this was the moment I'd been dreading. Putting the receiver to my ear, I said hello and heard Dad's voice on the other end. He was hardly able to speak as he told me that Mum had died peacefully in her sleep only a few hours before. We talked for a minute or two more, and he asked me if I could tell Barry. After I put the phone down, I stood in the chef's office for a while, trying to gather my thoughts. Even though she'd been so very ill, I couldn't take it in.

I stumbled out of the office and told Chef what had happened, and then set off to find my brother. While my body went through the motions of walking, my mind was in a whirl as I tried to understand what was going on. Mum was gone! My best friend in all the world, the one person who really understood me and had been there for me every day. What would life be like without her? It was almost too much to bear.

Barry had been working a different shift and I found him asleep in our chalet. Waking him up, I broke the news. 'It's Mum,' I managed to say, 'she's gone!', before I broke down and cried. Sitting side by side on his bed, we didn't speak. We took comfort from each other's presence and shed our tears together.

I don't remember much about the days leading up to the funeral; we must have travelled home together but I can't remember much else, let alone anything in particular about the funeral service itself. I do recall being back at the house afterwards, watching everyone and everything around me, as if I was not a part of it at all. The whole family was there, lots of aunts and uncles who I hadn't seen for a long time, and quite a few old friends and neighbours.

I clearly recall hearing Roy telling one of my cousins how Mum had arranged her whole funeral. 'She was a truly remarkable woman,' he was saying. 'As soon as she knew what was happening, she organized the whole thing: the hymns with the vicar, the flowers for the church and the arrangements with the crematorium. She even asked Mrs O'Toole next door to take care of the sandwiches and refreshments for the wake.' I was amazed. Even in the last days of her life, Mum was thinking of her family and what she could do to make her death as painless as possible for the rest of us left behind.

I could see Dad in the garden talking to his brothers and sisters, while Barry stood quietly to one side. Thinking of my promise to Mum, I went in search of June to make sure that she was OK. I found her sitting on a chair in the front room looking truly like a little girl lost, totally on her own, although she was surrounded by lots of people. As I stood there, I could hear some of my maternal aunts talking with Lesley and Sheila and realized they were trying to decide what to do with June – discussing matters such as where she would live. It seemed they felt that if she didn't go to Lesley or Sheila's, she would have to move in with one of them. In their opinion, Dad would never be able to care for my sister.

Walking over to June, I took her hand and asked her to come with me. Just before we left the room, I turned and asked for silence. 'Just so that there is no misunderstanding,' I declared, 'June is staying here. That's what Mum wanted, and that's what I promised her would happen. She is not leaving this house.' June and I then went for a very long walk and talked about Mum, finding warmth and comfort in our shared memories.

When we eventually returned, nearly everyone had gone, except Barry, Dad, Lesley and Sheila. One of them, I can't recall who, then said to me, 'You were always Mum's favourite. Did you know that?' There wasn't any jealousy or resentment in it, it was said as a compliment. I simply responded by saying, 'Who fancies a cup of tea?'

Mum was right: Dad did stop drinking from that day on, and he looked after June very well, becoming a proper father to her. Barry and I decided to leave Clacton and come back home. And between me, him and Dad, we shared the duties of looking after June, while Barry and I set up back in the aerials business together. Dad took over Mum's role in his own male way, and with three men in the house, June got a great deal of affection and attention. We all wanted to protect her and make sure that she was as happy as possible.

In 1975, Barry moved out, setting up home with his girlfriend Linda, and in September of that year they had a lovely son, Danny. We carried on working together, but I was beginning to feel restless, and a bit lonely, if the truth was to be known. I needed to go away on an adventure, and having lost my travelling companion, decided to do it alone.

Looking for inspiration, I found myself going into a travel agent's, and less than an hour later I emerged clutching tickets to Benidorm, flying out in the first week in April. I thought if I went so early in season, I'd have no problems finding a job.

Several weeks before I was due to depart, I bumped into my old friend Kenny Walker. I hadn't seen him since I left school, and got chatting. His sister Elaine and her best friend wanted to go and find work in Europe, but Kenny wasn't too keen on the idea and asked me to talk to them about it and tell them what it was really like.

Shortly before I left, I met up with them. I told them about all the adventures I'd had but also explained that it was far more difficult for young girls travelling and working abroad. But, despite Kenny's best intentions, they were not deterred, and asked me to give them a ring if I thought there was work there for them.

Two days later, I was taking off for Spain.

15. Solo in Spain

It was the first time I'd travelled by plane, and the first time I'd travelled alone, so I was a bit apprehensive, to say the least. Also, I'd never been particularly comfortable in my own company, so I wasn't sure how things were going to turn out.

Benidorm was bigger than Lloret del Mar, but similar in many ways. The coastline seemed to stretch for miles and, looking out to sea, I was reminded of all the times Barry and I had swum together, some four years earlier now. But being on my own just didn't feel right. I felt that everyone was staring at me – old Billy-No-Mates all alone! – and I found myself quickening my pace as if I was on my way to meet someone. How stupid was that?

I went to a few bars to ask if they had any work going, but it was too early in the season. Of course, I had to have a drink in each one, and so I found myself, a bit the worse for wear, nursing a drink in one bar, well past midnight, while the barman cleared away. There was only one other person still in the bar, a Scandinavian-looking man with long, almost white, blond hair.

I ordered one last drink and suggested the barman have one himself, and give one to the other guy. The blond guy raised his San Miguel in acknowledgement, and a short while later bought me one in return. I raised my glass in thanks, but by now, the beer was beginning to lose its appeal, so getting unsteadily to my feet, I decided to see if I could find my way back to my hotel.

I stopped to thank the man at the bar for the drink, not really in the mood for conversation, and especially not in a foreign language, but he caught me off guard by replying in a strong Yorkshire accent. It turned out he'd been born in Lancashire and was now working for a company building villas nearby, so we had a couple more beers and ended up chatting. The bar finally closed and I somehow managed to find my way back to the hotel, before falling into a deep sleep.

What seemed like only minutes later, a loud banging and shouting outside my door jolted me awake. A man was shouting in broken English, telling me it was a wake-up call. My head pounding from lack of sleep and excess of beer, I wondered what was going on. Was I dreaming, or had that stranger last night offered me a job?

Trying to work it out made my head hurt. I could hardly remember a thing from the previous night, but after I had taken a cold shower, half of me had a hazy memory that I'd agreed to be picked up at 7.30 that morning. The other half still didn't know what day it was.

I stood outside the hotel entrance in the early-morning sunshine, not at all sure what I was doing there. Dressed in a pair of tight white shorts and matching vest, with white sports socks and plimsolls, I must have looked as if I had just stepped off a tennis court.

As I sobered up, it was easy to convince myself it had all been a dream. But near to giving up and returning to the comfort of my bed, I heard a car horn behind me. Turning around, I saw a battered old truck parked down by the road. As the driver's window lowered, I saw a familiar head of white-blond hair. It was the guy from last night. 'Hey, Scouser, get in!' he called out.

There were six men in the back. A hand reached down towards me, and I heard a loud Cockney voice say, 'Come on, Scouser. Grab a hold.' Taking his advice, I found myself squatting on the dirt of the flat-bed truck surrounded by a lot of different British accents as everyone introduced themselves. The Scandinavian-looking guy was nicknamed Rubio, the Spanish for 'blond'.

I felt a right idiot with my lily-white skin and matching 'tennis' outfit. Who in their right mind would dress like that to go to work on a building site? They all looked the part, with their brown muscles and tattooed arms. God alone knows what they thought of me!

After forty minutes of being thrown around in the back of the truck and getting to know the motley crew, we arrived on site, somewhere up in the mountains. There was only one villa completed; several others were half built. As I scanned the scene in front of me, trying to take it all in, I heard Rubio calling out, 'Right, come on, Scouser, follow me!' Walking behind him to a large mixer, he asked me if I had ever mixed concrete before. This was not the time nor the place for bluff. 'Not to worry,' he reassured me. 'I'll show you how.'

I made and tipped concrete all morning, the hot sun burning down on me, then after a three-hour siesta, Rubio handed me a pickaxe and told me to get to work with a couple of the other lads digging a trench.

My first day was definitely an endurance test to see what I was made of. And if my aching muscles weren't proof enough, the blisters on my hands certainly told me how hard I had worked. It was way after seven by the time I was dropped outside the hotel. My body ached all over as I climbed out of the truck, and I was starving. Rubio pushed a bundle of pesetas into my hand. 'Well done, Scouser,' he said. 'Same again tomorrow?'

Entering the hotel, I had just one thing on my mind – food – so, afraid the restaurant would soon be closing, I decided to get my dinner straight away. There was a long buffet set up, so I joined the queue, holding my tray, and made my way along, piling it high with bread rolls and ham to make sandwiches for the following day, as well as lots of fresh hot food to enjoy there and then.

Sitting down, and oblivious to everything around me, I got stuck in. But after a few mouthfuls I noticed the restaurant was almost silent; there was no chatter of voices or clatter of knives and forks. Pausing, a forkful of food on the way to my mouth, I looked around and realized that every eye was on me.

Suddenly it struck me that the hand holding my fork was a thick grey white, as were my arms and my top. In fact, apart from two circles around my eyes, the whole of my body was covered in cement dust. I was a living statue! Too tired to care, I threw a smile in the general direction of my fellow diners, and continued eating. Within minutes, the noise in the restaurant had returned to normal, the evening's entertainment over and done with.

I sold my return ticket to stay working on the site for a while, and found a flat with one of the other builders, Cockney Steve. Barry, Dad and June thought I was mad to stay out there – there was plenty of work in England, after all – but it was something different, and I was having great fun. I got in touch with Elaine to tell her that there were hardly any jobs going, but she and her friend Gina had already booked a two-week holiday and were coming out at the end of April.

I'd agreed to meet up with them on their first night, so Steve and I took them on a tour of Benidorm, showing them where all the best bars and clubs were and introducing them to our English and Spanish friends. Both girls were very pretty, and I found myself protecting them from all the young handsome Spaniards. I hadn't planned on playing the big-brother role, but nor did I want them to get hurt by some hot-blooded local only interested in a one-night stand.

Towards the end of their holiday it became clear that they didn't want to go back to England. They wanted to find work and stay, living off their savings until they found a job. But finding an affordable apartment proved almost impossible, so Steve and I decided that we would share one of the bedrooms at our place and offer the other to the girls. It made good sense splitting the rent four ways, and the girls agreed and promptly moved in.

My interest in Gina started to grow. There was something special about her that set her apart from the rest of the girls in Benidorm. If anything, she was the exact opposite of everyone else: while the other girls wore the shortest skirts possible, hers were down to her knees; while their necklines plunged to their navel, her collars were done to the top – she had a Mary Poppins way about her. I found myself thinking about her more and more.

It all came to a head one evening. We were out at one of our favourite bars when I realized that she was being chatted up by a Spanish guy. It irritated me, and I desperately wanted her to know how I felt about her. Taking a deep breath, I made my way over and gently took her to one side. My heart was in my mouth and I just blurted it all out. 'As from tonight, I am not chaperoning you and Elaine any more,' I stated. 'You can see whoever you want!'

She just stood in front of me, a confused look on her lovely face. 'This isn't going well,' I thought, 'this really is not the way to tell a girl how you feel.' But I couldn't stop. 'I want you to know that I fancy you myself!' As I stood there waiting for a laugh of rejection, all I could think was that that was one of the worst chat-up lines ever! What an idiot!

But Gina gave me the most amazing smile I had ever seen in my life. 'I fancy you too,' she said. She said it so quietly that I could hardly hear. I just stood there, speechless, for once in my life.

When we left at the end of the night, I took Gina's hand in mine. Walking along, I really wanted to kiss her, but didn't know if it was the right moment. We walked a bit further and I couldn't wait any longer. I stopped and pulled her close to me. And I kissed her. That kiss sealed my future.

In early June, Gina and Elaine found a job working for an English couple who owned a café/bar. They took it in turns, one waitressing during the day while the other babysat Steven, the owners' four-year-old son, in the evening.

I was still as accident-prone as ever and moved on from the building site after one day the ground suddenly gave way beneath me, sending me flying into a small ravine several feet below. As I fell, my shin caught on a jagged edge that was sticking out of the rockface. The pain was horrendous, and it left a long, bloody gash up my leg. When the girls saw it, they insisted I get it treated, and after asking around, we were directed to a convent, where the nuns ran a small hospital of sorts. When one of them set to work dry-shaving my leg with a cut-throat razor, the pain was so excruciating I nearly hit the ceiling, and when they stitched me up, I had to be held down and the air was blue.

I had to find other work, and had heard about a new discotheque that was opening. The manager told me that the Spanish owner only employed local barmen, but if I wanted a job working on the door I could have one, as long as I didn't mind dressing as Charlie Chaplin.

I laughed. 'Of course I don't mind!'

He handed me a bowler hat and a thin cane and told me to be ready to start at 7 p.m. on opening night. I couldn't wait to get back home to share the good news with my flatmates. They all thought it was hilarious, and I spent hours practising Chaplin's walk, swinging the cane and tipping my hat.

On the big night, I wore black shoes, trousers and a waistcoat with a collarless white shirt, and Gina pencilled a black moustache on my face. The whole thing worked a treat, and the club was soon full, the success continuing night after night.

Elaine started to get homesick and decided to return to England at the end of July, leaving Steve, Gina and myself sharing the apartment. Gina chose to work evenings only, babysitting little Steve, which meant we had the days free together. We explored the whole of Benidorm and the surrounding villages on a little moped, having the time of our lives.

In August, some friends came to stay, and of course they wanted to go to Tramps. I was working the door the night they came, planning to join them once Gina arrived, when one of them suddenly ran out to me. 'You'd better get downstairs now. There's going to be trouble,' he said. 'One of the Spanish lads has just grabbed Ronnie's bird.'

I was surprised. There was hardly ever any trouble at Tramps. Heading down the stairs, I wondered which of the locals it could be, because by now I knew most of them pretty well. There were somewhere in the region of three hundred people in that night, but peering through the smoky atmosphere, I saw who he meant. It was Cossi.

Everyone knew him and he'd never been any bother before. He was slightly backward and a real loner, but I got on well with him and always let him in for free. I smiled at him and suggested we went somewhere else, but he didn't move and instead he spat straight into my eye. If it had been anyone else, I would have punched their lights out on the spot. But because it was Cossi, I just grabbed him and tried to move him out of the club.

Halfway up the stairs, he began to get violent. His strength seemed to come from nowhere, and he went berserk. By now I had him in a headlock. I felt like a cowboy holding on to a young steer by the horns as he tossed me all over the stairs. I couldn't let go, I had to get him upstairs, so I held on as best I could, determined to get him outside. Suddenly I felt a sharp pain in my chest and, looking down, saw a red stain spreading across my shirt. Cossi had sunk his teeth into me and was not going to let go.

Cossi had to let me go sooner or later – surely he had to breathe! As soon as I felt his teeth slackening, I loosened my grip. In a split second, he threw himself backwards with all his strength, sending me hurtling down the stairs. Cossi was the first to get up, running into the club and somehow managing to get over the bar. Within seconds he was hurling bottles of spirits into the dancing crowds. It was pandemonium.

Once we got hold of him, it took a few of us to overpower him and pin him to the floor. He was going nowhere now, at least not until the police arrived.

The full extent of the damage only became clear once the

lights came on. There were half a dozen or so young men and women with blood pouring from injuries caused by the bottles hitting them in the face and on the head. An ambulance arrived, and the police not long after, and they began to arrest anyone they could get their hands on, including holidaymakers who'd had nothing to do with it. I tried to intervene, to explain what had happened and to tell them that they were arresting the wrong people, but they threatened me with their truncheons and threw me into the back of a jeep.

After much confusion at the police station, I found myself locked up in a prison cell. A couple of hours later, two policemen entered and started to interrogate me. Their English was poor, but I could understand enough to work out that they were accusing me of having caused the trouble, picking on a man with learning disabilities. They were getting very angry and started to beat me with their truncheons, hitting my ribs and my legs. I tried to show them where Cossi had bitten me, but they weren't interested and just carried on lashing out. Curling myself up in a ball on the floor and covering my face and head with my arms, I could feel their boots kicking my back. The fear seemed to make the pain go away, and the only sound I could hear was their shouts of 'English pig'.

Some hours later the cell door opened. The nightclub owner had found an English-speaking lawyer to represent me in court. He came straight to the point: 'Listen very carefully to me, señor,' he said. 'You are in a lot of trouble and could go to prison if you do not listen to what I say and do what I tell you to do. Do you understand?' I mumbled a yes in reply. 'You do not tell the judge that you work at the club. You are here on holiday, and it was your girlfriend the man was annoying. Leave all the talking to me and do not say anything. Do you understand?' Again I said I did.

An hour later I was standing in the dock, numb with pain, tired from lack of sleep, scared by what was happening and terrified at the thought of spending the rest of my life in a Spanish jail.

Cossi was standing directly opposite me on the other side of the small courtroom. We stood as the judge entered, and the proceedings began. Of course it was all in Spanish, so I couldn't understand a word. Suddenly it was all over, and my lawyer walked over to me and told me that I was a very lucky man: I had twenty-four hours to leave the country. I asked him what was going to happen to Cossi: what sentence had he received? His answer was simple: nothing! Apart from being told to keep away from Tramps, he had been allowed to walk away free!

Gina and a group of friends were waiting for me outside the building looking anxious. When I told them what had happened, they couldn't believe it. Gina was happy to see me, but more concerned about my blood-soaked shirt and the teethmarks on my chest so, once again, I found myself being sewn together by my friendly Spanish nun!

Gina and I quickly packed up, saying goodbye to all the lovely friends we had made over the five months we had spent in Spain. Despite everything that had happened to me, that summer of 1977 was still one of the best summers ever. Mainly because I met Gina, the love of my life and the best friend that anyone could ever wish for.

16. New Beginnings

Our unannounced arrival home was a shock to everyone. Gina's parents were pleased to see her – though I'm not so sure what they thought of me having been chased out of Benidorm by a judge! I went back to live with Dad and June and picked up where I'd left off, working with Barry on the aerials, while Gina stayed with her parents and worked as a barmaid four nights a week, leaving her Saturdays free to help her father selling shoes on his market stall.

One Saturday near Christmas, I was on my way to put up an aerial on a house near Park Road Market, where Gina was working, and I decided to call and surprise her. She was hard to find at first, as a big crowd had gathered in front of the stall, but as soon as she spotted me, she called out. 'Jeff! Great to see you! Come and help me. I'm on my own – Dad's had to go for more stock!'

'Brown size nine and size four in pink,' one lady called out, and I found myself serving a customer straight away. The slippers were stacked high, and Gina and her father, Bob, were selling them cheap. I carried on serving until Bob returned and then set off to get on with my own work.

Picking Gina up at around 7.30 that evening, we went for a quiet drink and spent the evening talking about the markets. I couldn't believe how much I'd enjoyed helping her out that day. Memories came flooding back from when I was a young boy working with Mum on the market, and selling stockings out of a suitcase with Dad. By the end of the night, I'd talked Gina into going into business with me. I was convinced it was fate and meant to be, considering we were both from Liverpool market-trading families and that destiny had brought us together three thousand miles away, in Spain.

It was then that I came clean to Gina, telling her about my inability to read and write. I felt so ashamed and embarrassed at first but much better after my confession, and she was my right hand from that time on.

We spent a day visiting as many markets as we could, looking at all the competition and what people were selling. The possibilities were endless, but we wanted to sell something completely different from all the others. We eventually decided to go into business selling teenage girls' fashion. I gave up the aerial business, and by the time Christmas was over we had told everyone what we were going to do and registered J&R Fashions as our trading name – the R standing for Regina, Gina's full name. Bob gave us an old market stall and a canvas sheet he didn't need any more, and I already had a van. Now all we needed was something special to sell.

Not having a clue about where to go to find it, we almost fell at the first hurdle. However, our June had recently bought a checked shirt, which we both really liked, and the label inside said, 'Kumar Brothers'. We got their Manchester address from the phonebook and on Thursday 5 January 1978, a twenty-year-old Gina and I, a slightly maturer twenty-four-year-old, set off to Manchester, clutching hold of our life savings of £300.

The address was a huge former office block in the heart of the city centre. We made our way down a dark and dingy stairwell into the depths of a large cellar, where we were met by an elderly Indian lady, Mrs Kumar, the mother (and boss, by all accounts) of the two brothers who owned what turned out to be a whole-sale fashion company. We introduced ourselves as market traders from Liverpool, and she invited us to look at all the clothes that were bursting out of the hundreds of cardboard boxes laid out on the floor.

Walking slowly down the lines inspecting every item of clothing in every box was exciting at first, but after two hours or so we realized that most of the styles on offer were just not what we were looking for. We did, however, manage to find thirty-six checked shirts and twenty-four pairs of drainpipe jeans, which were just starting to come into fashion. Gina also liked the look of a cowl-necked jumper, so we chose a dozen in different colours.

Handing over all our savings to Mrs Kumar was worrying, to say the least. She informed us that Friday night at around seven o'clock was the best time to come, as that was when the big deliveries arrived from London with all the latest styles. We spent the whole drive back to Gina's house trying to convince each other that we had bought the right things.

The next day, we were over at Gina's parents' house, getting everything ready to sell. Robert and Brenda were a fantastic couple and really helped us out. They were the type of parents who would do anything for their children.

I arrived at Gina's at five in the morning to set out for our first Saturday's trading. It was still dark and very cold, and Gina was in the kitchen pouring hot soup into a flask, wrapped up in several layers of warm clothing, protection against the cold January air. We left, making our way to Paddy's Market, the same place I had started out with Mum.

Organized chaos greeted us: at least fifty vans were trying to find somewhere to park in the darkness of early dawn, their headlights blinding me as they bumped on and off the pavement. They were a law unto themselves, but they had obviously been here before and knew what they were doing. We parked a short way away from all the commotion. I couldn't help but feel a sense of urgency at the speed with which everyone was unloading their vans, and the noise of the metal bars hitting the concrete ground was deafening at times. I told Gina to stay in the van while I went looking for a space to set up.

Five minutes later, I returned: I had found the perfect spot. It didn't take us long to empty the van, both of us working as speedily as everyone else, and soon we'd piled everything up in the space I'd chosen. Putting a stall up for the first time is very similar to erecting a tent when you go on holiday: nothing ever seems to fit together. After an hour of wrestling with it, however, we eventually managed it, and stood back for a moment to admire our new business venture. I put my arm around Gina's shoulder and squeezed her towards me. 'This is it, love,' I told her, 'the start of something big.'

But our special moment was quickly cut short by the arrival of an angry man the size of a block of flats! He didn't mince his words: we had to move our stall or he would do it for us. 'What do you mean?' I asked. 'We were here first.'

'Don't be stupid,' he replied. 'This is my pitch and has been for years. You can't just set up wherever you like.' He stopped for breath. 'You have to go to the office and see the inspector if you want a pitch. You'd better hurry up and take it down – I haven't got time to stand here chatting to you all day. So move it, or I'll take care of it myself.' Not doubting his ability to carry out his threat, I accepted defeat and told him to keep his hair on; anyone could make a mistake.

Gina and I spent the next half-hour taking the stall down and putting everything back in the van. By the time I got to the office, there was a queue of at least twenty people waiting outside. I asked a man at the back what the procedure was for *this* market, as if I generally knew the score. He said the inspector would arrive at nine, and we had to follow him around the market. If any of the two hundred regular traders didn't turn up, he'd allocate their pitch, first come, first served. Anyone who didn't get a pitch just had to try again the following week.

By 9.30 all the available spaces had been filled and the inspector announced there were no more left, before heading back to the warmth of his office. The remaining small crowd dispersed as Gina and I just stood there looking at each other in disbelief. Our dream of a business together was becoming a nightmare. But there was no way I was going to give up that easily, so I returned to the inspector's office.

He was sitting behind a desk with a large mug of tea in one hand and a bacon and egg buttie in the other, just about to get stuck in. 'I'm sorry to bother you,' I interrupted him, 'but there is no way I can go home. My life's savings are stuck in the back of a van out there, and I need to sell today. Surely you must have some spaces available?' He didn't flinch. He'd obviously heard it all before.

Speaking with his mouth full, he replied, 'I told you no, and that means no. Now shut the door on your way out!' I couldn't bring myself to tell him he had egg yolk dripping down his chin and it was just about to land on his uniform, thinking it would be best if he found out for himself. So I quietly left, closing the door behind me. But I still wouldn't leave it, and so I searched up and down the place myself, finally finding the smallest of spaces around the back, where all the secondhand clothes were sold.

The inspector was rubbing his uniform with a damp cloth when I returned. He wasn't too pleased when I told him about my great find, though he seemed to change his mind when I said there'd be a fiver in it for him.

Gina and I made the best of a bad situation, making our first sale at 11 a.m. After that, there was a steady flow of customers, and by the end of the day we were pleased with the way things had turned out. As we drove home, Gina sat next to me counting the takings. Her smile was getting bigger and bigger the more she counted. 'Jeff, how much do you think we took?' she asked me. 'Go on, have a guess!'

'About £70,' was my estimate.

'No – double that!' She couldn't contain her excitement.

'£140? You've got to be joking!'

'That's right,' she said. '£140!'

That much money on our first day! I was almost singing with happiness. 'We made that much and from such a bad position? Yippee, we're going to be rich.'

The following Saturday, in a better location this time, we took £350, selling out on a lot of the styles we'd chosen. We were now up and running, but we still had a long way to go.

We'd taken Mrs Kumar's advice on board and arrived at her warehouse on Friday at 7 p.m. in the hope of finding some really good stock. The place was full of Indian and Pakistani traders standing around talking; there must have been thirty or forty people there, also waiting for the London deliveries, and ours were the only white faces.

Half an hour later, a trapdoor was opened on the pavement outside and men were unloading boxes off a huge wagon and sliding them down a chute into the cellar. As they landed with an almighty bang on the floor, Mrs Kumar supervised as two of her men opened the boxes, pulling out the various styles for everyone to see while she called out the quantities and prices. Within a split second, one of the other buyers put his hand up and said something in a language I didn't understand. A box was put to one side, exclusively for him. These were definitely big buyers, and they knew what they were doing, while we were small fish with only a little bit of money.

This went on for hours, until there were no boxes left. We got home at midnight, not a single sausage to our name, so I had to put my thinking cap on. The following Friday, I arrived half an hour early, with a big bunch of flowers for Mrs Kumar. She was taken by surprise, and the other traders stood around wondering what I was up to. Very quietly, I murmured in her ear, 'Please, Mrs Kumar, please give some small traders a chance to survive as well.' That simple token of a bunch of flowers clearly worked: from then on, Mrs Kumar always offered us first refusal, and we went from strength to strength.

The next obstacle we had to overcome was to establish ourselves as permanent stall holders on as many markets as possible in and around Liverpool. This proved to be quite difficult: firstly, you had to get there very early and sign on the casual list; then, after some months and sometimes even years, you would be offered a permanent pitch. Gina and I were lucky, as we started in January in bad weather, when a lot of stall holders stayed away, and in just five months we became established on four different markets.

Business was good, but it was still hard to find the right stock. We spent days walking around the Manchester fashion district knocking on the doors of the larger fashion labels, but it wasn't working. Once they heard we were market traders they would literally shut the door in our faces, saying they didn't want their brand being sold on market stalls.

Feeling rejected and frustrated, we decided to try and make our own styles. I placed an advert in the local paper for a pattern cutter and machinist working from home, and the response was very good. Finding a fabric merchant to supply us was a task in itself, but eventually we succeeded. I spent hour upon hour dropping off bundles of fabrics at machinists' houses and going back four days later to pick up and pay for the finished products. It was hard work, but it was the only way we could get what we wanted. The first style we put into production was a checked, pleated mini-skirt. In the first week, we sold almost sixty on our four stalls – at Garston, Speke, Park Road and Paddy's Market – eventually going on to sell around seven hundred in total.

Making our own styles worked well, and we shifed large quantities week after week. Gina and I were a real team and built up the business together, and in no time at all we had loads of regular customers. Mum had taught me how to survive on the markets and I hadn't forgotten what I'd learnt.

I clearly remember one particular Tuesday at Garston Market. As we started to set up, Gina noticed that the stall opposite was selling exactly the same coats as we were, but £5 cheaper. Gina wondered whether we should put the coats back into the van or reduce the price, but I told her we would leave them as they were.

The stall opposite was run by Isaac, an old Jewish man who had been trading from the same spot for years. He was more than established and was literally an institution to all his customers. We were amateurs, while he was the master, and the better trader by far – in fact, he was everything I wanted to become.

As we were packing up to go home, I heard Isaac calling me over. Thinking he was going to have a go at me for selling the same coats, I was a bit hesitant, but he called out, 'Hey, kid! I don't know what you've got, but whatever it is, you should bottle it and sell it!' Confused, I asked what he meant. 'I've watched you sell at least four of those coats, for £5 more than I'm selling them for, and I haven't sold one!' he explained. 'In all my years on the markets, I would never have believed it possible if I hadn't seen it with my own eyes. What an extraordinary gift you must have.'

I smiled and thanked him for the compliment and returned to help Gina pack up. It was a good thing he hadn't heard me telling my customers that my coats were perfects and not the rejects that are sometimes found on other market stalls! Only then did I appreciate how valuable all those years spent with Mum on the markets had really been.

Six months had now passed since we had started, and business was very good. June now worked with us on Saturdays, just like I had done with Mum. Gina and I had built up a good stock level and bought a larger van. Things were going well, so having worked non-stop for months, up at dawn and out in all weathers, we decided we could do with a holiday. We chose Benidorm so we could catch up with all our old friends and go back to all the places we'd gone to when we'd first met.

On our last night there I took Gina out to a beautiful restaurant overlooking the beach and we had a truly romantic candlelit dinner. We held hands and talked about the past year we'd spent together. I was madly in love with Gina and knew I wanted to spend the rest of my life with her.

As the evening was coming to an end, we walked back along

the beach, arm in arm. A familiar clear sky with bright stars glittered above our heads, and a full moon seemed to shine down just on the two of us. It was completely silent except for the sound of the Mediterranean gently washing up on the sand. The whole experience was magical. I stopped and turned Gina towards me. Holding both her hands, I got down on one knee in the sand and asked her to marry me. Giving me the most radiant smile, she softly said, 'Yes.'

Getting to my feet, I held her close in my arms, and we kissed for what seemed like the longest time ever. It was a totally spontaneous proposal, but it couldn't have been more perfect if I had planned it.

On returning to England, we couldn't wait to break the news that we were getting married, and both Gina's family and mine were more than happy for us both. A date was set for the following year, 19 May 1979.

Not long after we got back from holiday, Gina passed her driving test, which enabled us to put another van on the road. She now went off with Sue, her friend, to trade on four markets a week, while I managed to do five, with Alan, another friend of mine. The remaining two days were spent trying to find stock from all over Manchester.

If I had learnt anything in my short time in the fashion business, it was that buying was the most important part. Finding the right product to sell was the key to success. The teenage girls in Liverpool were some of the most fashionable in the country, and it was my aim to come up with styles they would buy. I had no other alternative than to go to the heart of the fashion industry, London, in search of new suppliers.

Leaving home at 4.30 a.m. dressed in a smart suit, shirt and tie, I set off in the van on the 500-mile round trip to the capital. With £2,000 cash in my pocket, I headed straight for the West End. Looking at the fantastic displays in the windows of the large fashion houses excited me, even though I was more nervous than usual. Having finally built up enough courage to go inside one and take a look, I opened the door and was greeted politely by an immaculately dressed woman in her forties or fifties. Still feeling nervous, and a little intimidated by her posh voice, I kept up the pretence of being a successful businessman.

'I'm looking to buy some stock for my company,' I said.

'Well, you have certainly come to the right place,' was her response. 'Follow me, I'll show you our latest collection.'

I followed her into a larger show room, where there were thousands upon thousands of the most fabulous garments hanging on the rails. In my wildest dreams, I could never have imagined a place like this. 'Is this the sort of thing you are looking for?' she asked. Speechless, I could only nod, silently saying yes to style after style. I wanted to buy them all.

After a while, she asked, 'Where is your shop?'

'Liverpool,' I replied.

'Whereabouts?' she pressed.

I started to feel very uncomfortable, knowing that she probably wouldn't like the truth. I carried on talking while a hole started to appear at my feet.

'All over really,' I answered. Clearing my throat, the hole got deeper.

'How many shops do you have?' She did seem interested.

'Several,' I replied. Knowing that she would go on asking, I carried on. 'They are not quite shops, though.' I paused for a moment. 'More like very nice stalls.'

'*Stalls!*' Her soft voice became a shriek of horror and I was quickly ushered to the door. As I stepped out into the street I heard her final comment: 'I am sorry, but we couldn't possibly supply the likes of stallholders. Good day!'

Turning around to protest, I was faced with the door being slammed firmly shut in my face. I tried a couple of other companies, but received the same response. I gave up and drove the 250 miles back to Liverpool feeling desperately disappointed and rejected. What was wrong with market stalls? That was how all retail had begun. Marks & Spencer started out as a small market stall, after all.

Gina and I enjoyed the market way of life. There was a real sense of being part of a small community, and most traders are some of the most genuine, kindest and hard-working people you could ever wish to meet – a very special breed. It's not an easy life, setting up shop in the early hours, come sleet or shine, working ten hours at a time, then taking your stall down at the end of the day, only to repeat the whole process all over again the following day. You need real dedication.

Gina and I worked hard that winter. The weather was nearly always horrible, and I got so fed up getting blown to bits in the wind and rain that I bought a large box trailer and converted it into a small mobile shop. The back and one side could be opened up to create awnings, and steps leading into the trailer allowed our customers to come in out of the cold. It even had a changing room in one corner, which gave people privacy when they wanted to try things on. Our market trailer was the first of its kind and was admired by all. I had plush carpets laid on the floor, and it soon became known as the 'Harrods' of the markets.

Mum, holding me as a baby, outside our house in Liverpool

Me, aged six

My beautiful mum, Elsie

'The Boss': my handsome father, Leslie

Dad, my sister Sheila
and brother Barry with
me, little Mr Muscles!

The four of us: (*l to r*)
Sheila, Lesley, me and Barry
on our first holiday in Wales

Setting up shop at Paddy's Market on a wet winter's morning in the 1950s

(*l to r*) Alan, me, Rubio, Steve and Reg on the building site in Benidorm, Spain

In my chef's whites in the kitchen at Butlin's

Gina and me with our first market van

Our first Girls Talk boutique, with customers queuing out of the door for leather pants for £1

My gorgeous bride
and I leaving St
David's church on
our wedding day

My daughters ready
for school: Katie,
aged seven, and
Faye, aged five

Gina, playing polo
on Tordia

Me, playing polo
on Rubia

Our Jaguar horsebox
in all its glory

Our first Tickled
Pink Collection in
1989 – neon paid off!

Nutria and I prepare
for battle: I am in
character as Sir Jeffrey
of Whitegate

Abbots Walk:
the big house in
the country

The entrance to my emporium, Jeff's of Bold Street, with the wishing-well behind me

(*l to r*) Me, Ian Yates, Katie, Faye, Gina and Trinny and Susannah, with my Gold Award for Independent Retailer of the Year

17. Three Wise Men

Another Christmas came and went, and our wedding day was drawing closer. We were working all the hours God gave, and not having much spare time, we still hadn't found a place to live.

One night, Gina went to visit a friend of hers who had just got married and moved into her own home. The next day Gina told me how gorgeous it was and that there was another house for sale nearby, so we made arrangements to visit it the following Sunday. It was situated in Whiston, on the outskirts of Liverpool, and as soon as we saw the house, we fell in love with it. It was a three-bedroom semi with a small front garden and a larger one at the rear, and after two hours I managed to negotiate a purchase price of £16,000. It was hard to believe that soon it would be ours.

On Saturday 19 May the weather was at its best, with not a cloud in the sky; a perfect day for getting married. Looking at my reflection in the mirror, dressed in a light-grey suit and white shirt and tie, I was proud of myself, and really proud that I was getting married to Gina. I did, however, feel a certain emptiness, as if something was missing, which of course it was – Mum. She should have been there to share in my happiness. If only she could have met Gina, she would have adored and loved her as much as I did. Taking comfort from looking up at the blue sky, I remembered her words and how she said she would be looking down on me – and I knew she was.

My thoughts were interrupted by Barry, my best man, calling up the stairs to tell me the hire car had arrived. A short while later, pulling up at the church, I noticed a group of women standing by the entrance. Not recognizing any of the faces at first, I thought they must be 'left-overs' from the previous wedding, but as Barry and I got closer they started calling out, 'Good luck, Jeff!' and 'All the very best!' Some of our regular customers from the markets had come to wish us luck, some of them from quite far away, and that made us feel even more special.

The small church was full. I saw a lot of familiar faces from my side, while Gina seemed to have an even larger gathering of friends and family, many of whom I had yet to meet. As I sat in silence, nervously waiting in the front pew, Barry broke the silence. 'Are you sure you want to go through with this?' he asked. 'Or should we just quietly leave, go and buy an old banger of a van and spend the next six months driving around Europe?' His comment broke the tension, and we both burst out laughing, making the vicar peer disapprovingly over the top of his glasses.

As our laughter faded away, the organ started up. Standing in front of the altar, I found the temptation to look over my shoulder too great to resist. Turning slightly, I watched as Gina walked slowly up the aisle towards me, a vision of loveliness in her wedding gown. I felt a lump forming in my throat as I glimpsed a sight of her face through her long veil. Her beauty was hard to miss. Close behind Gina were her three bridesmaids: her sister Susan, her best friend Wendy, and my baby sister, June. The rest of the day passed in a blur. One of the most important days in my life, but definitely the fastest!

We couldn't afford a honeymoon, or the time off work, for

that matter, but living in our new home as man and wife was special in itself. Like all young couples committed to sharing a future together, we had dreams of one day having children and enjoying the happiness that a family could bring. I had always had a burning ambition to better myself and now, with the prospect of a family of my own to provide for, it was even stronger. Being a loving husband and a caring father was very important to me. I had no intention of letting Gina experience the kind of life my mother had had. Nor did I want my children to grow up with an absent father. I was determined to ensure that my family was protected and brought up in a loving and happy environment.

We were doing very well on the markets, but I thought we could do even better. I didn't want Gina having to get up at four o'clock on freezing-cold mornings for the rest of her life. I wanted to make her life easier, and also to expand my business. The best way to achieve this, I felt, was to open a shop. So the next six months, in whatever spare time we had, we spent looking for and planning the perfect premises.

Every month we'd spend a day in Liverpool city centre, visiting the larger stores, studying their stock and their prices. We had to do our homework so we could be one step ahead of the competition. One day, we noticed a fairly small shop on Church Street, pretty close to some of the larger high-street stores. Not only was it empty, but there was a large board saying it was available to rent and giving the agents' contact details. Fired by my determination to fulfil my ambitions, I made enquiries and discovered they wanted £15,000 for the lease. It seemed like a good opportunity. Gina and I talked about it over the next few days, and we finally decided to see if we could acquire the shop.

Apart from needing to raise the money, I found my enthusiasm dampened by my lack of education and poor literacy skills.

I had to force myself to swallow my fear of being found out and ask for help from some 'educated' people. The three people I approached were my bank manager, my accountant and my solicitor. They were the only ones I could rely on for advice.

I set up appointments with all three for the following day, and set off, my heart in my mouth. By the end of the day, and after earfuls of advice, I was so depressed I felt like jumping into the River Mersey! Any dreams I had had been destroyed in a matter of hours by my three wise men. In short, I was told, 'Forget it.'

That evening, Gina and I had been invited to dinner at her parents' house. As we sat around the table, Gina, Bob and Brenda were all eager to hear my news. I spent the next hour or so explaining how disappointed I had been with the advice I had received. My bank manager had lectured me on the perils of the high street and said that, although I was a good market trader, this alone would not be enough for me to take on the big boys such as Marks & Spencer and C&A Modes. On that basis, he was refusing to lend me any money. My accountant had been more sympathetic but felt we did not have enough retail experience to take on a shop. In his opinion, we were being too ambitious and should simply continue with the market business.

My final appointment was with Alan Espley, my solicitor, who had helped us buy our house. Alan had explained in great detail the numerous pitfalls regarding a lease, how once you signed one, it was your responsibility. In essence, he said, if my idea for a boutique failed, I would still have to pay the rent. Like the others, he told me to stick to what we knew best – market trading.

When I had finished telling them all this, Bob wanted to know how I felt – what my thoughts were, now that I had received the professional advice. I told him I felt that they were wrong and that, in my heart, I believed that I could do it. 'I know we can compete with the big boys,' I said. 'Every day, our stalls are busier than all the rest – Gina and I have a gift!' With that, he rose and went over to the mantelpiece. He picked up a large envelope that was propped up behind the clock and placed it in the middle of the dining table.

'This envelope,' he said solemnly, 'contains the deeds to our house.' Gina and I sat in silence, looking at him. 'We've just finished paying off our mortgage after twenty-five years,' he went on, 'and have all the faith in the world in you two; that you and Gina can make it work.' He then passed me the envelope and told me to take it to my bank manager the following day to use as security against a loan. Words failed me. I looked at Gina, wondering if she was going to say anything but, like me, she was silent.

'Enough of the misery.' Brenda broke the silence. 'Let's have a cup of tea to celebrate.'

I took Bob and Brenda up on their exceptionally generous offer and, as a result, Gina and I were soon the proud owners of our first shop premises, on Church Street, Liverpool. On the day I went to pick up the keys, my solicitor mentioned something that took the wind out of my sails. He told me that Harold Bagenski, the previous owner of the shop, had said that I would only last twelve months. Apparently, I didn't have a clue what I was doing. If he couldn't make it work despite many years' experience in the menswear business, then there was no way that I was going to succeed specializing in fashion for teenage girls! I felt doomed before I had even got going. But putting the miserable thoughts to the back of my mind, Bob, Gina and I got stuck in to doing the shop up.

The shop was named after a song by Dave Edmunds, 'Girls Talk'. And once we had purchased the new stock and recruited four staff we were ready for business. On Saturday 26 April 1980, we opened the doors to the public. I had set up my stall very early that morning at Paddy's Market. Bob and my sister June were going to run it while Gina and I focused on Girls Talk.

By noon I was getting worried. The place was empty. We had not sold a thing. I found this hard to accept, because we were offering the same stock at the same price as we had on our stall in the market. As I paced up and down, all I could think was that I had set my sights too high. My father-in-law's house deeds! All the advice I had ignored! There was so much riding on the shop's success.

Gina knew I was worried by the shop's first day's trading so, as we settled down later at home, she decided to cheer me up with some good news. It was news which I had been waiting for, for some time. She was expecting our first child. Now our dreams had come true: the new member of our family was expected to join us in November. Everything was happening so fast.

The shop had only been open for a week when the strangest thing happened. I was upstairs sorting out some stock, whilst Gina had gone to the doctor's for a check-up. I was interrupted by one of the sales girls coming to tell me that there was a woman in the shop wanting to talk to me. Apparently, she had a message from my mother. I looked at her in disbelief. 'What do you mean? My mother has been dead for over three years.'

The sales girl shrugged her shoulders and replied that she was only passing the message on.

I headed downstairs but stopped halfway, when I spotted a petite blond woman standing in the middle of the shop with her back to me. The sight of her and her uncanny resemblance to my mother made me panic, so I immediately turned and ran back upstairs as quickly as I could. I stayed there for about fifteen minutes, not sure what I should do, trying to calm my breathing and a sense of irrational fear. Finally, I plucked up the courage to return to the shop floor, only to find that there was no sign of the woman. 'Where is she?' I asked the sales girl.

'Oh, she's gone,' she replied. 'But she did leave a message. She told me to tell you that your mother said not to worry and that everything will be all right.' When Gina returned from the doctor's, I told her about my visitor. She was intrigued and asked me why I hadn't spoken to the woman. She was right: all these years later, I still regret not having spoken to her. But I am also positive that my eyes were not deceiving me.

We soon got into a routine. I worked the four best market days and then helped Gina on the two remaining days at Girls Talk. The market stalls continued to be very busy, but the shop was almost too quiet for comfort. I suspected this was because no one knew we were there.

Except for Mr B, that is. He came in the day after the lady who had delivered the message from my mother. Once again, one of the sales staff came to tell me that I had a visitor, this time a man who wanted to speak to the new owner. He was standing at the shop entrance, a tall, well-groomed man wearing a long black overcoat and black leather gloves, which on a warm sunny day made him seem very odd.

'Hello, can I help?' I asked.

'If you're the owner, you can,' he answered in a rasping voice.

'I *am* the owner,' I replied.

'Good, then I will call every Friday at the same time, four o'clock. You got that?' He looked at me sternly, almost daring me to say no. I just looked at him blankly; he had to be some kind of nutcase. 'When I call, I want you to have an envelope with £200 cash inside. Do you understand?'

I was no clearer now than when he had arrived. 'Why would I do that?' I asked, confusion written plainly across my face.

'Don't be funny with me, kid, or you'll regret it. You're on my patch, and that's the way it works.' I could see he was getting angry.

'What happens if I don't?' I didn't want to ask, but I needed to know.

'I'll torch the place.'

'What do you mean, torch it?' I was still lost.

'I'll burn the place down!'

'Why would you want to do that?' I asked. He *had* to be mad. But I knew it wasn't a good idea to upset him.

'Because that's what happens if you don't pay, you idiot. See you next week.' And with that final comment, he turned and left.

I was shocked and did not know which way to turn. That night, on my way home, I stopped at my gym on the north side of the city to do my regular workout. One of my mates was lying on the bench pressing weights while I lifted them on and off for him. While I was telling him about my strange visitor at the shop and the demands he had made, the owner of the gym appeared and asked me to come into his office. He must have overheard me, because when I followed him in he told me to close the door – he had something he needed to discuss.

Johnny was in his sixties. Built like an ox, he was one of the fittest and strongest men I had ever met. I had been going to his gym for two years and got on well with him. We had sparred and worked out together, and he seemed to like me. After I had finished telling him what had happened, he said he knew Mr B and said that he too would be at my shop at four o'clock on the Friday. I told him I didn't want any trouble and felt sure that I could sort things out myself. Looking at me from across his desk, he quietly assured me that there wouldn't be any trouble, but that I would not be able to sort things out on my own.

The following Friday, Johnny arrived at the shop at about 3.30, as he'd said he would. I made him a cup of tea and we sat chatting in the staff room. At four o'clock on the dot the inter-com sounded: 'Jeff, Mr B is here to see you.'

Getting to his feet, Johnny told me to stay close and to leave all the talking to him. Mr B was by the door, dressed in the same black clothes as before but looking even more menacing.

'Hello, Johnny.' Mr B seemed to know my companion.

'Hello, Tony.' Johnny returned his greeting. These two were obviously men of few words. 'Tony, I am going to ask you to do me a favour.' Johnny got straight to the point.

'What's that?' Mr B asked.

Nodding his head in my direction Johnny said, 'This lad is family. I want you to leave him alone.'

'Can't do that, you know that. He's on my patch. You know how it works: I look after the south side and your family look after the north.'

Johnny seemed to be ignoring him, his quiet voice making it

difficult for Mr B to argue. 'I'm asking you to do me a favour on this one occasion. Just leave this lad out.'

Mr B said nothing for a moment, just looked Johnny straight in the eyes, one giant to another. Finally he spoke. 'OK. You owe me one,' he said. With that, he and Johnny shook hands and then embraced, before he turned and left.

I was mesmerized by what I had just witnessed. It had been like a scene from *The Godfather*, only this time set in my small shop in Liverpool.

For the next six months or so, every Friday afternoon at 3.30, Johnny would drop into the shop – apparently just passing by – for a cup of tea. Although it went unsaid, I knew that he just wanted to make sure Mr B never bothered me again.

In the twelve years I remained on Church Street, I never saw Mr B again and I often wondered why Johnny had gone out of his way to help me like that. At the end of the day, it was probably because he was a genuinely nice guy. Or maybe, just maybe, Mum had paid him a visit as well!

18. Mannequins and Nappies

I didn't have any money to spend on advertising so I had to come up with something fast. One day, I was walking through Church Street, not too far from our shop, when I noticed a crowd of people gathered around two black teenage girls dancing like robots to music from a ghettoblaster. Robotic dancing was the new thing at that time, and watching them, I had an idea: I could pay them to dance outside my shop. If they drew the same crowd, it would be good publicity. When I spoke to them, they were very keen, so I asked them to come to the shop at 9 a.m. the following Saturday.

That left me a week to turn my idea into reality. I had 2,000 flyers printed announcing the arrival of Girls Talk, then bought two white boiler suits and two baseball caps, and had them printed with the name of the shop in brilliant red.

The following Saturday the girls put on their outfits, adding black stockings over their faces and black gloves on their hands. They looked spectacular and once they had started their performance, a crowd quickly drew up, keeping Gina and me busy handing out the flyers. Within an hour, Girls Talk was packed with eager shoppers, all happily spending their money. And this continued for the rest of the day. Towards the end of the afternoon, however, my two robots came into the shop accompanied by two 'bizzies'.

'Excuse me, sir,' one of the policemen asked, 'are you responsible for these two young women?'

'Yes, I am,' I replied. 'Why? What's wrong?'

'I'm afraid we cannot allow them to continue their dancing,' he explained. 'It's against the law.'

'Against the law?' I was puzzled. 'They're not busking or doing anything wrong – just entertaining the shoppers as they pass by.' I really couldn't see what the problem was.

'If we let it continue,' said the policeman, 'soon everyone will be doing the same thing, and the area will become congested. I am sorry, sir, no more dancing, and that's final.'

The girls looked disappointed. The day had been going so well for all of us, and now it was ruined. However, by the time they'd changed out of their costumes, I had come up with a solution. 'Don't worry, girls,' I told them. 'Next Saturday you can perform in our windows!'

The following Saturday, I removed a mannequin from each window and Gina dressed the girls in two of our latest styles instead of their boiler suits. Once they had put the black stockings over their faces and the gloves on their hands, they looked just like the real mannequins in the window.

They were brilliant. They stood completely motionless in the window until somebody walked past or stopped to have a look, then they would make a small movement, scaring the life out of whoever was looking. It was hilarious watching people's reactions and listening to their screams of surprise. No one had ever done anything like this before. Within a very short time, a large crowd had gathered, and soon the tills were ringing non-stop as people started coming inside to spend their money. My idea had worked – I had got the customers through the door, and when they got there they loved what was on offer.

But then the bizzies appeared once more – in fact, it was the very same one as the week before. 'Sir, I don't know what it is you are doing, but whatever it is, you have to stop,' he said. 'You are causing an obstruction on the pavement outside.'

The penny dropped – but I had to smile at his blindness. Even this sharp-eyed cop had missed the obvious – my window was the stage for two living dolls!

'You can't be serious!' I protested. 'Last week you told me that I couldn't promote my business outside, and now you're telling me that I can't promote it from inside? How do you expect me to do it then?' I was irritated now. How could he be so narrow-minded?

'I don't know, sir. But I can't allow you to cause an obstruction.'

I muttered a few angry words under my breath as he left. This was too much – I was trying to make my business busy but the bizzies wouldn't let me!

As the weeks passed by, Girls Talk started to established itself, although the pressure was still there to do a lot better. If I was really going to compete with the big boys, I had to start thinking like them.

Now that we had shop premises, many more doors were opened to us. I started driving to London once a week to buy the latest styles from the larger fashion houses. The only drawback was that they were expensive, and I hated selling them at a similar price to my competitors. My aim was to sell cheaper than anyone else so, every trip to London, I spent hours searching for small factories.

Labour costs were low at these factories so I could keep my own prices down, and they worked really fast. If a buyer handed over a winning style on a Monday, it could be manufactured, delivered to the high street and on sale in the department stores by Saturday. The speed with which they produced finished garments was amazing.

My job was to find 'cabbage', an old trade term for leftover fabric or cloth. Most of the big fashion houses would design a garment, source and pay for the cloth, and then give the design and cloth to a known manufacturer on a cut-make-trim basis (CMT). They would pay the factory owner as little as they could get away with, but if he was clever, he would cut the cloth very carefully, allowing no wastage – hence the expression, 'Cutting your cloth according to your means'. It was accepted that any leftover fabric belonged to the factory owner, and he could often save between 10 and 15 per cent of the fabric, which on the basis of an order for 1,000 blouses, say, would leave you enough for somewhere in the region of 100–150 over-makes. Then, because the cloth was free, the over-makes or 'cabbage' could be sold at a very low price, which meant I could sell up-to-the-minute garments for much lower prices than the competition. 'Cabbage' was one of the fundamental reasons for Girls Talk's success.

One day I was in the stock room when I heard a shout from upstairs: 'Jeff, quick!' I ran to the sales floor, and found the customers and my sales staff standing immobilized, mouths hanging open in disbelief. 'Jeff, quick,' one of the girls shouted, 'Quick, he's taken it!'

'Taken what?'

'The till,' she replied.

'Which way did he go?' I demanded.

'That way,' someone said, and everyone suddenly came to life.

Dashing out of the shop, I found myself among the crowds,

but I caught a glimpse of a man two hundred yards away who kept glancing over his shoulder, and ducking and diving his way through the shoppers. Racing after him, I shouted, 'Stop! Thief! Stop him!'

As the gap between us shortened and he realized I was closing in on him, he suddenly hurled my cash register backwards over his head, sending it crashing to the ground and spilling the money everywhere.

For a split second I wasn't sure what to do – continue my pursuit or retrieve the till. I decided to carry on after him and leapt over the shattered machine. There was only one thing on my mind: to get my hands on this guy! But glancing backwards, I saw a crowd of people picking my money off the pavement. This brought me to a sharp halt and, turning around, I retraced my steps. People had taken fistfuls of notes.

'That's my money, leave it alone,' I shouted, snatching as much as I could from their clutches and stuffing it into my pockets. I then picked up the remains of the till and returned to the shop.

Apparently, the thief had just casually strolled into the shop, made his way to the cash register, picked it up off the counter and run out! Everyone who saw it had been stunned by his sheer audacity and had been frozen to the spot. Later, on contacting the insurance company, I was informed that, if any of the staff had been hurt by the thief, it would have counted as robbery with violence and they would have replaced the till and the missing £160. But as this had not happened, it was classified as simple shoplifting, which my insurance policy did not cover.

After that incident, the new cash register I purchased was firmly bolted to the counter!

At this time, Gina was blooming. At eight months pregnant,

she was in full sail and needed lots of encouraging to stay at home and rest. But being obstinate, she wouldn't listen and insisted on continuing to work in the shop. This particular Saturday morning, while I was at the market, she was serving a customer when two women in their mid-twenties entered and threw a carrier bag down on the counter. One of them, a blonde, demanded her money back. Gina picked up the bag and handed it back, saying, 'Do you mind? I'm serving someone at the moment, but I'll be with you in a minute.' Once she had finished, she turned to the young women who had been waiting. 'Now, how may I help you?'

Pointing to the bag, the blonde woman stated, 'I bought this last week, and it has already fallen to bits. I want my money back now!' Opening the bag, Gina was hit by a strong smell of alcohol, and on closer inspection, she found a stained blouse with its collar hanging off.

'How did it get in this condition?' she asked.

'That's none of your business,' she was told. 'It's faulty, so just give me my money back.'

Gina put the blouse back into the bag and handed it back to the customer. 'This is my business, and I'm sorry, but I am not prepared to refund your money, particularly as it looks as if someone has tried to rip the collar off.'

But the young woman was not going to give up. 'I'm taking this to the Citizens Advice Bureau, and we'll see what they have to say.'

'Please do,' said Gina, and the two of them stormed out of the shop.

Half an hour later, the phone rang, and Gina answered. 'This is the Citizens Advice Bureau here. We have just had a woman

173

come in with a blouse that she bought from you; we advise you to give her the money back.'

Before Gina could say anything, the line went dead. She thought there was something strange about it and when she mentioned it to one of the staff, she was told that the Citizens Advice Bureau was not open on a Saturday. She called to check, and just as she was putting the phone down on the recorded message, she noticed the two troublemakers walking back through the door.

Throwing the bag down on the counter again, the blonde arrogantly informed Gina that she should have had a call from the Citizens Advice Bureau. 'They told us that they have spoken to you,' she whined, 'and that you have to give me my money back.'

Looking her in the eye, Gina replied. 'I don't know which of your friends I spoke to, but it certainly wasn't the Citizens Advice Bureau, as they are closed all day Saturday.'

At that, both women began loudly cursing at her, angry at having been caught out. Gina came out from behind the counter and towards the door, to encourage them to leave the shop. Seeing her standing there in a well-filled maternity dress, the blonde leaned towards her and hissed, 'I'll put you and that baby through that window, you cow!', and her friend spat in Gina's face. Two of the staff ran over to assist Gina, and after much arguing, eventually managed to steer the two women out of the shop.

When I arrived at the shop at five o'clock that afternoon, Gina was in a terrible state. The staff told me what had happened and where they thought the women had gone. Taking one of the staff with me to identify them, I headed to a pub around the corner. We quickly spotted them sitting at a large table with some other men and women, all making a lot of noise. The pub was poorly lit and full of smoke, the loud atmosphere telling me that everyone there was well into a Saturday drinking session. Furious at what had happened, I didn't stop to think and stormed straight over. Putting my hands firmly down on the table, I leaned in close, eyeballing the pair.

'If you two come anywhere near my wife or my shop ever again, I'll put you through every window in this place.' My voice was so loud that the whole pub must have heard me, and the place fell quiet. 'Do you understand?' Thank God, no one said a word or did anything in retaliation!

In the early hours of the following morning, Gina woke me to tell me that her waters had broken and she was going into labour. I carefully drove her to the Oxford Street Hospital, where she remained in labour for a further thirteen hours before finally delivering our daughter. I was present when she was born. Four weeks premature and only weighing 5lbs 10oz, she spent the first week of her life in an incubator in intensive care. We found the whole thing terrifying. We had come so close to losing our baby girl. And all because of the distress caused by those vile women.

We named our precious little girl Katie May, the middle name after Elsie May, my mother. In the early months of Katie's life, Gina took her into work and breastfed her there. There was no alternative, as we couldn't afford any more staff.

Once Katie arrived, our luck seemed to change for the better. Over the next twelve months, our business went from strength to strength, and for the first time we began to enjoy the financial rewards of all our hard work. By the end of the year, we had saved enough money to pay back Gina's parents and move to a bigger house. To be honest, it wasn't so much a bigger house as more space outside we needed, to accommodate the large market trailer, the vans and Gina's car.

After looking for some time, we came across a Victorian house set in half an acre of land. It was a mansion compared to our last house, with six bedrooms and three bathrooms. Although structurally sound, it needed a lot of updating. It had been built in the late 1800s for Lord Latham, the then owner of most of the land in Huyton, and his coat of arms still remained above the front door. It seemed that Gina and I were the only ones mad enough to buy it, and in March 1981 we moved in. It was rather spooky at first, with its dark cellars and large staircase, which led up to an even larger landing. There were eight tall doors at the top of the stairs and, with its high ceilings and large windows, it seemed huge for two young people and a tiny baby. Even with Carla and Ranger, our two German Shepherds, we still all rattled around.

One day, I opened the door to find two policemen standing there. One looked me up and down before speaking. 'Morning, young man. Is your father at home?'

'No he isn't,' I replied. 'How can I help?'

There was a moment's silence. 'We need to speak to Mr Pearce.'

'Yes, that's me,' I informed them.

'I don't think you understand, young man. We need to speak to Mr Pearce, the owner of the house.'

'That's me,' I said with pride. After a short while, I finally managed to convince them that I was indeed Mr Pearce, whereupon they explained that they had come out because the alarm was going off in the shop.

They weren't the only ones who found it hard to believe that such a young family could own such a grand house. It took us a year to put our stamp on it and make it really feel like our home. In the middle of all this, Gina announced some more good news – she was expecting our second child. The pressure was now even greater than before to make a success of our business.

19. By the Seat of My Leather Pants

It was the early part of December 1982, and I was on my regular once-a-week journey from Liverpool to London with my part-time driver, George, at the wheel. I was looking for good-quality stock for the Girls Talk sale, which always started the day after Boxing Day. It had to be something different that would make us stand out from the rest of the competition. By five o'clock that day, I must have visited between twenty and thirty factories all over London, and I had managed to fill three-quarters of the van with pretty good deals. By now, we would normally be heading back for Liverpool, but something was bothering me: there was something missing, and I felt we could do better.

Then it hit me. I gave George instructions to drive us across London to Brick Lane, near Spitalfields Market in the East End, where I'd bought leather trousers before. Brick Lane was not for the faint-hearted; it was a maze of dingy streets and poorly lit, narrow alleyways leading off the main thoroughfare. It was a bit like how you imagined a casbah to be, with doors in the narrow streets leading to small factories. The dark alleyways outside were always full of shifty, slightly menacing-looking characters.

We arrived as it was getting dark, and I soon found myself face to face with Rashid, the owner of the leather factory I'd come to visit. He hadn't changed too much, and apparently neither had I, as there was a clear look of recognition on his face. 'Mr Jeff, greetings,' he said, gesturing towards his office. 'Please come, sit and have a tea.' That's how we'd always started off our business negotiations.

After we'd drunk our tea, he asked me what I was looking for. 'Girl's leather pants,' I replied, 'at a very cheap price. I need them for my sale.' For regular stock, I normally paid £35 per pair and then sold them for £70. But I now wanted to pay no more than £17 per pair, to sell at £35 in the sale.

'Impossible,' he said. 'I would go out of business, it would ruin me. Mr Jeff, the raw leather costs me that much! Are you mad?' He was good.

We continued in this vein for the next twenty minutes, me bartering for the best deal but making no real progress. So I decided to use my ace card. Putting my hand into the inside pocket of my overcoat, I pulled out £1,000 in used £20 notes bundled together with an elastic band. 'Rashid,' I said, pointing to the money, 'it's getting late, and I want to finish our business. I am quite serious about the leather pants, so if you want any of that money, show me some cheap stock.'

This had never failed to work in the past. There was no way he was going to let me go back to Liverpool with all those lovely pound notes. Grabbing the money off the table, he raised his tunic and stuffed it into a money belt around his waist.

'Come,' he said. 'Come with me, Mr Jeff.' I couldn't stop smiling as I followed him upstairs. The cash-on-the-table trick had worked again!

After climbing three flights of narrow stairs, Rashid led me into a small, dark room. In the corner was a pile of leather pants in all colours and sizes, literally just thrown one on top of the other. Pointing towards them, he said, 'You can have these for £20 a pair. Good-quality leather, nothing wrong with them.' I started to examine them carefully for serious faults such as rips and holes. Years in this game had given me an 'experienced eye' and I was not easily fooled. But this time around, the only problem I could find was that all the side zips were broken. After checking them all, I counted seventy-two pairs, a real treasure!

Throughout my inspection, Rashid had stood quietly to one side, his eyes never once leaving me. 'You must be joking,' I said. '£20 a pair when they're all faulty? They can't be worth more than a fiver in this condition!' I had found that starting at the lowest price was often the best way to plant doubt in the seller's mind and would help me get a price I wanted. 'The colours are horrible,' I continued, 'and the sizes . . .' I paused for effect. 'They are all big sizes!'

'There's nothing wrong with them,' countered Rashid, a note of anxiety in his voice.

'Nah, nothing good here,' I said, feigning disinterest.

'They look good to me.' Once again, Rashid sounded hesitant. '£15 a pair then,' he offered.

Putting on a poker face, I looked him straight in the eye. 'No, I'm not interested, and to be honest, I can't think of anyone else who'd be daft enough to buy seventy-two pairs of faulty trousers!' Putting my hand out towards him, I continued, 'I'm sorry, but if you could hand me my money back, I'm going to head off now. I have a long drive ahead of me.'

Rashid lowered his head to one side as if in deep thought. 'Make me an offer,' he said.

'£10 a pair,' I replied, 'that is my last and final offer. £10, take it or leave it.'

Poor Rashid – his face looked as if he had just received some tragic news. I started to make my way downstairs, still pretending not to be interested, when I was stopped by a shout: 'OK, Mr Jeff, all right, it's a deal.' He stood at the top of the stairs, a defeated man.

Within twenty minutes, my van was loaded and George and I were setting off for Liverpool. As we turned the corner, I started to laugh. 'What's so funny?' George asked.

'My mother taught me well,' I replied.

We finally got home in the early hours of the morning. Gina, who was now six months pregnant, had not been able to sleep and got out of bed as soon as she heard the van pulling up. Opening the door, I was greeted by a rather tired and slightly annoyed wife. 'Where have you been?' she demanded. 'Do you realize how late it is? I've been worried sick, thinking something might have happened to you!'

'I'll tell you all about it over a brew,' I said, and as we sat there sipping a hot cup of tea, I told her about the deal – and about what I'd decided to do with the leather trousers.

On the journey home, I'd been thinking, as usual, of ideas that would make us stand out from all the other shops in town. 'I've had an idea,' I told Gina now. 'Rather than sell these leather trousers at £35 a pair, making a £25 profit, I want to sell them for £1 a pair.' I paused, waiting for the explosion that I knew was coming.

'You can't be serious,' Gina replied, looking at me as if I'd lost my mind. 'Nobody sells leather trousers for £1 a pair. Think how much money we could make if we sold them for £35 each – about two and a half thousand pounds! And they would still be a fantastic bargain; half the normal price. You just can't be serious.'

'Just think of the publicity,' I argued. 'Selling leather trousers for £1 a pair would make us the talk of the town. It'd never be forgotten.'

I could see it was going to take a while to bring Gina round to my way of thinking. In the meantime, I found a local man to replace all the broken zips. He charged £1 per pair. I couldn't help smiling at the irony of it – he was charging the same price for a zip as I planned to sell the trousers for!

It took a few days, but I eventually managed to get Gina to agree that the loss more than justified the potential publicity. We knew it was a gamble, so to try and minimize the risk, I placed an advert in the *Liverpool Echo*, which appeared on 24 December, wishing all the Girls Talk customers a merry Christmas and thanking them for their support over the past year. And of course the advert was also publicity for our sale on 27 December. It stated that, in addition to all the fabulous half-price bargains that would be on offer, we were also going to be selling leather pants, reduced from £70 to £1. If anything was going to grab their attention, it was going to be that!

On Christmas Eve, we started reducing all the old stock and introducing the new stock brought in for the sale. We had eight staff working for us by now, all lovely young girls, and naturally enough, they each wanted a pair of the leather pants. I explained to them, however, that I would rather wait and see what happened on the first day of the sale; they agreed that this was fair. In the afternoon, with everything ready for the after-Christmas sale, I told the girls to go home and wished them all a Happy Christmas, and started closing the shop down for the next two days.

Overcoat on, shop alarm set, I locked the front doors and was just about to pull down the steel shutters when I noticed a young woman sitting on the ground with a blanket around her shoulders. I asked her if she was all right, wondering what she was doing there.

'I'll be all right if you've got a black pair of size ten, leather pants for just £1!' she said.

I looked at her, still not sure what was going on. 'Yes, we will have leather pants for £1 in the sale, and I'm sure there's at least one pair of size tens!'

'That's good,' she said, pulling the blanket further up around her shoulders and huddling down into the blanket. This was frustrating. I wanted to get into my car and home, and yet I was standing here having a conversation with some strange young girl who was sitting outside my shop in the middle of winter with a blanket wrapped around her.

'How did you find out about the pants?' I asked, wondering if the *Liverpool Echo* had made a mistake and put the wrong date in the advert.

'*The Echo*,' she replied.

'Well, when did it say the sale was starting?'

'The day after Boxing Day,' she answered.

I couldn't help myself, this was totally weird. 'Well, then why are you here, sitting outside the shop with a couple of days to go before the sale starts?'

'I want to make sure that I get a pair of leather pants for just £1,' she said.

By now it was dark, cold and starting to snow. It was also Christmas Eve, a time when people are usually at home with their families, getting ready to enjoy Christmas.

'You can't be serious,' I said. I was getting irritated. She was just not listening. Injecting a more forceful tone into my voice,

I told her, 'I have got seventy-two pairs of leather pants. Go home now and then come back at five o'clock on the morning of the sale. That's all you need to do!' She didn't move. 'You must be mad,' I finished. I couldn't think of anything else to say, other than goodbye, and headed off to the car park.

When I drove past the shop ten minutes later, this solitary figure was still sitting there. She looked so sad, alone on a cold, dark night, with wet snow all around her. In the car, I couldn't stop thinking about her, comparing the situation with my own.

I knew Gina and Katie would be waiting for me. It was so wonderful coming home any day of the year. But at Christmas it was even more magical. As I opened the front door, Gina welcomed me, with Katie in her arms, and gave me a hug and a kiss. Katie was just over two years old, a great age for climbing all over me and calling out, 'Daddy.'

Putting Katie on my back for a piggyback, Gina and I headed for the kitchen, while I told her about the girl who had set up camp outside our shop. I don't think she really believed me, as she laughed and looked out the window, noticing that the snow was starting to stick. 'I'm sure she'll have gone home by now,' she said. 'Come on, dinner's ready. And Jeff? Will you stop talking about work!'

We had a lovely dinner, settling down in front of the fire and watching television afterwards. But hours later, I found myself still thinking about the girl outside the shop. Was she still there? Was she all right? So once Katie was tucked up in bed, I told Gina that I was going back to the shop.

'I feel like Ebenezer Scrooge,' I said. 'Here we are, all nice and cosy, and she could still be out there in the freezing cold. If she is, I'm going to promise her a pair of leather pants on the day of the sale, and then send her back home. The only way I'm going to be able to enjoy Christmas with my family is if I know she's OK.' I gave Gina a kiss, and set off, promising that I wouldn't be much longer than an hour.

The weather outside was bitter, the snow now turning to sleet. As I turned the corner and got closer to the shop, I could see boxes lined up on the ground outside. Pulling up alongside the pavement, I couldn't believe my eyes. There were now twelve people, all sitting inside cardboard boxes to try to keep warm.

As I stepped out of the car, the girl who had been there earlier shouted out, 'That's him! That's the owner of the shop. The man I was telling you about.'

Suddenly, I found myself being bombarded with questions: Did I have a size fourteen in brown? Had I a size twelve in black? Were they really £1? The noise and the commotion were starting to worry me. The last thing I needed was the police to turn up, thinking there was trouble. Holding my hands up, I raised my voice so as to be heard. 'Calm down, everyone. I've got seventy-two pairs of pants in all different colours and sizes. You don't have to stay here. Come back on the day of the sale. It's not starting for three days!' I pleaded and pleaded with them to go home. But no, they were determined to stay put! It seemed there was nothing I could do.

Getting cold myself now, I decided to get back into the car. Looking at them all huddled together in now-wet boxes, I couldn't help but feel sorry for them, at the same time thinking that they had to be mad to stay out all night in the freezing cold. With these thoughts in my mind, I started the car and headed back out of town. Driving home, I spotted a fish and chip shop near the city's Adelphi Hotel, so I went in and ordered twelve portions of fish and chips and twelve cans of Coke and drove back to give them to the people in the queue, asking each one to go home as I did. Still, no one moved.

Finally, admitting defeat, I wished them all a Merry Christmas and left.

After breakfast the following morning, I was still wondering about the people outside the shop. The weather had changed for the better and the sun was shining. Thinking to myself that, it being Christmas Day, they must surely have gone home by now, I called Gina's brother, Robert, who lived quite close to the shop, to ask him to drive past and see if there was anyone outside. A short while later, he rang me back.

'What on earth is going on?' he asked. 'There must be around eighty to a hundred people queued up outside!'

I was astounded. 'Are you sure? There can't be that many!'

'Well, I didn't count each individual one,' he replied. 'I just estimated, that's all. But it's certainly close to a hundred.'

I thanked him and hung up. I was starting to panic. This was all getting out of control. I only had seventy-two pairs of pants. There were still two days and two nights to go. How many others would start queueing up? How was I going to cope? What the hell was I going to do?

When I told Gina, she was silent for a moment or two. 'You idiot,' she finally said. 'What are we going to do now?'

I started to think positively about ways of cashing in on what now seemed to be something remarkable. It was no small achievement, getting people to give up their Christmas holidays to camp outside a shop for three nights and three days, just to buy a pair of leather pants for £1. One publicity stunt had led to this bizarre situation, and here was the perfect opportunity for another. But it had to be really good. Something really different.

As I sat there, sipping on yet another brew, it came to me. I needed to speak to Paul Feather, a guy I knew, who was the owner of an up-and-coming hotel and catering business. I told him what I had in mind, and sure enough, he was up for it.

On Boxing Day morning, there were about 150 people outside the shop, all sitting in a long line, their backs against neighbouring shopfronts. They were all chatting to each other, seemingly enjoying themselves, as if it were a trip to the sea-side or some great camping adventure. It really was quite something to see, and we just sat there, staring out of the car window, at a loss for words.

Soon afterwards, the Paul Feathers Catering van pulled up and two of his staff began unloading some heated trolleys, similar to the service trolleys you find on aircraft. Gina and I went over to help serve all the people on the pavement with tea, coffee and bacon butties.

Everyone was in good spirits and kept asking about the leather pants. I'd been in contact with Radio Merseyside, Radio City, the *Liverpool Echo*, the *Daily Post* and Granada Television, among others, and they'd all turned up, so after everyone had had something to eat and drink, I was kept busy giving interviews. We ended up on air, live, with BBC Radio Merseyside. Radio City had us on their news updates every hour on the hour, and the newspapers were interviewing people in the queue and taking lots of photographs. It must have been at least 3 p.m. by the time we were finished.

I had also been giving some thought to 'security' on the day of the sale itself. Gina had organized extra sales staff but the problem would be crowd control. The thought of hundreds of stampeding young females was a daunting one for the even the biggest and bravest of men. I would need men for the door.

I managed to get hold of John, my brother-in-law, and then Paul, Phil and Albie, three mates of mine. All four of them were tall and well muscled. We agreed that in order for them to look the part they would need long black overcoats, white shirts and black dickie bows, and all four of them spent the evening tracking down the appropriate clothing in order to be ready for the eight o'clock start the following morning.

Gina and I were too tense that night to sleep much, and it was almost a relief when the day of the sale dawned. Getting up early, we were ready to go by the time Bob and Brenda arrived to look after Katie. Leaving shortly after 7 a.m., both of us were apprehensive about what would be waiting for us.

On our way into town we passed the Army & Navy Stores near the Adelphi Hotel and saw lots of people queuing up outside. It was a relief to see that we were not the only shop with a long line of people outside it. But as I drove off down Ranelagh Street, I found myself almost following this long human chain, around the corner and the whole way down the road, until it came to an abrupt halt – outside our shop! The Army & Navy Stores queue wasn't theirs, it was ours! I hadn't counted the number of people as I drove past, but there must have been close on a thousand.

It was a terrifying thought. We weren't one of the large department stores, which could handle such a large volume. We were small, modest, humble . . . even our doors suddenly seemed too small to cope. My mind was racing as I passed the shop on the way to the car park. My four 'security guards' were positioned outside, looking very professional and well turned out. But I feared they weren't nearly enough to cope with the throngs of people looking for a bargain at Girls Talk.

I needed an army, not four brave lads and a handful of sales assistants. All I could foresee was riots, people getting hurt, ambulances pulling up, the shop getting damaged. It was almost too much.

I looked at Gina. Her face showed the same amazement and disbelief at the spectacle before us. All we could do was look at each other in horrified silence. What were we going to do? I think we both felt like turning the car around and heading home.

Gina looked petrified and close to tears. Taking a deep breath, I said, 'Come on, love, let's go face the music, this is not going to go away. I'll think of something on the way over, I promise you. It'll be all right.'

As we walked along, I held her hand tightly, trying to give her a sense of strength and togetherness. In reality, I was the one quaking inside, and I was feeling as guilty as well. I alone was responsible for creating this mess, and it was up to me to sort it out. Keeping my eyes pinned on the shop entrance, I focused on John, Paul, Phil and Albie as if they were rocks in a stormy sea. My head and shoulders tense, I stared straight ahead, unable, unwilling to look towards the long queue of people just in case somebody recognized me and called out my name.

The boys were like the Four Musketeers, standing bravely solid against a large force of the king's troops. The only difference was that the 'troops' in this case wore skirts and carried handbags as opposed to knee-high leather boots and swords. They greeted us both with a cheery 'All right, boss,' but as my mouth was dry, I was only able to mutter a strangled 'Morning' in response.

Fixing a smile as if nothing was wrong, I pulled out the keys and, with a trembling hand, started to open up the security shutters. As I did so, an unusual noise caught my attention. Turning in the direction it was coming from, I saw to my utter amazement about forty people standing outside Chelsea Girl, clapping and throwing comments in our direction. Chelsea Girl was the biggest fashion store in Liverpool at that time and was very successful. It was like the grand lady of fashion compared to the younger Girls Talk. The people gathered outside were the sales staff, and they were clapping at us, cheering us in our success and wishing us luck. Just then, the manageress, who I admired very much, called over to me: 'Well done, Jeff. Good luck with the sale!' The sense of pride I felt at that moment was overwhelming. I would love to have savoured the moment a little longer, but it was time to open up.

I didn't feel any better once I was inside looking out. I really did need an army of men – and the only available army I could think of was the police. So at about 8.20 a.m. I rang Cheapside Bridewell, the main police station in Liverpool. The phone was answered, and I introduced myself, explaining that I needed to speak to someone in charge as a matter of urgency. But when I explained the situation, the policeman on the line just wouldn't take me seriously.

Time was ticking away, so I tried again. It must have worked, as I heard the phone being dropped on the desk. When he came back on the phone, the tone of his voice had changed, and he asked my name again, and my telephone number, and instructed me to wait by the phone.

Within ten minutes it rang. It was the sergeant-in-charge. I repeated the story for the third time, stressing my concern that something could go terribly wrong, that the situation could get out of hand and people perhaps get hurt. His response was music to my ears. They would be here as soon as possible.

In no time at all, a police van had arrived. The sergeant looked very impressive, and he'd brought five officers with him, who would spread out along the queue in an effort to keep everything under control. He also told me that he was sending for reinforcements as the five were not nearly enough. The sheer number of people lined up was causing problems. The weight of bodies leaning against plate-glass shopfronts was causing the windows to bow inwards, and there was a fear of glass breaking and people being seriously injured. Furthermore, people were blocking the shop entrances, making it impossible for staff, let alone customers, to go about their business.

Nine o'clock came, the police reinforcements had arrived, and a degree of control had been established. We were ready to start trading. On my suggestion, we were going to start by letting customers in one at a time.

The doors opened, and that very first girl, from all those many nights ago, came in. I couldn't help but like her, and served her as quickly as possible. As she paid for her trousers, I gave her a lovely jumper worth about £25 by way of a thank you for her perseverance.

We continued in this manner, one shopper at a time, for the next hour. At the end of it, I could see that this method was not going to work, as we had only served seven people, and the queue was still endless. Taking me to one side, the sergeant muttered in my ear. 'Excuse me, sir, for being blunt, but are you taking the mickey? At this rate, we'll be here until midnight, and my men and I have better things to do. You had better get a move on.'

I returned to the floor, trying to speed things along as quickly as possible, until all the leather pants had been sold. It was now 11 a.m. Walking over to the sergeant, I shook his hand, thanked him for all his help and told him what a relief it had been having him and his men there. 'Without wanting to presume too much,' I added, 'would it be possible to leave two police officers with me for an extra half-hour, while I walk up and down the queue telling everyone that all the leather pants have been sold?'

I felt sure that, once everyone knew that all the pants had gone, the crowds would disperse and everything would return to normal. Funnily enough, though, most of the people in the queue still stayed the whole day. We took more money in sales that day than we had ever done before – £25,000. The staff, although tired, said they had loved it, and even my four muske-teers seemed to have enjoyed themselves. By the day's end, Gina and I were exhausted. But as we walked back to the car hand in hand, the adrenalin and elation put a real spring in our step.

The next day, Tuesday 28 December 1982, I picked up a copy of the *Liverpool Echo*. I couldn't believe my eyes. We were front-page news. The headline read:

THE BIG SALES SPREE

and there were two large photographs of the shop! Our little boutique was now a household name on Merseyside.

We did the same thing the following two years, and again dominated the front page. The third year, Girls Talk even shared it with a photograph of Diana, Princess of Wales, holding Prince Harry at his christening.

Some years later, a journalist on the paper told me that in the 130 years the paper had existed, there had only ever been three people who had achieved front-page headlines on three consecutive occasions: Jack the Ripper in the late 1800s; Prince Charles – and me, a young Scouser possessed with a vivid imagination.

20. A Licence to Print Money

Those headlines turned Girls Talk into Liverpool's number-one fashion boutique, with queues at the tills a daily sight. And the phone didn't stop ringing, with garment manufacturers wanting to supply us for a change! I received a telegram from the previous owner of the shop congratulating me on the phenomenal success we had achieved, which I thought was brave of him, considering his earlier comments about me not lasting more than twelve months. I also found myself having to refuse invitations to lunch from my bank manager as I was far too busy.

Life was good, and became even better with the birth of another special little girl on 25 March 1983. Faye Louise weighed in at 9lb 10oz. Gina and I were so proud of our two precious daughters, and so thankful for being blessed with two healthy baby girls.

Shopping for fashionable clothing for Katie and Faye was proving difficult, and Gina and I were amazed that there wasn't a boutique specializing in trendy clothing for children. So when a shop became available four doors away, we jumped at the chance and opened Kids Talk. It took off like a rocket, and in less than a year it became as popular as Girls Talk.

Eventually, the time came when I had to make a very important decision – to give up the markets. It was sad leaving them behind, as Gina and I wouldn't have been able to have achieved what we had without them. I made sure that all our regular customers knew where to find us, as they had become friends over the years. Saying goodbye to all my fellow traders was just as hard.

Having experienced success, I felt the urge to expand, so I started looking further afield, away from our shops in the city centre. Having visited Chester, a city popular with shoppers and only an hour's drive away, I decided to concentrate my search for premises there. After weeks of having no luck trying to find the right-size shop in the right position, I approached another retailer, who had the perfect site right in the middle of the main shopping street in the town centre. This was where all the large multiples had their stores – just where I wanted to be. The negotiations went on for several hours, at the end of which I made him a substantial offer, which he would have been mad to refuse. It was another gamble on my part, but I believed, as always, that I was capable of making it work.

It was a very hot summer in 1985 when Gina and I opened the doors on our newest venture. The premises were big enough to accommodate both Girls Talk and Kids Talk, and so we were able to provide a new shopping experience for young mums with small children. Our quarter of a million pound investment soon became *the* place to go for fashion in Chester, and in no time was as successful as our other boutiques in Liverpool.

Sometimes I had to pinch myself to make sure that I wasn't dreaming. Our success was so phenomenal. We now had four shops on the high street that were doing exceptionally well. I always believed my mother was looking down on me, though it was such a pity she wasn't there to share in our success.

Finding winning styles week after week was a problem. *Top of the Pops* was one of my favourite ways of coming up with bestsellers. Whatever the pop stars were wearing, the public wanted it the following week.

One Thursday night, Wham! were on with 'Wake Me Up Before You Go-Go!' and George Michael was wearing a large white baggy T-shirt with 'Go-Go' printed on it. The following morning, I was immediately on the phone to our suppliers looking for XXL plain white T-shirts. I was in luck, as they had them for £1 each, so I ordered a thousand. The supplier was based in London so I asked him to put them on the next Euston to Liverpool train then ring me to let me know what time they were due to arrive.

It was now ten o'clock, and the next thing was to find a local screenprinter. I rang all the people I knew but kept drawing blanks. In desperation, I rang Liverpool University's art department, chatted to a very helpful lady, and asked if she knew of any students that could do it. She said she'd try her best to find someone.

Not convinced that I'd find anyone now, this late on a Friday afternoon, I headed to the station to pick up the T-shirts. A short while later, returning to the shop, I found two dodgy-looking characters dressed like tramps waiting to see me. 'Can I help you?' I asked.

'You're looking for someone to print something,' one of the youths mumbled.

This was not quite what I'd had in mind, but I asked, 'Who told you?'

'The bird from the uni,' said the other one.

'Right, OK.' Taking a T-shirt from the box, I asked. 'Can you print "Go-Go" in big black letters on the front of this?'

'No probs.'

I stood there wondering what the hell he meant.

'No probs.' The other one said the same thing.

'What does that mean?' I asked.

'We can do it!' Right! I was now getting the hang of his business negotiations.

We agreed a price, and I gave them £50 for materials and an extra £10 for a taxi, which I loaded with the T-shirts, and waved them goodbye. My staff told me I was mad, saying I wouldn't see the students, my money or my thousand T-shirts ever again, but I simply said, 'Oh ye of little faith.'

The following morning, I arrived early at the shop and found the two young men standing outside. Both of them had their arms full of T-shirts hot off the press. They had worked through the night and had printed five hundred! I put the T-shirts on the mannequins in the front window, and they sold like hotcakes. By the end of the day, we had sold out. And all this less than forty-eight hours after I had seen George Michael wearing one on *Top of the Pops*.

That year, we sold 250,000 T-shirts in every possible print you could think of. 'Frankie Says Relax' was our bestseller, particularly in the smaller sizes for kids. There was a £3 profit on every T-shirt, which made us a cool £750,000 on a moment's inspiration. My two dodgy-looking friends printed every one and went on to be very successful printers in their own right. However, my biggest thanks still have to go to George Michael, for helping me revolutionize the printed T-shirt business!

Gina and I became very wealthy, and along with the money came all the trappings. She now drove a black Mercedes sports car, while my choice was a Jaguar. One evening, arriving home in the dark after work, I was going through the large metal gates at the bottom of the driveway when a man suddenly jumped out from behind the hedge, his face appearing at my window. It frightened the life out of me, until I realized it was an old friend from years ago – John. Lowering the window, I was about to say hello when he said, 'Jeff, I don't know what you're doing, but they're on to you.' He was speaking very quickly and quietly. 'They're tapping your phones and following you!'

When he paused for breath, I managed to ask him, 'Who?'

'The bizzies. They're asking informers to grass on you!'

Suddenly he was gone, disappearing into the darkness without another word, leaving me very confused. John knew, and associated with, a lot of real villains in the city, but he was a pretty straight guy himself.

I went indoors and told Gina what had happened. Her response was to tell me not to be daft, John had most probably been drunk. 'Gina, I'm telling you, he wasn't drunk. Something must be going on!'

Having my phone tapped and being followed, if true, really worried me. I walked over to the phone and picked up the receiver, listening intently, but could hear nothing unusual. I called Gina's parents, and when Bob answered the phone, I heard a strange sort of *beep-beep, click-click* before I heard his voice saying hello. 'Sorry, Bob,' I said. 'It's Jeff here, I think I've dialled your number by mistake.'

I told Gina what had just happened, trying to convince her that our phone was being tapped, but she wasn't having any of it. 'Who do you think you are? James Bond?' she said, but I was still feeling anxious when I went to bed.

The following morning, I kept checking my rear-view mirror as I drove to work to see if I was being followed. I was becoming paranoid, imagining that someone was tailing me. However, once in the office, the day-to-day routine pushed it to the back of my mind until Gina called me at around noon. Once again I heard that *beep-beep, click-click* noise, and this time Gina heard it too. I put the phone down and went to Kids Talk, where I called my solicitor. 'Stay there, Jeff,' he said. 'I'll pick you up shortly.'

Ten minutes later, I got into his car, and he drove me to Cheapside police station, where he had made an appointment for us to see a CID inspector.

At the station, my solicitor told the inspector that I had reason to believe I was being followed and that my telephones were being tapped. The inspector had a file in front of him and, when he opened it, he confirmed my suspicions. I nearly fell off my chair with shock. Flicking through the file, the inspector started to talk.

'Six weeks ago, we had a tip-off that Mr Pearce could possibly be laundering drug money through his shops. We therefore had no alternative but to carry out a thorough investigation into these allegations, and had to inform Customs & Excise and Inland Revenue. We followed Mr Pearce to London in the early hours of the morning on numerous occasions, and yes, we have been tapping his phones. These were serious allegations. But I'm pleased to inform you that we are more than happy with Mr Pearce's business activities and can see nothing suspicious going on. We are therefore now closing the file.' He apologized for any inconvenience but explained that tip-offs like this could not be ignored.

When I thought about it later, I figured the only reason it had happened was the speed with which Gina and I had expanded our business and the wealth we'd accumulated in such a short time. Someone must have been very jealous: we must have rattled somebody's cage somewhere along the way.

There was a hilarious end to the story though. While the investigations had been going on, I happened to be involved in the *Liverpool Echo*'s annual fashion show, and I had had the idea of giving each customer a £1 voucher to spend in our shops, so I'd instructed our printer to produce green £1 notes. They were only printed on one side and they had 'The Bank of Girls Talk' rather than 'The Bank of England' on them but, otherwise, they looked just like the real thing. We'd run out, so I'd asked the printer to print me an extra thousand, unaware that my phone was being tapped. He agreed to do it, but they never turned up. It wasn't until a couple of weeks later, when I called to pay him, that I found out why he hadn't delivered them.

'Don't talk to me about printing money!' he exclaimed. 'Not long after I spoke to you on the phone, the police burst in and arrested me, keeping me in a cell overnight until they had searched my shop and house! They thought I was forging real bank notes!'

I didn't have the heart to tell him that it was all my fault!

That wasn't the only problem wealth brought, though. As a child I had dreamt of one day of owning a Rolls-Royce. All the other kids would laugh at me and taunt me, saying, 'You're poor, you are, Pearce. You'll never own a car like that.' On the day my dream came true I drove my new Rolls-Royce Silver Shadow out of the showroom and straight to the neighbourhood where I grew up as a child, and drove up and down the streets. As the young boys stared, I smiled and gave them a wave. I thought to myself, were they thinking what I did when I was their age?

One afternoon Gina told me that she was just going to nip

to the butcher's to get some mince meat, so I volunteered to take her, finding any excuse to drive my new toy. As I waited outside I noticed the butcher admiring the graceful lines of my elegant car. When Gina returned, she told me that my luck was in. 'We're having fillet steak tonight,' she exclaimed. 'There was no way I was going to ask for half a pound of mince after having got out of a car like this!' It was the best-looking car I had ever seen. But it made me feel uncomfortable driving it. When I stopped at traffic lights, I felt like a horse with blinkers on, unable to look at motorists alongside in case they thought I was looking down on them. Instead, I would sit behind the wheel staring straight ahead, feeling very self-conscious. And if I saw someone I knew at a bus stop, if I offered them a lift, I was being flash; if I didn't, I was a snob. It made me realize another valuable lesson that Mum had taught me: it was OK to admire someone and what they had achieved, but envy was a different matter. It was a no-win situation, so the car had to go. I took it back to the showroom and, fortunately, they still had my Jag. Exchanging the Rolls for my old car, and losing £2,000 in the process, I drove away a happier man. I had only had the Rolls for seven days, but at least I could say that my dream had come true.

Gina's dreams also came true one Christmas morning. Katie and Faye opened their presents on our bed, and then it was Gina's turn. The first box she opened contained a pair of jodhpurs and a riding hat; the second had a pair of black riding boots and a crop. After a little bit of encouragement, I managed to get her to try them on. Puzzled, she said, 'Are you getting kinky in your old age?'

'Not yet!' I assured her. Standing in the bedroom, dressed in her full riding kit, she certainly looked the part. The only thing missing was the horse. I suggested that she open the curtains, pretending I wanted to see what the weather was like. Suddenly there was an almighty scream: 'Jeff, there's a silver-grey horse in the garden!'

Now standing beside her, I whispered in her ear, 'Happy Christmas, Gina. Her name is Foxy Lady, and she's all yours!' I could hardly get the words out for the tears running down my face.

Gina had often told me that, when she was a little girl, she had dreamt of owning a horse, and that it had to be silver-grey. Suddenly she was off, out of the bedroom and running out into the garden, Katie and Faye watching. By the time we'd all got dressed and gone outside, Gina had disappeared. We found her trotting up and down St Mary's Road, riding like a true professional. Foxy Lady was to change our lives, as she was the first of many.

By the middle of 1986, J&R Fashions had expanded to seven properties, with four retail shops, two distribution warehouses and a head office, stretching from Warrington to Chester. This, with the weekly trips to Manchester and London, meant I was spending too much time driving. So one day I marked out X's on a map showing where all our properties were located then dropped my pen in the middle. It landed on a place called White-gate, in Cheshire. The following day, Gina drove out that way with a friend to have a look around and see if there was anything for sale, and that evening she showed me some property details she had picked up. One of them was perfect, a magnificent country house by a small lake with ducks swimming on the surface. It was called Abbots Walk. We went to see it a few days later, and bought it there and then.

We were all sad to leave our home in Huyton. Although it was old and somewhat eerie, the four of us had grown to love it. If we could have picked it up and transported it to Cheshire, we would have.

We set off in convoy to our new home on a fresh November morning in 1986. As we drove into the village of Whitegate, the first sight that greeted us was the magnificent steeple of the sixteenth-century church. Opposite it, we made our way down a narrow lane with old oak trees on either side, their branches forming a thick canopy overhead and almost blocking out the daylight. This tunnel of trees led all the way to Abbots Walk, our new home.

When we arrived, Gina gathered up Katie and Faye and went off to show them the ducks, while I went to chat to our removals men. Suddenly I heard a woman's voice shouting loudly. Turning around, I saw Mrs Woods, the lady we had bought the house from, having a go at Gina and the girls. I went over to see what was wrong, and she soon let me know what the problem was: she wanted us to leave the property, as it didn't yet belong to us. 'Go on,' she screeched. 'Get the hell out of here – now!'

We had no alternative; she was hysterical and totally unwilling to listen to reason. So our convoy was once again on the move, ending up in the car park of a large country pub some two miles down the road, the only place big enough to accommodate us. I rang my solicitor and told him about the unpleasant reception we had received, and he called back after a few minutes to inform me that the property would not legally become ours until noon, but from then on we were entitled to tell *her* to 'get the hell out of there'!

When we arrived back at five past twelve, there wasn't a soul to be seen. The front door had been left ajar, and that was it. Gina and I had left a bouquet of flowers and a card wishing the new owners of our old house success and happiness there. What a contrast to the reception we were getting. Still, they do say, 'There's nowt so queer as folk!'

That wasn't the only time that day that expression rang true. We spent the rest of the day familiarizing ourselves with the house and its grounds and unpacking, and were just enjoying a well-deserved cup of tea in the kitchen when I heard the sound of a car pulling up on the gravel drive. I looked out of the window and saw a man of the cloth getting out of the car. 'Gina, quick, go and fetch Katie and Faye. It looks like the vicar is here to welcome us,' I said.

We picked up the girls and opened the front door, cheerful smiles on our faces. 'Hello, vicar,' we chorused.

'Are Mr and Mrs Wood still here?' he enquired. His tone was almost stern.

'No, I'm sorry, you've missed them,' I replied. 'They've already left.'

'Oh dear. I called to say goodbye.' He was obviously disappointed.

Gina and I stood there, still smiling, waiting for him to say hello and to welcome us to his parish, but he turned his back on us, walked away and drove off without so much as another word. We were speechless, standing in our doorway in total disbelief. He hadn't even said hello!

And that wasn't the end of it. There was to be a third strange occurrence. That Sunday morning was too good a day for staying indoors, so after breakfast I suggested we take the girls and dogs for a long walk. Gina suggested that we go through the woods, which were just past our boundary fence. We wrapped ourselves up well with hats, gloves and scarves to protect us from the cold, and set off. We felt like explorers, while the dogs looked more like wolves sloping through the undergrowth, picking up the different scents of the wild foxes and rabbits that lived there.

We must have covered six miles or more by the time we got back to the house and were all ready for a hot drink. Just as I was about to take my first sip, the phone rang. I picked up the receiver. 'Hello?' I said. A well-spoken lady asked if I was the new owner of Abbots Walk. 'Why, yes I am. How can I help?' I answered.

'My name is Nancy Wright, and I own the farm just next to you. We're all members of Neighbourhood Watch here in Whitegate,' she explained. 'And if anything untoward or suspicious happens we immediately ring around to inform our neighbours. I just wanted to tell you that there are lots of gypsies in the area, and in fact I saw some on my land this morning.' She went on to describe the people she had seen in great detail. She told me where she lived and where she had seen them. Looking out of the kitchen window, I could just make out the farm where she lived.

'Oh yes, I can see your place now,' I told her. 'I'll make sure to keep my eyes open.'

I put down the phone and turned to Gina and told her what the woman had said.

I took it all very seriously and immediately went upstairs to look through the bedroom windows, which gave me a bird's-eye view of the whole area, to see if I could see anything suspicious. Disappointingly, there was nothing. As I headed back downstairs,

I thought back to the description Mrs Wright had given me of the travellers she had seen. She had mentioned a gang with children and wild dogs. Stepping over Carla and Ranger, who were lying sprawled full length on the kitchen floor, it dawned on me. 'That cheeky cow was describing us!' I called out to Gina. 'We're the bloody gypsies she was talking about!'

'Give over, Jeff,' Gina replied. 'Don't be silly.'

'I'm not. Look at the evidence.' I was taking this very personally. 'She said she saw a man and a woman with children and dogs on her land this morning. That was us – we were walking close by there today. What's more, we were dressed more like townies than people who live in the country – I was wearing a black leather coat and a black wool hat!' Gina started to laugh. 'I don't know what you're laughing at,' I told her. 'Your choice of clothing wasn't much better!'

Within a few seconds, we were all laughing at the silliness of it all, including the girls, who loved the idea of being gypsies. A few days later, however, we did go out and buy ourselves Barbour jackets and green wellingtons. We didn't want to be mistaken for gypsies again!

It took many years for our neighbours to accept us city slickers, and in the beginning it was very hard. It was like being stranded in the middle of the back of nowhere. If Katie and Faye had not settled so well into their new school, Gina and I would have most probably returned to somewhere nearer Liverpool. But we persevered, and eventually we felt at home there. We bought Katie and Faye ponies for their birthdays, and I ended up with a mad Arab horse called Diego who spent most of his time throwing me to the ground. On the odd occasion when I did manage to stay on, we would all go out riding together as a family. I even began to feel like a real lord of the manor.

Now that we were comfortably off, I kept my promise to my dear mum and made sure that Dad and June did not want for anything. I could never bring myself to call him Dad, though, always referring to him as 'the Boss'. I came to love my father over the years, and we became good friends. And even though he never said it, I knew that he loved me and was very proud of all that I had achieved.

21. Sport of Kings

In May 1987, on a glorious Saturday afternoon, I was driving along the A49 on my way home, only a mile away from our house, when I noticed a sign at the side of the road saying, 'Polo: 3 p.m. today'. Glancing at my watch, I saw it was ten past three, so I pulled off the road into a large field, where there were lots of horseboxes lined up, and dozens of horses tethered alongside them. Ahead of me there were cars parked in a long line, with people standing around watching the game, so I did the same, and quickly became absorbed in the game. I had never seen anything like this before. I hadn't even heard of polo. It's not exactly the sort of thing a boy growing up in Liverpool would have heard about. The horses thundered past, their hooves pounding the turf and sending vibrations through the ground. I was fascinated. There and then, I just knew I wanted to play this game. But how did you learn? Who should I ask?

A short while later, a bell sounded and the players rode off the field, heading towards their wagons to change their horses. I was close enough to see that the horse's flanks were heaving as they struggled for breath, their sides lathered in sweat – and the riders looked just as hot. Within minutes, most of the players had returned to the field, except for one rider, who remained seated on his fresh horse at the edge of the field. Thinking that this might be a good opportunity, I approached him. Screening my eyes from the sun with my hand, I said, 'Excuse me,' in my best English, trying to hide my Liverpool accent. 'How do you learn to play polo?' I stood there, smiling and waiting for him to reply.

'F*** off' was the response, the tone loud and clipped. 'Can't you see I'm bloody playing? Just f*** off.'

I stood there, gob-smacked to hear someone swear at me in the posh accent of a High Court judge when I was asking a simple, polite question! Then the man kicked his horse hard in the ribs and galloped back on to the field.

Despite the man's rudeness, however, I was still determined to learn how to play. Polo appealed to me on several levels. It was played on horses, and I was just starting to learn to ride; it was a team game, which I always loved; and it was played with a ball. What appealed most, however, was the adrenalin rush: such was the air of excitement and danger, you could almost smell it on the horses and riders as they charged past in full play.

The man who'd been commentating on the microphone looked more approachable, so I decided to go and have a word with him. 'Dingo,' he advised. 'He gives lessons. That's his box over there.' Thanking him, I went off in the direction of his horsebox. Getting closer, I could see a man kneeling down and washing his pony's legs. Once again in my best, most polite, English, I asked if he was Dingo, and said that I would like to learn to play.

'For God's sake, f*** off!' he said. 'Can't you see I'm busy?'

I just turned and left, walking back to my car. I was astounded. I had only spoken to three people, all very posh, and two of them had told me to eff off. In the world I grew up in, that was fighting talk.

I told Gina all about the game and how great I thought it was, and she was keen to see for herself, so the next day, we packed up a picnic and I took her and the girls to watch. After a while, she seemed to be as engrossed in it as I was. While we were sitting watching, Katie and Faye had found some other children to play with, and they were running around having a good time.

A little while later, Katie came over to us, bringing one of her little friends with her. 'Daddy, Daddy, this is Sarah. She's in my class at school! She's my friend. Her daddy plays polo, and he's over there!' She had no idea what she'd done: I now had an opening! Gina and I went over to introduce ourselves and started chatting about schools and children, but I soon turned the conversation to polo.

They were nice people, and Geoff, Sarah's father, had only just started playing himself. After a while he stood up and announced that he was going on to play. Gina and I remained with his wife, watching the game and chatting. At the finish, they invited us into the club house for a drink and introduced us to a couple of other members. It was a brilliant end to a great afternoon.

The following weekend, we went back, and this time I got talking to a man called Steven Leung, who had been a member of the club for the past two seasons. He gave me an insight into the people that played there, laying on his accent thick to demonstrate his point: 'Me Chinee man. They no like me velly much. You long-haired Liverpool man. They no like you either.' And so was born a long-lasting friendship.

Gina and I were determined to learn how to play. We joined the club and bought two ponies from fellow members. They were 'schoolmasters' – experienced horses that know the rules better than the rider does. We paid £3,000 for each one. But within a week, both ponies had gone lame. And they hated getting into the horsebox I'd bought too. I'd paid £2,500 for it, and it too turned out to be 'lame'; it was always breaking down. In hindsight, we were a bit naive. We had been led like lambs to the slaughter!

Polo is a complex and dangerous game, with rules that are hard enough to understand without having to master all the skills of horsemanship required. By the end of the season, I was frustrated. We were always put in the last two chukkas with the junior boys and girls aged between twelve and sixteen. Having forked out well over £10,000 and gone through a lot of hassle, I was no closer to knowing how to play.

One day, I overheard the experienced players talking in the clubhouse about Argentina, and how it was the best place to learn and to buy young ponies cheaply. I remembered that I'd met an Argentinian, known as Manuel, at the club, when he'd been on a promotional visit to the UK. He'd given me his business card with details of the polo school he ran there, but I hadn't thought much of it at the time and had filed it away. A few days later, I talked to Steven Leung about going over to Argentina, and he thought it was a great idea, and asked if he could join me. It was agreed there and then that the two of us would go together.

I would like to point out that when I booked the flights, I knew nothing about Argentina. I had no idea where it was, let alone that we had recently been at war with the country over a remote group of islands. I was always so busy working I never had a chance to watch the news, and of course I had never read a newspaper in my life. It turned out, it was the other side of the world – or else we'd chosen the longest possible route. We changed planes four times and spent several hours sitting in airport lounges waiting for connecting flights. It took us over thirty-six hours to get there.

We arrived in Buenos Aires at 10 p.m. local time. It was dark outside, and there was nobody there to meet us. The airport emptied, and still no one turned up. After an hour or so, Steve and I agreed to call Manuel. It was a very bad line, with much crackling and interference, making his English even harder to understand, but eventually I managed to catch the words 'José', 'outside' and 'waiting'. I left the airport building and began to look for a man called José. There were several taxi drivers lounging around smoking, one or two guys sitting in cars, and others just hanging about. What was I supposed to do – walk up and down, asking for a José who knew Manuel? For all I knew, José was the most popular man's name in Argentina and they could all be called bleeding José.

For some unknown reason, my attention was caught by an old, dirty grey truck parked some way away. 'I don't believe it,' I muttered. 'What's the betting that's bloody José?' Tired, frustrated and annoyed, I ran over to it. There was a man sitting behind the wheel, his chin resting on his chest and a straw cowboy hat pulled down over his face. He was snoring loudly, and to someone as tired as me, this was like a red rag to a bull. I rapped loudly on the car window, shouting at him to wake up. Waking with a start, he leapt out of the car, bumping his head on the car roof and landing at my feet. 'José?' I demanded loudly.

Nodding his head frantically, he replied, '*Si, señor. Si, señor.*'

'Manuel Llinas?' I asked.

'*Si, señor. Si, señor.*'

This was hardly informative. No matter what I said, he would just say, '*Si, señor. Si, señor.*' At this stage, I was so fed up I just pointed to a blurred mass of human beings and suitcases in the distance. It was Steven's problem now.

Without waiting for me, José had jumped in the truck and reversed at high speed back to the airport terminal. I was chuckling to myself at the thought of Steven and José communicating with each other – one in heavily accented English and the other with a vocabulary limited to '*Si, señor*'! They must have managed somehow, however, because when I joined them we were all set to leave.

Steven held the door open for me and suggested I sit in the middle. More fool me. I found myself sitting on the hardest seat, more like a wooden plank really, wedged between a large Argentinean 'bandit' and my snoring Chinese travelling companion. The gear stick was between my legs, which made changing gears an embarrassing operation for both José and me. The handbrake was also limiting my leg room, and in the end I found myself sitting with my legs cramped up against my chest.

Stormclouds were gathering and it was beginning to rain. As we headed inland, the tarmac turned to dirt track and the road became bumpy, nothing but mounds of hardened dirt dotted with small rocks and large potholes. The rain was lashing down now. The headlights gave off only a faint beam, and the windscreen wiper was hopeless. However, José seemed to know the road well, clinging to the edges of the track and avoiding the danger zones. Suddenly, the truck swerved, heading into the darkness. Alarmed, I looked over to see what our driver was doing. Lulled like a baby by the swaying of the truck, José, like my Chinese friend, was asleep! I thumped him in the ribs and shouted his name. Grunting, he opened his eyes and straightened the truck and we continued on.

The rest of the journey continued as a white-knuckle ride. Steven, oblivious to it all, lolled against me, his weight bearing down on my shoulder, his snores rumbling in my ear. José lit cigarette after cigarette, filling the cab with foul-smelling smoke. Each time his head fell forward, I'd thump him awake. I was not prepared to die in the middle of nowhere, squashed between an overweight Chinese man and a chainsmoking Argentinean with a gear stick rammed up against my bollocks.

Waking up the next morning, I was disoriented, and still in the clothes I had been wearing since leaving England. I wandered out of my room, to find Steve sitting enjoying breakfast as if he had lived there all his life. I joined him, and while we were eating, Manuel arrived and told us what our schedule for our two-week visit was going to be. Each morning we'd ride over to the main house, then we'd spend two hours learning how to stick and ball, standing on chairs following Manuel's instructions on how best to hit the ball. After a break for lunch, we'd head back out to the polo field to learn the correct way to ride a polo pony. This would involve taking a horse from a standing start into a full canter within seconds, stopping and turning the horse on a sixpence and, most importantly, 'riding off' an opponent. This is one of the most important aspects of polo. If an opponent has the ball and is heading towards your goal, you either 'ride him off' (come up alongside him and lean your horse into his horse, steering him away from the ball), or you 'stick him' (use your stick to stop his stick from hitting the ball). After that, there was time for a dip in the outdoor pool, before the big polo game at four o'clock.

I couldn't wait to get started. For the first time, I would be playing polo as it should be played. I had a quick shower and changed into my gear, then we were mounted and heading over to the big house. We weren't the only pupils, there were people there from all over the world, and once introductions were made, we got down to the serious part of the day. We all got on well, sharing jokes and stories of our mistakes over lunch, swimming mid-afternoon and entering into the competitive spirit of the four o'clock game.

That wasn't the end of the day though. There'd always be at least ten of us for dinner, gathered around a large table formally set with gleaming silverwear, crystal glasses and crisp white linen, and after we'd eaten, the table was cleared and covered with green fabric so it looked like a miniature polo field. Manuel would then talk us through the rules of the game, moving small models of horses about to show us what he meant.

A few days before I left, Manuel took me shopping for equipment. I had a pair of boots specially made for myself and Gina, both with our initials engraved on the sides. Then I bought two sets of six polo sticks, and two small sticks for Katie and Faye. I also snapped up four complete saddle sets with matching bridles. The quality was so good and the prices so low, I couldn't resist. Essentially, I bought anything to do with polo, completely forgetting that I was going to have to get it all home! Steven had left to visit his family in Hong Kong.

Manuel drove me to the airport himself. We talked about me buying a couple of young horses and discussed prices and transportation. He said that if I came back he would take me all over Argentina looking for good ponies and would help organize their transportation back to England. Shaking his hand, my last words to him were, 'I'll be back.'

When I arrived at Heathrow, I went straight to the luggage carousel. I only had an hour to get over to another terminal for my shuttle to Manchester. I was soon surrounded by everything I had bought, fifteen packages in total, in every shape and size. I stacked them on the trolley, trying to get them to balance and stay on, but as everyone who has pushed a luggage trolley will know, they have a mind of their own, and this trolley was no exception. I was trying to head towards the Green Channel, while my trolley wanted to go to the Red!

In the event, sheer determination won the day, and I managed to get down the 'Nothing to Declare' route without any further mishap. Walking past those customs officers is an uncomfortable feeling at the best of times, but I knew I was pushing it with this load. I had nearly reached the end of the corridor, when a voice called me back. Reluctantly turning around, I headed over. One thing I knew, it wasn't my appearance that had caught his attention. I'd wanted to look my best for Gina, so I was dressed smartly, in a pair of chinos, a white shirt with blue and red striped tie and a very smart navy blazer with brass buttons on the cuffs and front and an embroidered badge on the breast pocket.

The customs officer started to open up my luggage, revealing saddles and bridles, and everything else I had bought. The smell of new leather, and the contents of the bags, plus the fact that I was returning from South America were grounds enough for suspicion.

'Well,' he asked, intrigued by the contents, 'where have you been, sir?'

'Argentina,' I replied, trying to look as calm as possible. Someone had once told me that nervous people blink a lot, so I most probably stood there looking like a glazed idiot, trying hard not to blink at all.

'What were you doing there, sir?' he asked.

'Playing polo,' I answered.

Stopping what he was doing, he looked at me more closely. 'Hmmmm, playing polo,' he mused. He paused for a moment before adding, 'With Prince Charles, I suppose?'

'No, not this time,' I said, desperately hoping to gain a bit of respectability.

Throughout our conversation, he had been staring at the badge on my blazer, and his next question threw me a little. 'Playing for England, were you?'

The penny dropped, and wanting to make the best of the situation, I crossed my fingers and replied with a simple 'Yes.'

'Did we win?' he asked.

By now it was obvious what he thought – he thought I was a player with the English polo team!

'Of course,' I muttered, pretending to be modest.

The officer turned to a colleague on a nearby desk, and called out, 'Hey, Billy, we beat those Argies again.'

I was so embarrassed, I just wanted to get away. If only I could just say, 'Beam me up, Scotty,' and find myself being transported to another planet. Glancing down at my watch, I must have let out a quiet groan of despair.

'What's the matter, sir?' he asked.

'I've missed my shuttle,' I replied, my disappointment clearly written all over my face. 'It was the last to Manchester tonight.'

He looked at me for a split second then turned away, picking up the phone and talking to someone on the other end. I was in for it. Certain he was going to arrest me, I had visions of spending a night in a cell. Why oh why hadn't I been a little more honest and gone through the Red channel? 'You stupid Scouser,' I thought to myself. 'You stupid git.'

I must have been standing there in a daze, because the next thing I was aware of was a small buggy pulling up alongside me. Moving out from behind the desk, the customs officer started to load my luggage on to it. 'Give me a hand, sir, would you please? They're holding the plane for you. This man will take you there.'

He shook my hand and apologized for the delay. 'Anyone who plays for our country is all right by me,' he said. 'Good luck, sir.' I thanked him for all his help, while at the same time feeling a little remorseful. I'd been so lucky. I hadn't been completely honest, and had got away with it.

Gina and the girls were waiting for me in Manchester when I arrived. Seeing their faces was the most wonderful feeling in the world; I was overwhelmed by my love for them all.

I was so excited about Argentina and talked so much about it that my enthusiasm rubbed off on Gina. Her parents offered to look after Katie and Faye, and within four weeks, we were both on our way there. It was a big thing, as it was the first time we'd ever left the girls, but they were more than happy to stay with their grandparents. We stayed as Manuel's guests in the main house, and we were the only ones there, which meant we had more intense, one-to-one lessons in the morning, then played polo in the afternoon. It was lovely having Gina there, riding along by my side every day and having her there to share it all with me.

Manuel kept his word and drove us all over the place looking for ponies. He advised us about bloodlines and training, and we finally chose six youngsters, paying £1,000 each for them. It was £3,000 per pony to fly them back to England, but similar ones here would have set us back at least £8,000 each, so they were still a bargain. When I arrived home, my time was taken up with building six new stables and overseeing the creation of a polo ground so we could practise everything we had learnt and ready ourselves and our ponies for the coming season without having to leave our home. And that winter I bought a brand-new horse-box and had it converted to accommodate our new ponies.

As usual, however, I was starting to think about business opportunities: it would be great to share the cost of the coming polo season with someone. I needed a sponsor, and after giving it careful thought, I decided to approach Jaguar. It seemed like an obvious choice, as I had bought four of their cars over the years. I arranged a meeting with their sales director and presented him with a proposal outlining my ideas. The horsebox, the ponies' saddle cloths, horse rugs, leg and tail bandages, and the players' polo shirts would all be in racing green and, where possible, would have the Jaguar logo and name emblazoned across them. In addition, Jaguar would sponsor an annual silver-cup competition, providing a marquee, and laying on a champagne lunch for VIP guests. At the same time, they could display their latest cars around the polo ground.

The meeting went well and the sales manager was enthusiastic. We went through the figures and he told me he'd get back to me in a few days. Sure enough, he called me back and gave me the good news. I was now the official captain of the Jaguar House Polo Team. It was up to me to bring it all together.

On a sunny Saturday afternoon in May 1988, almost a year to the day after I had first turned into the polo ground to watch that very first time, Gina and I were back. We'd made a major financial investment (something in the region of £100,000) but, although we were a bit nervous, we were looking forward to a good season. We'd certainly come a long way in the past twelve months. Arriving at the polo ground, the painted horsebox looked magnificent, and made quite a few heads turn. However, it was nothing compared to the commotion caused when our six ponies trotted down the ramp. A crowd gathered on the terrace of the club house to watch, and some of the comments carried over to us on the afternoon breeze.

'Who the hell is that?' asked one man.

'It's that Jeff Pearce fellow,' commented another.

'The long-haired Scouser,' said a third. 'Last year, he had two knackered ponies and he couldn't even play!'

There were a lot more comments along these lines, but we didn't care, we were here to play polo. And it wasn't surprising, all the fuss that was made: sponsorship was unheard of in those days. And the horsebox did stand out!

That first afternoon, the club manager put me in a decent match. The first three chukkas, I played reasonably well, and in the fourth, our team was awarded a penalty. The rule in polo is that the better player always takes the penalties, and in this case it was Dingo, who was a three-goal player.

In polo, there are five different types of penalty hits, and for each one the players have to be in certain positions. I didn't know where to position myself for this particular shot, so I decided the best thing to do was to ask Dingo. Riding over to him, I said, 'Where would you like me to be positioned for this penalty?'

'Off the f***ing ground. I hate it when people like you don't know the rules.'

Again, I couldn't believe what I was hearing. I rode over to where one of our other players was standing, reining up alongside him, but although the game continued, I couldn't stop thinking about Dingo's comments. I was furious.

At the end of the game, I rode up to the horsebox, handed over the reins and ran, raging, towards Dingo's dark-green horsebox a hundred yards away. It was difficult running in boots and knee pads, and by the time I got there I was red-faced, puffing and panting, I looked up to see Dingo standing at the top of the ramp of his wagon. I felt dwarfed in comparison, but there was no turning back.

I ran up the ramp like a charging bull, my head hitting him straight in the groin. The force pushed him backwards, and the two of us were carried towards the rear of the wagon, ending up on the floor, fists flying, covered in manure and hay. We scrapped like a couple of raging terriers and, in between punches, I told him exactly what I thought of him. Someone must have called for help, as two male grooms arrived on the scene and pulled us apart. We were still snarling at each other and punching the air with our fists.

The club manager had been attracted by all the noise and commotion and came over demanding, 'What the hell is going on?'

'It's between him and me,' I said, still staring at Dingo.

'It's not,' he said. 'I will not tolerate this kind of behaviour in the club.'

He took me into the club house, telling me to sit down and wait. A few minutes later, he returned with the club president and official steward for the Hurlingham Polo Association, the governing body of the sport in the UK. They don't come much bigger in the polo world.

He and the club manager positioned themselves directly

opposite me, two judges facing the guilty party. The club president spoke first. 'This type of behaviour is not acceptable,' he said. 'This is a gentleman's club, and gentlemen do not resort to street fighting to resolve issues. There are established procedures for resolving issues, and we adhere to those procedures. The penalty for fighting is instant dismissal from the club, revocation of your membership.'

I looked at them both across the table. I appreciated that there were rules, I said, and was willing to abide by them, but I thought it only fair that I was given a chance to explain my side of things. I told them that I had been sworn at three times now, each time just for asking a simple question. They were shocked by what I told them, finding it hard to believe that one of their 'gentleman' members would behave that way. I was asked to wait outside. It was Dingo's turn to go into the clubhouse now.

I couldn't believe what had happened. What had I done? Six new horses? A new wagon? All that money spent on the stables and polo ground? My sponsors and all the money that they had spent – what were they going to think? I felt pretty lousy, but I still felt right was on my side. Just because I was from humble beginnings did not mean that I was a lesser person and could be spoken to like that.

After ten minutes, I was called back in, and the club president gestured me towards him, saying that Dingo had something to say.

'I am sorry,' he said. 'Will you accept my apology?' I couldn't ignore his outstretched hand and returned his handshake.

The manager clapped us both on the back. 'Come on, you two,' he said, 'that's the end of it. No more swearing, and certainly no more fighting.' Dingo and I shook hands again, and we all smiled. The club president even put his hand on my shoulder, took me to one side and apologized for the 'welcome' I had received!

A couple of years later, I went with the club manager to Guards Polo Club at Windsor for a special four-week course on becoming a Grade One umpire. As well as enjoying every minute of it, we both passed with flying colours. I got on well with him, and some time later, he invited me to play in a team against Prince Charles. Unfortunately, Prince Charles fell off his horse and badly injured his arm a few weeks before we were due to play. The match was cancelled, but I did end up umpiring the game that took its place that day in the grounds of the club president's fabulous home, Hembury Hall. Princess Margaret was presenting the prizes, which was definitely a highlight, as one of them was for me!

The rest of that season was a great success. Jaguar were more than happy with their sponsorship deal, and agreed to finance the Jaguar polo team the following year. Gina and I were eventually accepted and made to feel very welcome in the polo world.

22. Tickled Pink

By thirty-five, I was a millionaire living the dream, with everything I could possibly wish for. I had a gorgeous wife and two lovely, healthy daughters, a large house in the country, stables for our horses and garages full of new cars. I also had a successful business that was doing unbelievably well. Girls Talk and Kids Talk had become so popular we had queues at the doors every Saturday. The power of our brand names had become phenomenal, with teenagers saying that if it wasn't from Girls Talk or Kids Talk, it wasn't fashionable.

Karen Foster had joined me in 1985 and was now area manageress, looking after all our shops. She knew how Gina and I worked, and how much importance we put into attention to detail. She was absolutely fantastic at her job and took a lot of pressure off us. So did June, my sister, who was now the manageress of my first shop, in Church Street.

I knew everything was in good hands, but I just could not just sit back and enjoy what Gina and I had built up over the past ten years. I was a workaholic. It wasn't in my nature to sit still; I was only happy when I was running at 100mph. Perhaps it had something to do with my childhood, or my mother urging me to better myself. Or maybe it had something to do with Mrs Jones, my teacher, and her comment on the day I left school that no good would ever come of me.

I was still driven, wanting to achieve more. But I still could not read or write, and I lived with the shame and embarrassment of it every day. I had organized my life to try and hide it from the world, avoiding anything that would expose me, like writing a cheque or reading a menu, but it was always there. I felt like a criminal, always on the run.

I remember seven-year-old Katie and five-year-old Faye asking me to read them a story one night, and passing me a book of nursery rhymes. It had lots of pictures and large writing. I was terrified and began to panic. Looking at the pictures I made up the words. They started giggling and said, 'Daddy, you're being silly, it doesn't say that.'

That innocent comment from my young daughters nearly destroyed me. I was their father and I couldn't even read them a simple bedtime story. If I could have traded in all my wealth there and then, just to be able to read the simplest of words, I most certainly would have.

Gina was very happy and contented with everything, but I was beginning to realize I needed a new challenge. One night, we sat and talked for hours about different business ventures. After a couple of weeks, we'd narrowed it down to two: property development or launching a new clothing brand into the fashion industry, this time producing and selling our own brand to other retailers. After discussing it for some time, we finally agreed to stay in the fashion business – 'Better the devil we knew . . .!' We decided to set up a new fashion company, designing all our own styles under our own label, specializing in teenage girls' clothing. It was all very exciting.

The first step was to choose a name, one with global potential that would appeal to the female market. We chose an old English expression, 'Tickled Pink'. I applied to register the name as a brand, and within a few weeks, it was accepted. The next step was to find suitable premises. London would have been ideal, but it was too far away; I didn't want to be away from my family for long periods of time. Basing ourselves in Manchester made better sense. It was only an hour or so from home, and the shops in Liverpool and Chester were about the same distance away. And it was the UK's second busiest city for fashion after London, and there were lots of companies supplying the trade in the area.

I soon found the perfect place – a 2,500-square-foot show-room in Stephenson Square, near Manchester's Piccadilly, surrounded on all sides by other fashion houses. Ironically, it was also just around the corner from my old friend Mrs Kumar.

Wasting no time, we opened on Sunday 2 October 1988, just in time for the busy Christmas trade. I put a full-page four-colour advert in the *Drapers Record*, a weekly fashion-trade magazine, inviting everyone in the fashion business to the grand opening. We served pink champagne and pink cakes, and over a hundred inquisitive customers turned up, among them some nervous competitors, who seemingly anticipated I would be a threat.

We had spent a lot of money on the new showroom, framing the windows with ultra-modern pink-neon lights and dressing the mannequins in up-to-the-minute styles. To begin with, we sold other companies' designs, and even a little bit of 'cabbage', as we needed six months to organize our own designs. I wanted to get the showroom up and running before introducing our own label.

We started off as wholesalers, essentially a cash and carry, which meant that shop owners from all over the north of England could call in once a week to buy their stock, paying for it there and then. I took on new staff, and having learnt the power of media and advertising from the very beginning, I set up a campaign to market the brand, starting with a front cover on the *Drapers Record*. It was a full-colour photograph of a top model wearing Tickled Pink's newest look. It cost a fortune, but it was worth it, because it generated a buzz; everyone in the fashion business was talking about Tickled Pink, wanting to know who we were and where we had come from.

Gina and I set about putting a spring/summer collection together for 1989, with Kirsty, a young fashion designer we'd taken on straight from university. We wanted to be different from our competitors, to stand out, so we decided that our very first collection was going to be all fluorescent colours – neon pink, yellow and green. Bright! This was a brave decision. Other companies had tried and failed miserably. What we did that was different, however, was to trim the bright colours in black.

There were ten styles, the tops and T-shirts all bearing the Tickled Pink logo embossed in black. We had five different styles of 'bottoms', including black lycra cycling shorts. To complete the collection, we added a washed-out-denim range with three-coloured neon cotton embroidery on each piece. The samples were so fabulous, we decided to put ourselves under even more pressure by producing all the styles for younger girls aged between two and twelve. This had proven so successful in the past that it was worth taking the risk.

Once all the final designs were completed, I set off all over Europe looking for factories to produce them. A daunting task for anyone. But for someone who could not read or write, a nightmare. I ended up in Greece, where they specialized in manu-facturing light-weight cottons and lycra. I felt it would be best not to put all our eggs in one basket, so I chose three factories:

one to manufacture the cotton garments, one for the lycra and a third to produce the washed-out-denim collection.

Ten days later, having worked at least twelve hours a day with the respective factories on the designs, I placed orders for 60,000 garments, the value of which came close to £300,000! Many saner people would say I was crazy to take such a big risk so early on, and in our first season. However, if I had learnt anything in life, it was that there are 'ditherers', there are 'doers', and there are those with 'lots of balls'! I was aware that I stood to fall at the first fence, losing a lot of money and possibly ruining the Tickled Pink brand overnight. But I also knew we stood to make a huge amount of money if we had got things right.

Being successful in the fashion business requires spending all your time gambling on your judgement and instinct. It's all a numbers game, and not for the faint-hearted. As long as you win more than you lose, you are doing all right. I never felt the need to gamble on horses, cards or anything else: my life and business were a perpetual gamble.

As soon as I got back to the UK, I had to open three irrevocable letters of credit from my bank, guaranteeing the Greek factories money. Without this, they wouldn't start producing our designs, and the clock was ticking away. There was no going back now. I had once again put my neck on the proverbial block and could only pray that my gamble paid off.

All the stock was due to arrive at the end of February, so I booked a stand at the Birmingham NEC fashion trade show and produced a glossy brochure featuring the collections. Tickled Pink was definitely a 'family' business. We had Katie and Faye modelling the clothes for the kids' range, and professionals for the teenagers.

Our merchandise arrived from Greece on time, and the show-room looked fantastic with all the new neon styles. Despite all this, I still had a sick feeling that the collection would not be as successful as we had prayed for.

We set up our stand at the NEC the day before the show opened. I'd had a large, electric fluorescent sign made with 'Tick-led' in blue and 'Pink' in pink. It hung in the middle of our stand, with mannequins on either side, dressed in our new designs. By the time we had finished, we were exhausted but proud at how brilliant it looked, and returned to our hotel, full of excitement at the thought of the following day. We had attended enough exhibitions in the past as buyers, but this time we were there as exhibitors!

The next morning, we were feeling more nervous than ever. Would the buyers like our styles and the bright neon colours? And would they actually place any orders for immediate delivery? We were taking a risk. Nearly all the other companies exhibiting were ahead of the game, showing styles for autumn delivery, some six months ahead, while we were showing for that season.

Nine o'clock sharp, when the main doors opened, thousands of buyers rushed in, and within what seemed like minutes, we had a large gathering around our stand asking questions about Tickled Pink, wanting to know how long we'd been established, and how competitive our prices were. They loved our styles, and we spent the next eight hours doing nothing but taking orders. We were literally mobbed, and it was impossible to leave the stand. The show was supposed to close at 6 p.m., but we still had people on the stand. At 6.30, one of the security guards had to show us out through a back door. It was mad. Absolutely, wonderfully mad!

Gina and I were in a state of shock. All the buyers wanted our concept in their shops straight away. At the end of the show, we had sold over 25,000 pieces and opened 67 new accounts all over the UK. We had sold over a third of our initial 60,000 in the three days of the show. We were also inundated with enquiries from fashion agents wanting to carry our samples and represent Tickled Pink in their regions. They had noticed our stand was one of the busiest at the show and wanted to be involved. Gina and I took their names and phone numbers and I told them I would get in touch.

Back in Manchester, we found out that the showroom had also been very busy with cash-and-carry customers, and that the Girls Talk and Kids Talk shops had sold out of certain styles in just a couple of days. Some of the most popular styles had to be repeated from Greece to keep up with demand; an extra 20,000 pieces in all. By the end of August, we had sold every last piece. Tickled Pink was up and running, the decision to do the children's sizes proving to have been a good one. And it didn't stop. Over the next few years, we went from strength to strength, becoming the fastest-growing brand at the time.

In order to keep up with demand, I invested every penny we had in Tickled Pink, and we still ended up having to borrow large amounts of money from the bank. The more accounts we opened, the more stock we had to carry. We now dealt with factories all over the world, and I found myself travelling to Hong Kong, Thailand and China at least once a month.

We no longer needed the cash-and-carry business, as all our work was forward orders. And with the volume and size of our clients, we soon outgrew the Manchester showroom. We rented larger premises in Runcorn, a brand-new 40,000-square-foot warehouse, and based all our operations there.

We were now supplying over six hundred independent shops throughout the UK and parts of Europe, and had customers which included most of the high-street big names, such as House of Fraser, John Lewis, Selfridges, Dickens & Jones and Harrods. It had only taken us two years to win the top accounts in Europe.

I now employed thirty-eight staff in total, with another seventeen sales representatives out on the road showing our latest collections. The children's range had expanded into boyswear for two- to ten-year-olds too. As young boys would not want to be seen in the Tickled Pink brand name, we kept the initials and registered Tom Pepper, which had a more boyish feel to it.

We also had to protect these two prestigious brands, selling them only to the exclusive top-end department stores and upmarket boutiques. I therefore insisted that the larger, price-conscious department stores such as C&A Modes would only be allowed to stock the styles under our Girls Talk and Kids Talk labels – which they did, successfully, the biggest single order being half a million pounds. We now had four in-house labels all under one umbrella. My job now was to control the production in twenty factories all over the world.

23. Two Wrongs Don't Make a Right

I was riding on the crest of a wave by the time we entered 1992. Tickled Pink was heading for its best season ever, with £2 million worth of forward orders on its books, and all four brands were performing well on the high street. I was proud of what we had achieved – and all in two and a half years. My long-term plan was to build up to £5 million worth of forward orders per annum before selling Tickled Pink to the highest bidder.

We had spent eight months in lengthy negotiations with a large manufacturing company who had offered me a £3 million buyout over three years. This sum was based upon my forward orders and, more importantly, my contacts book, a valuable list of customers that would expand any company's penetration into the retail market. We were three days away from completing the deal when the news hit the press that the chairman of the company concerned had been arrested for embezzlement. Of course, the deal fell through.

As if that wasn't bad enough, weeks later, something even more catastrophic occurred: the recession hit the high street. I well and truly found myself in the wrong place at the wrong time. Consumers stopped spending. Fashion, often regarded as a luxury, was one of the first areas to be hit, and hit hard. The speed of the knock-on effect was frightening. Our big department-store buyers were having their budgets cut in half, forcing them to reduce their orders by half. The six hundred small independent shops we were supplying were cancelling orders left, right and centre. It was a nightmare. By now I was working on orders six months in advance, and I was heavily committed to factories all over the world. They in turn had large quantities of garments in production, and there was no way of stopping them.

While I was putting out fires on one side, the bank decided to light more fires on the other, demanding that I reduce my overdraft limit of £570,000. Typical! Just when I desperately needed the overdraft, they wanted to take it away. It was like being given an umbrella when the sun was shining, then having it snatched off you at the first sign of rain.

As the recession worsened, many of the small independent shops we were supplying were seriously struggling to stay in business; almost one a week was closing down. The bank kept increasing the pressure, and I was left with no alternative than to put my shops on the market. The timing could not have been worse, as property prices were starting to fall, to the lowest they had been for many years. My only consolation was that all my shops were in prime locations.

First to go was the Chester shop, then Kids Talk in Liverpool, and finally Girls Talk on Church Street. That hurt the most, as it had always been my favourite and had been a part of our lives for so long. Both Gina and I felt as if we were losing an old friend. In total, we managed to raise £200,000, which enabled us to reduce our overdraft limit, leaving us with £370,000 to trade with.

The loss of our retail business was hard to take, but I was convinced that Tickled Pink was the way forward. I was optimistic about the future with the brands we had created and the accounts we had opened; all we had to do was ride the storm.

We kept on going, constantly tightening our belts, and hoped the recession would soon come to an end and I could find a new manufacturer to buy us out for the £3 million we'd been offered.

By the middle of 1992, we were still doing reasonably well, and were on target to make a profit, albeit a small one. However, it was still a profit and I was quite pleased we had managed to survive when so many of our competitors had gone out of business. Then, once again, disaster struck. Black Wednesday! Like a hurricane flattening everything in its path, this was a day of untold devastation and ruin.

On 16 September 1992, the European Exchange Rate Mechanism fell apart, with a catastrophic effect on the pound. In a bid to prop it up, the government announced that interest rates were going to rise to 15 per cent. The banks got into a blind panic, pulling the plugs on any small business they could get their hands on: I knew mine was not going to escape.

A few days later, I received an extraordinary phone call from my bank manager. He didn't sound his usual polite self. 'I want you in my office at ten o'clock tomorrow morning,' he demanded. I was thrown by his abrupt manner, and hung up. The following day, I received a letter from him apologizing for his tone the day before. He asked me to be 'kind enough' to make an appointment to see him as soon as possible. Accordingly, I arranged to meet him at two the following afternoon, but before I hung up I was told to bring the company chequebooks, which made me feel uneasy.

The next day, I arrived on time and was escorted to his office.

He stood up and shook my hand, then indicated that I should sit in the chair opposite. He then got straight to the point: 'Have you brought your chequebooks with you?' he asked.

'Yes,' I replied, opening my briefcase and placing them on the desk in front of him. He reached out and slid them across the desk into a drawer. And then locked it.

'As from today,' he informed me, 'we are no longer prepared to finance your business.'

I was shocked. 'You can't be serious!' I said. 'You have enough security to cover my loan.'

'Not any more,' he replied. 'Property prices have halved since we last agreed your facility. I'm sorry, Jeff. My instructions are from head office.'

'Please,' I said. 'You can't do this to me.' Reaching into my briefcase, I pulled out my paying-in book. 'Look. On Monday I paid in £30,000.' I was desperately trying to reason with him, thinking that he would see sense. 'We have half a million pounds still owing to us,' I continued.

Before I could finish, he interrupted me. 'Yes, and we believe you won't realize more than a third of it in the current economic climate.'

'I won't receive a penny of it if you won't let me keep trading. What about the stock we own in the warehouse? It must be worth at least £150,000, and I only owe you just over £370,000!' I was begging as if for my life.

'I'm sorry. It's out of my hands.' He wasn't interested.

'Well then, what do you suggest that I do with no chequebook? I have staff wages to pay!'

'I suggest you go into voluntary liquidation,' was his unfeeling reply.

'Why on earth would I want to do that?' I demanded. 'After sixteen years of breaking my back to build up a business from nothing?' I was beginning to shout with frustration.

Getting to his feet, he walked to the door and opened it. Looking at me, he said, 'There is no more that I can say or do in this matter. Goodbye.'

I don't remember walking out of there, but I do remember being violently sick in the car park as the reality of it all hit me.

And after the vomiting came tears. How on earth was I going to tell Gina? And what about my staff? Some of them had been with me for years. My mind was in turmoil, trying to come up with answers. Sitting in the car, I was desperately searching for a way out of this mess; I had been in tight spots before and had overcome them. But this time it was no good; this was far, far worse. The more I thought about it, the more I realized that there was no way out. I felt like I was caught on the back of some horrendous monster that was carrying me away, with no means of controlling it and no way of getting off.

On my way back to the office, I rang Jaguar House and asked how much my Jag was worth.

'£16,000 is the best I can do,' I was told. I had paid £34,000 just two years before. Talk about adding insult to injury! Left with no alternative, I instructed him to bring the money in cash to my office the following morning.

That night, I sat down with Gina and explained everything. We talked into the early hours, and I told her I felt I had failed her and had let her down badly. She tried to comfort me by saying that it wasn't my fault. But it didn't make me feel any better.

The next day, I gave each member of our staff £500 from the sale of my car and told them that Tickled Pink was over. There were lots of tears shed that day, including mine and Gina's, as our staff had been so special. The atmosphere had always been fantastic. Everyone had loved working there. For it to have ended in such a cold-hearted way left us all feeling devastated.

Karen Foster stayed with us, and it was up to the three of us to try to raise as much money as we could for the £150,000 worth of stock that had been paid for and was now sitting in boxes in the warehouse, and to recover as much of the half a million pounds still owing to us as we could as quickly as possible. The bank held a charge over our house as security against my overdraft facility, so if we didn't get the money back, it wouldn't be long before they forced us to sell our home, the only property we now had.

After three weeks of doing everything we possibly could, we managed to raise £40,000 for our remaining stock. That was it. The huge loss in value was due to the fact that it was now a buyers' market and the major fashion clearance companies could offer peanuts for it. Collecting the money still owed to us was just as difficult. I spent day after day driving Gina's car all over the country, personally calling on all our customers and demanding payment. Getting blood out of a stone would have been easier, for the recession had also hit them hard and they were struggling to survive themselves.

One look at their shops told me all I needed to know: I had little or no chance of walking away with the money I was due, whether it was £2,000 or £10,000. By the time I had finished debt-collecting, I had managed to claw back £100,000. We had to kiss the rest of it goodbye. We paid the £140,000 we had raised into the bank, but were still short by £230,000. And now the bank was charging me £1,000 a week interest on my remaining overdraft facility, making themselves an additional £52,000 a year! I begged them on numerous occasions to freeze the interest on the outstanding loan on the grounds that I no longer had a business and had already paid them some £300,000 in interest and bank charges alone over the past four years, but they refused to listen or to help. Instead, they demanded that I sell my house to pay off the balance of the debt.

A few years earlier, our house had been worth half a million pounds. But with the fall in property prices, I would be lucky if I raised enough to clear my outstanding debt to the bank. The 'For Sale' board went up outside Abbots Walk, and I had to put my beloved Tickled Pink into voluntary liquidation. When I contacted an accountancy firm in Liverpool to arrange an appointment, I was advised by the gentleman I spoke to that it would cost me £4,000, and it had to be paid in cash on the day of the meeting. More money to pay out! With more problems than pennies, I had to borrow the cash from my old friend and former driver, George Haynes.

As we walked into the accountancy firm's offices on the day of our appointment, something was annoying me. I wasn't at all happy with their payment terms. So before our meeting I quickly removed £1,000 in notes from my briefcase, rolled it into a small bundle and shoved it into my coat pocket. Gina wanted to know what I was doing, but I just gave her a wink and opened the office door for her.

Our liquidators' greeting was very direct. 'Good morning, Mr Pearce. Have you brought the £4,000, as requested, to start this process?'

'I'm sorry, but I've only been able to raise £3,000,' I explained, placing three £1,000 bundles on his desk in front of him.

'OK, that's fine,' he said, and locked it in a drawer in his desk. He turned to us both, offering us a seat. 'Let's get on with it, shall we?' He asked me half a dozen or so questions then got to his feet. 'Mr and Mrs Pearce, I suggest that the two of you go and have a long lunch somewhere nice and come back in about three hours, by which time I will have gone through all your accounts and will have a much better idea how to proceed.'

As Gina and I walked out of the building we were greeted by a blast of cold air. It was a crisp autumn's day so we decided to head down to the Pier Head on the River Mersey to get some fresh air. The last thing we wanted at that point was a long lunch. Neither of us had eaten a decent meal since the whole nightmare had begun, some four weeks earlier. We both felt sick to the stomach, literally nauseated by what had happened to our lives. Everything had been turned upside down, and we felt a huge sense of loss, as if a loved one had died. For fifteen years we had grown our business bit by bit, nurturing it from a small market stall worth a couple of hundred pounds to a company turning over millions. Holding hands, we killed time in silence, an unnatural feeling of quiet between us, tinged with apprehension as to what was coming next.

As we neared the accountancy firm's building on our way back, trying to lighten the moment, I pulled the £1,000 out of my pocket. Showing it to Gina, I said, 'I haven't lost my touch yet, even with all this aggro going on around me.' The humour did us both good, and we laughed heartily.

Back in the office, we were told, 'Mr and Mrs Pearce, there is something terribly unusual about your accounts.'

We looked at him in disbelief. 'In what way?' I asked, but I didn't really want to hear his reply.

'You don't owe anyone any money. There is a small amount of VAT and PAYE still owing, but that is hardly worth talking about.' He paused for a moment, looking at us both. 'In fact, there is only the bank to settle with, and they hold the deeds to your house as collateral. So you now stand to lose your home.'

He sat back in his chair, removed his glasses and continued in a quieter tone. 'Most companies I come in contact with in liquidation situations such as this would have paid off their personal guarantees, that is, their bank loans, rather than paying their creditors. But your accounts show that you have paid the factories which you dealt with well in excess of the outstanding balance you owe to the bank. And you have done this recently.' He fell silent, waiting for my reply.

I chose my words carefully. 'Two wrongs don't make a right,' I explained. 'Just because the bank have shafted me doesn't mean that I have to shaft somebody else.'

He looked at me in surprise, then smiled at my summary of the whole affair. 'Right. I cannot see any need to hold a creditors' meeting and will therefore tie up all the loose ends before writing to you in due course.'

Walking us to the door, he thanked us for having chosen his company to handle our affairs and shook hands. As we left, I couldn't help but think that must have been the easiest £3,000 he had ever earned.

24. A Silent Prayer Answered

Gina and I shared the car home together, but little else. We were both lost in our thoughts, and conversation seemed unimportant. I had made eighteen successful business decisions in my life, but the nineteenth collapsed like a house of cards and cost me everything.

It all boiled down to one thing: the fundamental difference between being a retailer and a wholesaler. As a retailer, you get credit from your suppliers but don't have to give credit to your customers. However, I was a wholesaler, and therefore did not get credit from my suppliers but had to give it to my customers. It was a no-win situation.

I felt a strange sense of relief in a way now that these last few months were over. But I was deeply scarred inside by what had happened and the way I had been betrayed by the bank. What it had done to me was immoral and cruel. In fact, comparing the bank to some of the more colourful characters I had met in my life, I could honestly say that there was indeed greater honour amongst thieves. The greatest sense of betrayal however was my own. I had placed my family in a privileged world where they could have anything money could buy, and now I had taken it all away. I could never forgive myself for losing our home, and now I felt sick at the thought of having to remove Katie and Faye from the private school which they loved so much.

My ambition had brought us to this point. And my ambition

had lost it all. My need to succeed and my desire to prove my worth had put my family in this situation. It was unforgivable. At forty years old, I was a failure, lost, with nowhere to go, a man alone. I silently said the first of many prayers to my mother, asking for help.

The next couple of weeks were living hell. Despair drove me almost to the point of suicide. Trapped in this nightmare, all I could do was hope that my mother could hear me. One night, as I lay in bed, it happened.

'Stop crying and feeling sorry for yourself. You did it once before, and you can do it again.' Her voice was so clear it shocked me into sitting up. 'You can do it. You can do it.' She was repeating this simple phrase over and over in my head.

Glancing at the clock on the bedside table, I saw that it was 5 a.m. Confused and uncertain as to what was going on, I went into the bathroom and splashed some cold water on my face. Suddenly it all became clear: Mum wanted me to go back to the markets and start all over again.

My brain kicked into action. Questions struck me, and answers followed. What day was it today? Friday. Where did I go on a Friday? Park Road Market. Did I have stock? Yes, in the garage left over from the liquidation . . . and so it went on. Like a man possessed, I threw on some clothes, waking Gina in the process.

'Jeff, what are you up to?' she murmured.

'I'm going back to do it again,' I answered.

'Do what?' She was sitting up now.

'I've got to go, I'll see you tonight.' I hurtled down the stairs, grabbing my keys on my way out. I opened the garage and threw box after box into the back of the wagon. Slamming the back doors closed, I headed out on to the main road.

I had only gone a short distance when a flashing red light on the dashboard caught my attention. Glancing down, I saw the diesel gauge was on empty. This was all I needed! Pulling into the nearest service station, I jumped out and felt for my wallet, but – shit! – in my haste, I'd forgotten it. With not a penny in my pocket – nor, for that matter, in the world – and no time to spare, I put £10 worth of diesel in the tank. I walked up to the window patting my pockets, creating the impression that I was panicking and looking for something. 'Sorry,' I said. 'I seem to have come out without my wallet.'

'Well, that wagon's not going anywhere, mate,' the cashier replied. This was not going to be easy.

'Don't be silly, it's only £10,' I argued. 'I'll call back later with it.'

'Against the rules, mate. Can't let you do that.' Time was ticking on.

'Look,' I said, undoing the strap on my Rolex and handing it over. 'Take this as security, with my name and address.'

He picked up the watch suspiciously, looking at it closely. 'How do I know this is worth ten quid?'

I sighed. 'What difference does it make if it isn't?'

'A lot,' he replied. Taking a pen and paper, he made a careful note of my registration number and contact details. I was half expecting him to take my fingerprints, the way he was carrying on.

Climbing back in the cab, I thought about what he'd said. Worth a tenner? What a cheek! Gina had paid three and a half grand for it. Still, I had the juice, and I was on my way, foot to the metal, anxiously heading towards Liverpool, back to where it had all begun. After fifteen years' absence, I was curious about how I'd be greeted by my former colleagues. As I got closer to the market, I could feel how familiar it still was, and as I pulled into the busy car park, it almost seemed as if I'd never been away.

The traders were busy, rushing around, putting up their stalls. Time was of the essence – the quicker they were up, the sooner the traders could empty their vans and set out their goods ready for the day's trading.

Weaving my way through the bustle, I headed for the market inspector's office to see if there was a pitch available; I was desperately hoping it would be someone I knew. Luckily, it was. Ken had been the first inspector I had met, all those years ago. 'Hi, Jeff!' he said. 'What are you doing here?'

'It's a long story,' I answered, 'and I promise I'll tell you later. But right now, I need a pitch.'

'It's going to be hard,' he said, 'this close to Christmas, but let's see what we can do.' Picking up his clipboard, he headed outside, telling me to follow. I silently sent a word of thanks to my mother for the words of wisdom she had given me when I first started: 'Look after people as you move up the ladder of success, because you never know who you might meet on the way down.' If ever there was a true saying, this was it.

Ken turned to me. 'Right, Jeff, where are you parked?'

I pointed to my wagon, some twenty yards away.

'A horsebox!' he exclaimed. 'What are you selling? Horse meat?' Then he read the words on the side: '"Jaguar Polo Team"?! Polo horses in Toxteth? That's a first!'

He instructed me to turn the wagon around, dropping the tailgate on to an empty space between two stalls, and to trade out of the back.

'Thanks, Ken,' I told him. 'I owe you one!'

As I set up my pitch, I couldn't help but notice that my arrival with the horsebox had caused a bit of a commotion. Several other traders were standing around watching, and the buzz of conversation was getting louder and louder. One of them must have recognized me, as I heard him telling the others, 'You know who that is, don't you? Jeff Pearce, that's who.'

'Get away with it, he's a millionaire. He wouldn't be here. Not nowadays.'

I heard my name being called out, so I stopped and looked up. There was a chorus of disbelieving voices: 'It *is* him. What are you doing here, Mr Big Time?'

'The same as you, lads: trying to make a living,' I answered, but they wouldn't give up.

'Don't be daft,' they said. 'We have to be here. You don't.'

Like a helpless fish, I felt hooked. Slightly irritated by their comments, I just said, 'Look, lads, if I didn't need to be here, I wouldn't be. So back off and leave me alone!' That did it, and they took the hint and left.

Once I'd cleared the boxes out of the wagon, I realized there was horse manure all over the floor. I needed to get it sorted so that customers could come inside and try things on. I borrowed a brush and shovel, and a can of air freshener to get rid of the smell. At least the boxes held a pleasant surprise: they were full of good-quality jumpers I'd personally designed some six months earlier.

It didn't take me long to get back into character. 'Come on, girls,' I called out. 'Hurry up and take a look. They're first-class and going fast. Step up and have a look! A tenner a piece or two for fifteen! Don't be shy, come and buy! Jeff's my name, fashion's my game.'

To draw a crowd is difficult, but to keep it is an art. You have to create a feeling of excitement and desire amongst the punters. Never sell to them, let them buy from you. The banter amongst the people on the market went back and forth, Liverpool humour at its best. One woman called out to her friend, 'Go on, Mary! You've always wanted a roll in the hay! Get in there, you dirty mare!' and everyone burst out laughing.

In no time, my hands were full of £10 notes. My fellow traders looked on in awe; I was tossing garments at the customers as quickly as they could call out the size and colour they wanted. By the end of the day, I was exhausted, but my bulging pockets were clearly telling me I had 'done the business'. Not forgetting to call in at the office to pay my rent, I slipped Ken an extra tenner and thanked him for his help. 'No problem, Jeff!' he answered. 'Same again next week?'

'Yes, please,' I answered, smiling.

As I set off on the one-hour journey home, I felt good about myself for the first time in ages. I couldn't wait to tell Gina the good news and I sang along to familiar songs on the radio all the way home – not forgetting to stop off at the service station to redeem my watch, of course.

Gina was sitting with Katie and Faye, helping them with their homework. She gave me her usual kiss hello, asking where I had been all this time. Emptying my pockets on to the kitchen table in a big heap, I just said, 'Gina, we're back!' The four of us then set about counting the money. There was £750 – enough, I reckoned, to get us back into business.

Lying in bed that night, I couldn't stop thinking what a difference one day had made. In less than twenty-four hours my life had gone back fifteen years. Events had fallen into place in the most bizarre manner, and being back amongst my customers had restored my self-esteem. I now had a purpose again. I was ready to continue on my journey.

I have never been a religious or superstitious person. But my belief that my mother was looking out for me became even stronger that day when I returned to the markets.

25. Jeff of all Trades

During the couple of weeks after Tickled Pink was forced into liquidation, the telephone at home never stopped ringing. Factories I had dealt with were offering to back me in a new business, one managing director even wanting to go into partnership with me. It seemed to prove that honesty was indeed the best policy. Thanking them, however, for their kindness, I declined their offers. Gina was my partner in business, as she was in my life.

My first priority was to get some money coming in regularly, so I sold the horsebox and bought a decent van for the markets.

That first month back was the worst, as I had to listen to the snide comments of the other traders. They all felt that I'd had my chance to make it big, and that I'd never be able to do it again. As far as they were concerned, I was now there to stay. I was also made to feel as if I had let them down in some way. Everyone had looked up to me and talked about my success, and it gave them hope of doing well themselves one day. Now that I had failed, their dreams were shattered too.

The fashion wholesalers in Manchester were more sympathetic and accommodating. Mrs Kumar, who had supplied me all those years ago, gave me as much credit as I needed to get me started again.

My next priority was to find a home for my family. I didn't want to uproot Katie and Faye from their school if I could help it, nor did I want to return to Liverpool. There were also their pet ponies and our eight polo ponies to think about, not to mention two dogs and a cat. I would have to find a way to make the ponies pay, or I'd be forced to get rid of them.

We needed something with a bit of land, and it had to be cheap. At first, Gina and I looked for places to rent but, unfortunately, there was nothing out there. The situation was urgent: the bank had sold our home and given us notice to vacate.

The only property available was an old run-down veterinary practice which had several acres of land and twelve stables. And it was situated right next to the Cheshire Polo Club.

I convinced myself and Gina that I could turn it into a polo school. We could even take on liveries, looking after people's horses. I had become a highly proficient horseman over the years, and it seemed to be a perfect solution. The only drawback was that it was on the market for £200,000!

After having been turned down by every mortgage company I approached, I sold my four best ponies for £20,000, and used the money as a deposit on a loan with a French bank. Even though their interest rates were much higher than everyone else's, it was the only bank I could convince to lend me the £180,000 I needed. At this point, we were as good as beggars, and therefore could not be choosers.

Packing up all our personal belongings in the run-up to leaving Abbots Walk was very sad, particularly for Gina, as she had loved that house. She never said anything, but I did notice tears in her eyes on several occasions. All I could do was give her a hug, promising that everything would be all right and things could only get better.

On the day we moved, we were faced with the problem of getting the horses to the new house. Without a horsebox, the only alternative was to walk them along two miles of narrow country roads.

I was at the front, with two polo ponies on lead ropes, while Katie, now eleven, and Faye, now nine, followed in the middle with their ponies. Gina brought up the rear with the remaining pair. It was a dangerous journey walking along the winding lanes with so many animals, and my stomach felt tight with tension. Gina suddenly called out to me, 'Jeff, we really do look like gypsies now. I wonder what our new neighbours will think when they see us turning up looking like this.' I couldn't help but laugh.

With much shuffling back and forth, we eventually moved into Stone House Farm. Katie and Faye immediately ran upstairs to claim their bedrooms. Faye opened her window and it fell crashing to the ground. I soon realized that the 150-year-old farmhouse was in need of a little more than a coat of paint!

There was no central heating, for example, only coal fires to keep us warm. It was like going back in time to my childhood. But it didn't really bother us; we were together as a family, and that was all that mattered.

That year soon passed. Five days a week, I would travel to Liverpool in the early hours of the morning to set up my market stall. Gina would follow to help me after dropping the girls off at school, and Karen Foster, our devoted friend from the Girls Talk days, was now working with me again.

When I wasn't trading, I was teaching aspiring men and women how to ride horses and play polo. I became the Cheshire Polo Club's official coach, with my own polo school. Who would have guessed that when I first went to Argentina to learn how to play, I would one day end up teaching it myself!

I found myself doing everything and anything to make money

to pay the bills, which never seemed to end. Isn't it funny how you never seem to notice the postman coming every morning when times are good, but when you're broke you seem to see him all the time.

Bob Broster, a good friend of mine, offered me a job jousting at big county shows, an offer I couldn't refuse. It involved riding out in front of thousands of spectators, dressed in shining armour, and charging towards another 'knight', lances at the ready.

I was often sent crashing to the ground at speed, and the armour didn't make for a soft landing! I may have been battling as a knight, but I was also fighting for survival, more than happy with the £300 I earned in a day.

All was beginning to go well, and I was managing to keep the wolf (and the dreaded postman) from the door. Then, one day in September 1994, I received a call from Pinewood Studios asking if I was interested in doing some work as an extra in a film they were shooting in Wales. Apparently, I now had a good reputation as a stunt rider, and they were offering £100 a day, and £50 to cover the costs of the horse. The caller asked if I knew any other riders, and Peter, a young man I was teaching to play polo, sprang to mind. He didn't own a horse, but I could lend him one of mine and, in return, collect an extra £50 a day.

Gina said she would look after the markets in my absence, so I borrowed a horsebox and, before we knew it, Peter and I were setting off to Gwynedd in North Wales.

When we arrived, there were hundreds of horseboxes and rows and rows of makeshift stables. Large white tents had been put up across acres of farmland, and in the distance there was a huge construction of a castle with a moat and drawbridge. This spectacular site was mind-blowing.

We slowly made our way through the hive of activity, eventually signing in at reception, where we were given a stable number and told to report to wardrobe. The costumes had been designed by Giorgio Armani and were amazing: royal-blue tunics with layers of armour that glistened in the midday sun, a thick leather swordbelt and knee-high suede boots.

There were 260 horsemen in total, and we were playing knights of the realm in the army of King Arthur. Some of the horses didn't take kindly to wearing their armour, especially over their heads, and at times the field was full of knights being thrown off their horses in every direction. Poor Peter was in a terrible state, frightened to death, and even though I was more confident, I spent the next three hours hanging on for dear life while my horse reared and kicked to throw off its costume. At one point the man who seemed to be in charge of managing all the horses came up to me and asked what breed my horses were. 'Argentinian polo ponies,' I replied. When I said that I played, he smiled, and said, 'You'll be all right then. Get back in line.'

Later that afternoon, a helicopter appeared in the sky above. Everyone watched it land, and there was a huge cheer as Sean Connery emerged and waved to the hundreds of extras standing on the hillside. Half an hour later, another helicopter arrived, and Richard Gere stepped out. Word spread like wildfire, and I soon discovered we were about to appear in a £60 million blockbuster called *First Knight*.

The horsemen were instructed to form a long line, two abreast, to wear stern expressions and ride with our backs straight and our chests out. Most importantly, we had to keep our eyes firmly fixed on the head of the rider directly in front of us. The director then called out, 'You're the King's men going into battle, so act like it.'

Everything was going well until we were told to go into a rising trot. The instructions were clear: we had to rise up out of our saddles, then sit back down in unison, repeating this every couple of seconds. All 260 of us had to be in harmony. We practised for one hour and then we were told that, when we arrived at the throne where King Arthur was sitting, one column was to turn left, the other right. We all got into position and waited for the call of 'Action', then off we went. Peter and I were towards the back, and I could sense that he was not in time with the rest of us: as we were rising up, he was sitting down. He was also shouting out, 'It's hurting me.'

'What is?' I asked.

'Your sword!'

Taking my eyes off the rider in front for a split second, I looked down and saw, to my horror, that my sword had disappeared inside Peter's boot. And the more I tried to free it, the more he cried out in pain. We were now getting closer to where the two columns would separate. But we were stuck together like Siamese twins. Within seconds of us seeing the colour of Sean Connery's eyes, I managed to undo the buckle of my belt, releasing the sword, and turned sharp right. How Peter managed not to kill our precious 'king', I'll never know!

Everyone watched in disbelief as Peter then carried out an Oscar-winning performance of his own. His pony bolted off at great speed across the countryside while Peter held on for his life, with a large metal sword sticking out of his boot!

The next day, it was my turn for action.

All the horsemen had been in the saddle for several hours,

trying to perfect our departure out of the castle gates and over the drawbridge to the fields beyond. We must have done it a dozen times, but still it wasn't right. We were being put back into position one more time – and it's not easy to get 260 horses exactly where you want them – when a message that had been passed down the line finally reached me: 'Where's the polo player?'

Peter called out, 'That's you, Jeff, They're asking for you.' I shushed him to be quiet, thinking we were going to be thrown off the set. Then the man who had called me over on the first day came riding up the long line of horsemen calling out, 'Where's the polo player?' I thought we were about to be sent packing, so I tried to shuffle further towards the back, but then the man recognized me and pulled me out of the line.

'Come with me,' he said, setting off at a gallop. When we arrived at the front, he explained what was going on. 'It's Richard Gere's horse,' he said. 'Every time he rides over the drawbridge, it shies away from the big arc lights that are positioned along the way. I want you to ride directly behind him and, as he gets closer to the light, I want you to push your horse up to the back of his so that it has no time to shy away. Can you do it?' He knew, as I did, that polo ponies are bred for that sort of work.

Before I knew it, I was being introduced to Richard Gere, but I could sense that the clock and the pounds were ticking away and that this was no time for idle chitchat. We all got into position once more. But this time my heart was pounding faster than ever with the extra responsibility. 'Action' was called, and we set off out of the castle gates. As we hit the drawbridge, my eyes focused on the bright lights in the distance. As soon as I felt the time was right, I signalled my horse to move forward and push the horse in front. To my relief, I heard a voice on the Tannoy saying, 'Well done, everyone. That's a wrap.'

We had two weeks filming in Wales, and at the end of it, the guy in charge of the horsemen was taking his six best riders to Scotland to appear in another movie. He invited me to join them, so I rang home to tell Gina the good news.

She listened quietly, then said, 'Get your arse back here right now. If you think for one minute that I'm going to look after the business, the farm and the girls while you go galloping around a field with a bunch of movie stars, you've got another think coming!' Her choice of words was so funny I burst out laughing. The next day, I set off for home, where I truly belonged. Two weeks later, I got a phone call from the stunt team to say they were having the time of their lives – riding alongside Mel Gibson in *Braveheart*.

26. The Human Spirit Shines Through

Despite really enjoying working with horses, I soon realized I would always be scraping a living. It was too hit and miss. One week I would have half a dozen clients to teach; the next two weeks, nothing. Our small market business was subsidizing everything. It was a tough decision, but I had no other alternative but to close the polo school and concentrate all my efforts once more on building up the fashion business.

By now I knew my strengths, and I certainly knew my weaknesses. My strength was the vast knowledge of the fashion business I had acquired over the years. I knew in my heart I would be a great asset to any of the big names on the high street and I would have jumped at the chance to prove my worth. But, unfortunately, the reality was quite different. Who in their right mind would employ someone who could not even read or write? The truth was, I was unemployable. I would have to go it alone.

One night, I was talking to Gina after dinner and jokingly said, 'Put me in a field with lots of women and I'll make a lot of money!' Then it dawned on me. 'That's it!' I cried out. 'The county shows where I used to joust. They get thirty thousand visitors through their gates – at least ten thousand must be women.'

The next day, I made enquiries and, as luck would have it, our local Cheshire Show was to be held in two weeks' time. For £300, we could have a space to sell our clothes.

Even better, the show took place on a Tuesday and Wednesday, so it didn't interfere with our market days. £300 seemed like a lot of money, but I decided it was worth a go. All I needed now were the styles that would appeal to the female country set. The art of successful retailing is in the buying. Anyone can sell, but not everyone can buy.

I had always kept a keen eye on the fashion icons of the day, and Princess Diana was one of my favourites. It wasn't difficult to understand that, whatever Diana wore, these ladies would certainly wear, too. I'd always had a good relationship with many fashion manufacturers, and they were happy to give me sixty days' credit on the extra stock I needed.

On the first day, Gina, Karen and I took £3,000, and on the second, £4,000. The female customers absolutely loved our styles.

As we were packing up, I got chatting to a married couple who sold leather handbags. They told me they were going to travel through the night to go to the Royal Lincolnshire show, which started the next day.

Gina and I discussed it that night and, just after midnight, I too was setting off on the 200-mile journey to Lincolnshire.

I arrived around 5 a.m., and the place was buzzing. The office had just opened, so I made my way inside. After much begging and pleading, I finally managed to obtain a space. Erecting my stall, I felt like the poor relation next to all these other, professional traders, who had gleaming white marquees, with brand-new caravans parked alongside. I felt slightly embarrassed at first with my feeble set-up. But I convinced myself that it was the product I was selling that would determine how successful I would be, not the look of my 'premises'.

I spent the next three hours setting up shop and displaying my stock. It was a little harder than usual, trying to do everything on my own. But by the time the thousands of visitors had passed through the turnstiles, I was ready to do business. In no time at all, the Lincolnshire women were buying like there was no tomorrow. They absolutely loved my selection of clothes. But, even more importantly, they loved my prices.

I always believed in the three 'right's: the right product at the right price to the right customer. The rest is easy after that. My fellow traders stood gazing at the sight before them: a strange one-man-band set-up that would have looked more at home in a foreign bazaar. What they found hard to accept was that my small, humble stall was packed with customers giving me lots of money. I soon became the hot topic of conversation.

By 7 p.m., it was all over. I was well and truly exhausted. I'd had no sleep for close on thirty-eight hours. I put the remaining stock back in the van and crawled in after it on my hands and knees and lay on the floor. It was very dark and claustrophobic with all the garments touching my face. But exhaustion got the better of me and I fell fast asleep.

I was awakened next morning by the sound of the other traders readying themselves for the day ahead. With a towel over my shoulder and a toilet bag under my arm, I went in search of somewhere to freshen up. The only place I could find was a public Portakabin which, being in desperate need of a good clean, was not a pretty sight or smell. Trying my best not to breathe in, I washed and shaved in freezing-cold water – a far cry from the life I was once used to! Fortunately, there was a decent catering wagon close by, so I didn't go short of tea and sandwiches.

I took £6,000 at that show, and it definitely put a spring back in my step and gave me the energy to drive non-stop back home to my family.

Throughout the summer, there is a county show almost every week in some part of England. I found out where they were and criss-crossed the country, selling lady's fashion. The profits soon came rolling in, which enabled me to buy a good-quality second-hand marquee and a large box wagon. With my own caravan in tow, I was now as organized as my fellow traders. Everything was coming together, but I desperately missed my three girls.

In the school summer holidays, Gina, Katie and Faye would accompany me – it was a real family affair. Working through the day together and spending our nights in our small caravan, we often laughed ourselves to sleep. We were now really experiencing the travellers' way of life!

Despite everything else I was doing, I still managed to retain my market stalls in Liverpool. But it meant working all the hours God sent. In the winter months, when the summer shows had finished, I did indoor events such as the Horse of the Year Show at Olympia in London, and the Ideal Homes Exhibition at Earls Court. I also did the BBC's *Clothes Show*, which was held at the NEC in Birmingham. You name it, and I most probably did it. Anywhere I could find lots of women, I'd be there with clothes for sale.

I maintained this hectic pace for seven years, in order to pay the mortgage and my daughters' school fees. It was very important to me that Katie and Faye had a good education. I certainly didn't want them to suffer like I did.

*

The wintry weather came early in the year of 2000. It was the first Thursday in September, a day I will never forget. Karen and I were trading at Speke Market on the outskirts of Liverpool. The weather that day was cruel. Huge winds and driving rain were making it impossible to trade but, like always, I would not give in. Standing there like Jesus on the cross, my arms stretched wide, holding on to the stall's canopy, I was fearful of the gale force winds blowing my hard-earned business away. Heavy rain was running down the canopy that was protecting all my stock from being destroyed. The water ran down the back of my neck and the inside of my sleeves, soaking every part of my body. Even my shoes were soon full of water, but I couldn't let go. I held on for a good two hours, before the winds dropped slightly, allowing Karen and me the time to pack everything away into the wagon.

I arrived home that day without a penny in my pocket, only bundles of soaking-wet stock. Gina tried to salvage it, washing and ironing some fifty garments. At times like this, the markets were a cruel way of earning a living.

The next day, I arrived at the market at 5 a.m, as usual. But this time Karen was standing there waiting for me, which was odd, because she normally arrived at around eight. As I pulled up, she climbed into the passenger seat. I could tell by her expression she was upset.

'What's wrong?' I asked.

'Jeff, I've been awake crying all night,' she replied. 'I can't bear to see you struggling like this any more. You deserve better. I've had the pleasure of working alongside you for sixteen years now, through the Girls Talk and Kids Talk days, even the tough Tickled Pink times. But to watch you yesterday, struggling like that, was just too upsetting. You must get another shop. That's where you truly belong. You're far too talented to end up working like this. It's tragic. It has to stop.'

I was totally shocked by Karen's emotional outburst. I just sat there, not knowing what to say. But I knew she was right. As that day's trading came to an end, her parting words were, 'Jeff, please do something and get off the markets.' Deeply affected by her pleas, I decided that, instead of going straight home, I would drive into the city centre to see if there were any suitable shops available – more out of curiosity than anything else. Parking my wagon, I walked along Church Street, where my old shop used to be, but there was not one 'To let' sign in sight. Making my way back, I found myself in Bold Street.

In bygone days, this had been Liverpool's most prestigious shopping street and was regarded as the equal of London's Bond Street. But over the years it had sadly declined, both in character and in the amount of high-class premises on offer.

I noticed one shop had a 'To let' sign above its entrance. On close inspection, it looked ideal for selling fashion. I wrote down the agent's phone number and went home. That night, Gina told me she agreed with everything Karen had said. Their comments were making me re-think things.

It had been seven long years since the bank had destroyed my spirit. Maybe now was the right time to start again? I rang the agent and was informed there was a long list of applicants who were interested in the premises, and that I was wasting my time applying.

Over the years, I'd had many doors closed in my face, and my response had always been the same: never give up. When I told the agent I'd previously owned several shops in the city, he was intrigued and asked which ones.

When I told him, he said, 'I remember you. You're the one that had thousands of customers queuing up outside your shop every Christmas.' Eighteen years had passed since then, and he still remembered. 'What's your name again, sir?'

I answered, and before I could say another word, he continued, 'Mr Pearce, I am sure our clients would be more than happy with you as their tenant. When would it be convenient for you to view the premises?'

Gina, Karen and I visited the premises the following day. The shop consisted of 1,000 square feet of selling space on the ground floor only. A little small, I thought. But it was a start.

Rather than pay the £20,000 key money, I managed to negotiate a deal whereby I would use this money to refurbish the shop. A few weeks later, I collected the keys.

Over the years, I'd become pretty good at DIY, more through necessity than anything else. I worked all day and most of the night for two weeks until the shop was ready. My suppliers were once again more than happy to finance the £40,000 worth of new stock I needed to kickstart my new venture, now named Jeff's of Bold Street.

On 22 September 2000, I opened the doors to the public. The *Liverpool Echo* ran a double-page spread headed, 'Mr Fashion is Back!' And from the start, our new business was thriving.

Gina and a few staff ran the shop while Karen and I continued on the markets. I didn't want to give them up just yet in case something went wrong. With the run-up to Christmas, the sales went better than I could have imagined. That Christmas was the best Christmas for a long time, and I felt I had regained my usual high spirits once again.

As we moved into January, the strangest thing happened. The

agent who had arranged the lease on the new shop called in to see me and asked if we could talk somewhere private. 'Mr Pearce,' he said, once I'd taken him into my office, 'I'll get straight to the point. Can you raise £400,000 in the next ten days?'

I nearly collapsed with shock. But at the same time, trying my best to look calm, I asked, 'Why?'

'There's a freehold property for sale not more than a hundred yards from here that just might suit you.'

Part of me wanted to burst out laughing, because I didn't have a pot to piss in, never mind £400,000. But I was also intrigued. 'Where is it?' I asked.

'If you can spare the time, I can show you right now.'

As we left the shop, I grabbed Gina's hand and said, 'Come with me.'

The three of us made our way to a large property a few doors away, and the agent unlocked the door. Gina and I stood anxiously waiting to enter. The moment he turned the lights on, I knew this was the sort of building I had always dreamt of owning. My very own department store!

The property consisted of five floors, each with its own 1,500 square feet of selling space. It was perfect, except for one small problem – money! It needed at least £100,000 spending on it before it could be opened for business. And the purchase price alone was £400,000. Add to that the £200,000 which would be needed for stock, and it came to close on three-quarters of a million pounds!

My mind was full of different emotions; first excitement, next disappointment. There was no way Gina and I could possibly afford something as big as this. I thanked the agent for showing us round and kept my pride by telling him I'd think about it.

'Mr Pearce,' he said, 'I don't mean to push you, but the property is worth a lot more than £400,000. The owner is only prepared to sell it for that price if the deal is done within ten days.' Little did he know there was more chance of me flying to the moon than there was of me raising that sort of cash.

Gina and I spent the whole evening talking about the possibility of owning such a great store. In the twenty-two years we had been partners in business, and in life, we had never made an important decision without both of us being in complete agreement. I have always been a risk-taker and a true optimist; I truly do believe in fate and destiny making your own luck in life. My wife, on the other hand, is much more cautious and wise. But it's true what they say: opposites attract and can work well together.

In the early hours of the morning, after Gina had gone to bed, I masterminded a plan to raise the money to buy the property. It involved borrowing money off friends and, unfortunately, it involved the dreaded bank once again. It meant our home, which had now doubled in value, would have to be put up as security.

I had always felt personally responsible for losing our family's home the last time. Gina knew me better than anyone. She had faith in me and believed I would make a success of the new shop. So, with her blessing, I set the wheels in motion.

On 29 January 2001, just ten days after first setting eyes on 80 Bold Street, we signed on the dotted line and borrowed half a million pounds to buy and refurbish it. We'd done it, but the bank had tied me up in so many knots I could hardly move! My suppliers, on the other hand, offered me as much stock as I needed on a handshake.

Gina continued to look after the first shop at No. 72 – not to mention everything else. She truly was my rock in a stormy ocean, and I couldn't have done it without her endless love and support. While I did my two best market days on Friday and Saturday, the other five days were spent in the new shop playing Bob the Builder.

Our new premises had been built a century earlier. The best way to describe what I had let myself in for was opening a very big can of worms. The monumental task of refurbishing the building was proving very difficult: the more I tried to fix something, the more it went wrong. I very soon realized it wasn't a £100,000 shop refurbishment that was needed, it was a £250,000 rebuild!

Walking around the place for hours and noting all the problems, I finally realized there was only one option – I had to knock it all down and start again. Hiring ten of the strongest labourers I could find, we set to work gutting the whole of the inside. This involved dropping all the internal floors, leaving only the roof and four walls standing. I must have filled over fifty large skips with rubble.

Every time Gina popped in to see what progress I was making, the terrified look on her face was far from reassuring. On one occasion, she said, 'Do you know what you're doing? It looks like a bomb's just hit it!' But the driving force within me was irrepressible. Working seven days a week, I lived on five hours' sleep a night. With the pressure well and truly on, I knew no other way.

Hidden in the basement was an old Second World War air-raid shelter, which took up quite a lot of space, so I decided to demolish it. In the process of demolition, the men discovered what they thought was a small rat hole. We filled it in; but a few days later, it had reappeared. Hoping to kill any rats that were down there, I forced a pole down the hole. But suddenly I found myself flat on my face and the pole had disappeared!

After a few seconds' silence I heard the sound of the pole hitting water. Grabbing a torch and shining it down the narrow hole, I saw the beam shining back at me, as it reflected off the water at the bottom of this now seemingly endless shaft. Panicking, I thought, 'Blimy! I've hit the River Mersey,' and was assailed by frantic thoughts of the building collapsing around me.

I cleared the rubble beneath my feet and found a large stone slab, fear giving me the strength to push it to one side. As I shone the torch in front of me, I got the fright of my life, the shock sending me staggering several feet backwards. I lay down on the floor and inched forward on my belly, determined to discover what it was I had unearthed.

It was the darkest, blackest hole I had ever seen. How I hadn't fallen down it I'll never know. But peering over its edge, I was amazed to see a 30-feet deep, perfectly rounded shaft carved out of solid sandstone.

I was so intrigued I called the Liverpool History Museum to see if they could tell me anything. When their official arrived a few days later, he advised me to close down the site pending further examination by their archaeologists. Later, I was informed that the 'rat hole' was actually a well dating back to the early seventeenth century.

Never one to miss an opportunity, I removed my builder's hard hat and donned a marketing one, ringing all the newspapers and radio stations. The next day my find was front-page news – one paper headlining it, 'Well, Well, What Have We Got Here?!'

alongside a picture of me looking down the well. The media informed everyone they would have to wait till the grand opening of Jeff's of Bold Street before they could see the 350-year-old well close up. I was on a roll: the story had generated loads of great publicity for us. I even appeared on the *Nine O'Clock News*!

Some days later, I had a brainwave. I'd make the well a feature of the store by building it up through the basement to ground-floor level. When I did my calculations, I realized that the well would end up pretty much dead centre of the shop at street level, making it a truly remarkable centrepiece.

I built it brick by brick. It took two weeks to complete, and I'm so glad that I did it. Even to this day, visitors to Liverpool still make their way to Bold Street to see my great find.

When I was a child, my mother often told me stories about Bold Street and of how the posh ladies of the day would shop there, dressed in all their finery. They would arrive at their favourite stores in horse-drawn carriages or chauffeur-driven motor cars. The street was renowned for its millinery, quality tailoring and high-class furniture stores. There were also lots of tea rooms, where the ladies would sip tea from bone-china cups and gossip.

Inspired by my mother's stories, I based the image of my new emporium on the olden days, and went in search of anything that would fit that image. I found Edwardian and Victorian fittings and artefacts in old schools and churches that were under demolition, and I positioned each treasure with the same love and tender care as it would have originally been installed a hundred years before.

On the first floor, I re-created a Victorian tea room that would accommodate thirty-six customers. It took a lot of time and patience to scour the country for all the right silverware. I even had black and white Victorian uniforms specially made for the waitresses. Striving for perfection and authenticity, I put my heart and soul into it.

It took eight months in all to complete the restoration work on the new Jeff's of Bold Street store. Miraculously, I also managed to finish it on budget. We then moved out of our small shop four doors away, and on 10 September 2001, Gina and I, along with our daughters, Katie and Faye, June, Karen and fifteen staff, were ready to open the doors to our new venture. Needless to say, Gina and I both had our fingers firmly crossed!

27. Someone to Watch over Me

The store was an overnight success, and it became busier and busier as word spread. Customers travelled from miles around to experience the new Jeff's of Bold Street. We had an exquisite bridal gowns department, and the very best in special-occasions wear, with its own VIP lounge and personal-dresser service. This was a very exclusive area, for which I created a gold-card membership which afforded members personalized assistance as well as complimentary champagne on ice. Celebrities and some of the most important people in the country became customers. We also had a smart casual-wear department, and sold shoes, handbags and accessories for every occasion. Altogether, we had three floors covering all the latest fashions.

A commissionaire dressed in traditional uniform greeted customers at the entrance. In no time at all, we became known as the Harrods of Liverpool, and the shop tills were ringing to the tune of £40,000 a week. Soon afterwards, I finally ended my long career on the markets.

After the store had been open a few weeks, something happened that seemed to defy all logic. The commissionaire brought into my office a dark-haired, well-dressed man carrying a briefcase who told me that he wanted me to pay him £700 a month to protect me from shoplifters and ruffians. I gave him short shrift and told him I didn't want or need his protection, but a week later he came back, this time carrying a large black bin bag. He deposited the contents on my desk – close on £1,000 worth of lady's fashions, all with our price tags on them! 'You see, Mr Pearce,' he said courteously. 'I think you really do need our security.'

I was angry and accused him of running a shoplifting gang, but he denied this and said that his men had simply retrieved the garments from well-known thieves they'd had under surveillance. I didn't believe him, but I was also worried about the effect it would have on my business if the thefts continued. I asked him to give me some time to think it over, and he handed me his business card.

That evening, Gina suggested that we go for a drink before heading home. We were just walking into a bar in the city centre when suddenly I felt a hand on my shoulder and heard a surprised voice crying out, 'Jeff! Jeff Pearce!' Turning to see who it was, I recognized Alan, an old school pal I hadn't seen for thirty-odd years. We chatted, and he decided to come inside and have a drink with us. As we were talking, I mentioned my visitor and said I was being blackmailed. I then showed him the business card the man had left with me.

Alan didn't say anything, he just took out his mobile phone and dialled a number. Then, without altering his affable demeanour, I heard him say, 'Hey. Don't go near Jeff's of Bold Street any more. He's mine. I look after him. If I hear of you bothering him again, I'll blow your legs off. End of.'
Turning to me, he said quite calmly, 'Jeff, you'll have no more trouble from him, my old mate.' Then he handed me his own business card. When Gina looked at it later, we realized that he was in the security business too!

The timely meeting with Alan was uncanny. Was it coincidence?

Fate? The supernatural? Call it what you will. That night, I lay in bed thinking about it and was reminded of another incident some weeks earlier during the refurbishing of the store. Bernie Snagg, my old friend from the ice-rink days, now a skilled carpenter, had just spent the best part of a week laying 1,500 square feet of wide pine boards on the ground-floor sales area. I'd reclaimed this beautiful old wood from a demolition job in North Wales. Bernie was just finishing off, when he found he was two lengths short. This was annoying; there was no way I'd be able to find a similar width of wood. However, without knowing why, I went up to the top floor, just to see if I could find anything to suit. To my great astonishment, I immediately found two lengths. And when Bernie placed them into position they fitted perfectly!

'I don't believe it,' he cried. 'It's spooky working with you.'

Perhaps the next incident will explain these mysterious happenings. Shortly after my chance meeting with Alan at the city bar, I was working the sales floors, running up and down the stairs, serving as many customers as I possibly could, when one of the tea-room staff beckoned to me. Asking what she wanted, she informed me that the lady and gentleman sipping tea at the gallery table had invited me to join them. I was often invited to join customers, so I made my way over and introduced myself. While the gentleman poured me a cup of tea, the lady gazed at me intently, and then spoke. 'I have been blessed with a gift, you know. I have watched you walking around the store for some time now. Did you know that you have a guardian angel following you everywhere you go? A petite fair-haired lady?'

Quietly, she waited for my reaction, but I simply smiled, thanked her for her kind words, then stood up and headed for the privacy of my office, where I sat at my desk reflecting on what the lady had said. I had always believed my mother was looking over me from above, but I never imagined she would be literally shadowing me! There is rarely a day goes by when I don't think of her. But I wasn't prepared to discuss my private thoughts and feelings about her, even with the gifted lady. I already knew I'd had the most remarkable mother. I now knew for certain she had kept her promise to watch over me.

Incredible though it may seem, Jeff's of Bold Street became the most talked-about store in the fashion business in just twelve months. So much so that we were invited to attend *Drapers* Annual Awards, the Oscars of the fashion industry.

It was held on the night of 14 November 2002, and the champagne flowed as we sat at a table at the rear of the Dinosaur Room in the Natural History Museum in London. We had been shortlisted as a finalist in the Independent Womenswear Retailer of the Year category, one of the hardest categories of all, there being literally thousands of very good womenswear retailers from across the UK and the Irish Republic to choose from. Our relatively small business in Liverpool was up against some very tough opposition.

Katie and Faye were there to support us, along with some close friends. I was too nervous to enjoy it though. My mind kept on wandering back to my childhood and the beginning of my career. By contrast, now, here I was sitting in the same room alongside all the top names in the fashion business, household names like Philip Green, the billionaire who controlled most of the big names on the high street, such as Topshop and BHS; George Davies, the mastermind behind Next and George at Asda;

and Stuart Rose, the managing director of Marks & Spencer, to mention just a few.

The awards ceremony was hosted by Trinny and Susannah, the TV fashion-guru presenters, and it covered seventeen different categories. The Independent Womenswear Retailer category was a prestigious award, given towards the end of the evening. And sitting there waiting for the announcement was nerve-wracking.

Finally, it was 'our' turn, and as they called out the nominees, I held Gina's hand tight. Everyone's attention was fixed on the stage except for mine. I just couldn't look and simply stared at the table instead. As the envelope was opened a silence fell; not a sound could be heard.

'And the winner is . . .' There was a long pause. 'Jeff's of Bold Street!'

I leapt to my feet with excitement, lifting Gina with me and embracing her tightly. Beckoning to Katie and Faye, the four of us walked to the stage, applause ringing out around us. It seemed like such a long way as we snaked our way through the forest of tables.

On the stage, a two-foot-tall, maroon-velvet statue shaped like a mannequin was placed in my hands, and we all received a congratulatory kiss on either cheek from Trinny and Susannah. As we stood there, with the press taking photos, I realized that this was the moment I had been dreaming of for most of my life. To receive recognition from my peers for being the best womenswear retailer in the whole of the United Kingdom and Ireland was something special – particularly in the presence of my family.

Back at our table, our friends were more than pleased for us and continued the celebrations with more champagne. An announcement was then made of a further two Gold Awards still to come, the first being Fashion Retail Personality of the Year. Six of the very top names were shortlisted, and Philip Green was announced as the winner.

Finally, Eric Musgrave, the editor-in-chief of *The Draper* (formerly *The Drapers Record*) announced the most prestigious award of the evening. It was the highlight of the whole event – the Gold Award for the Independent Retailer of the Year. The nominations had been selected from all the winners of the independent retailer categories and were regarded as being the best of the best. As the award was being explained, Gina noticed that I was staring at the gold statuette standing alone on the stage. I was lost in a world of my own.

'Stop it, Jeff,' she interrupted my thoughts.

'Stop what?' I asked, dragging my eyes away from the stage.

'Stop building your hopes up. We're far too small to win a gold award. They're for the big boys,' she said. Then, placing my statuette in front of me, she added, 'We came here to win this, and we've won it.'

'Of course,' I said. 'I'm just excited. Can't you see? I *am* happy we're taking this home with us!' I picked it up to admire it. But Gina was right: she knew me well enough to know what I was thinking. I wanted that gold award more than anyone else in the room. My desire was greater and came from the heart. Suddenly, my thoughts were interrupted by the announcement from the stage.

'And the winner is . . . Jeff's of Bold Street!'

In disbelief, I nearly dropped to the floor. The expressions on everyone's face made me realize that it was true. We had won the fashion industry's highest accolade!

As the audience stood and applauded, the girls told me to go up on my own. It didn't feel right, however; this momentous occasion had to be shared with the ones that I loved. I insisted that they came with me.

Making our way to the stage for the second time was proving even more difficult, as we were now receiving a standing ovation. The continuous backslapping from fellow guests and the shaking of hands made me feel like a film star on the way to collect an Oscar.

If this was a dream, it was the best one I had ever had. Can you wish for something so much that it becomes true? Or was it a genuine acknowledgement of my hard work and determination? Being applauded by the top people in the fashion industry meant more to me that night than all the financial rewards I'd received in my whole business career.

Before I stepped down from the stage, I walked over to the microphone, raised the gold award high above my head and said, 'I owe this to two remarkable women: my mother for teaching me how to survive in the rag trade, and my wife for putting up with me for so long in this fascinating business that I love so much.' I couldn't have said another word, I was so overcome.

In the taxi back to the hotel, Katie and Faye summed up the evening beautifully. 'Dad, it was the same as you receiving your cap and gown. You were recognized by the fashion business for your outstanding contribution. We are so proud of you.' Their words made me feel incredibly special. It was the perfect end to a perfect evening.

The following day a photograph of all the winners appeared on the front cover of the top fashion industry glossy magazine. I was positioned at the front holding my gold award, with Gina,

Katie and Faye surrounding me. Inside, the article stated, 'Jeff Pearce is a paragon of independent retailing.' We didn't understand the word 'paragon', so Gina looked it up and said, 'It means you are a flawless diamond weighing at least 100 carats.'

It was only after receiving this wonderful recognition that I felt able to face the demons that had tormented me every day of my life. When I admitted to the world that I couldn't read or write, I was flooded with an enormous sense of relief, as if a massive burden had been lifted from me. I no longer felt that I had to constantly prove myself. Despite being severely dyslexic, finally, I felt equal to the person standing next to me.

Epilogue

The store continued to be successful over the next two years. I ploughed all the profits straight back in to pay for the £200,000 worth of stock we now carried. Then, in 2004, I started to notice that the takings were dropping below the £20,000 a week we needed to pay the interest on the loan and all the running costs.

The harder Gina and I worked to bring the takings back up, the more they fell. At the same time, the bank was contacting me more frequently and asking me to provide monthly forecasts on the store's takings. In short, they wanted me to give them the good news which I didn't have.

History was repeating itself – we were heading into another recession, and I started having sleepless nights. This time, however, I was not prepared to watch all my hard work disappear in front of my eyes. So I quickly put Jeff's of Bold Street up for sale with a price tag of £1 million. Almost immediately, we had interested parties wanting to purchase it, and I struck a deal whereby they paid the full asking price for the freehold and we were able to rent the premises back at a favourable rate. We were then able to continue trading without all the financial worry. What a lucky escape! I was no longer faced with the threat of the bank destroying our lives. And on the day we repaid the bank, Gina and I felt free.

Despite all my successes in the fashion trade, if you were to ask me what are my proudest moments in life I would say, without doubt, watching our two girls, Katie and Faye growing up into well-balanced young women. They too spent their childhood years growing up in the rag trade. When old enough they were out in all weathers helping us make a living. I instilled in them the same work ethic that my mother had given to me and they too excelled in their chosen fields.

At school Katie was head girl. She also captained the hockey and netball teams and later studied law at Nottingham Trent University. On completing her degree she decided to follow her passion and became a drama teacher, which she enjoys so much.

Faye, equally, proved her determination and talent. She became head of sport at school and played hockey for the Cheshire County Team as well as running for the North-west of England, like her sister. She later studied Fashion Design at Edinburgh University, achieving a First before completing her Masters at the Royal College of Art in London. She is now a fashion designer for a large American company, thus keeping the family tradition well and truly alive.

I carried out my mother's last dying wishes and looked after my baby sister June as if she had been my own child. As for my father, I also kept my promise and cared for him for thirty-two years. As time passed, he became my best friend and I loved him dearly, and he did eventually tell me how proud he was of me. I held his hand as he took his last breath at the age of eighty-two and, to ease his conscience about how he had treated my mother, I told him that she was waiting to welcome him with open arms.

As for my mother's predictions for me all those years ago, two were indeed correct. I have had a very happy life and I have been successful and wealthy. All that remains is, will I be famous? And in answer? I can almost hear my mother's voice singing to me 'Que sera sera, whatever will be, will be,' as she put me to bed when I was just a little boy.

The only regrets I have are that my beloved mother never met Gina, Katie or Faye, nor shared in the success I made of my life with me. And that Gina, my beautiful wife, has had to work so hard. My overly ambitious drive must have been difficult to live with at times, and I could not have achieved what I did without having her by my side. She is one in a million, the same as my mother was.

When I retired at the age of fifty-three I felt a burning desire to write my story. But there was one major problem. I could only read and write like a seven-year-old. I tried asking others to do it, but it just didn't work; it was no longer my story. Gina, as ever, gave me encouragement and words of advice – she insisted that I was the only one who could tell the story as it was, and that I had to write it myself. The thought terrified me. I felt that I would be leaving myself wide open to public humiliation and scorn; but part of me had to acknowledge that what she said was true.

I started small – writing ideas on bits of paper which I stuck on a board. It was hard going; putting my thoughts down on paper was a totally unnatural thing for me to do. I then began to write each story, staying up until the early hours. Each and every word was a struggle – written, rubbed out and written again – and even after doing my best, I knew it was still wrong. Writing frustrated the hell out of me, and made me hate my dyslexia even more.

Gina was the only one who could read my writing – she'd had many years of practice with the notes and love letters I'd written her – so she volunteered to type up my notes. But as my obsession with the book grew so did the volume of work I produced, until it was too much for Gina to cope with. I eventually found the perfect partner to help me, Kit Knowles. She was a star and would sit with me for hours and hours at a time; thank God she had the patience of a saint.

Over the next three years, with great optimism, I sent out chapters of my book to numerous literary agents and publishers, and received fifty-one rejections in return, almost one for every year of my life. But I didn't give up. I even printed a small run of my first draft for friends and family, and received such encouraging feedback that I persevered with my work. Almost four years after I started, I received a call from an agent out of the blue, telling me he had found a publisher who was interested in my story.

I often wonder whether my inability to read and write hindered me through life – or was it the spur that motivated me to succeed, to try and try again? Whatever the answer, obstacles are there to be overcome, and the important thing is to believe in yourself. After all, who would have thought it possible that a man who had lived in fear of the written word every day of his life, would then rise to a new challenge, overcoming his illiteracy and ending up writing this book? Whenever I think of these things, I always come back to the belief that it was my mother who had a lot to do with the success I made of my life. As well as giving me all the love I could ask for, she showed me that the harder you work, the more likely it is that you will achieve your dreams. And that sometimes, rags really can be turned into riches . . .